THE AESTHETICS
OF MURDER

Parallax 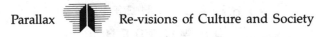 Re-visions of Culture and Society

Stephen G. Nichols, Gerald Prince, and Wendy Steiner,
Series Editors

THE AESTHETICS
OF MURDER

A Study in Romantic Literature
and Contemporary Culture

JOEL BLACK

The Johns Hopkins University Press

Baltimore and London

© 1991 The Johns Hopkins University Press
All rights reserved
Printed in the United States of America

The Johns Hopkins University Press
701 West 40th Street
Baltimore, Maryland 21211-2190
The Johns Hopkins Press Ltd., London

∞

The paper in this book meets the minimum
requirements of American National Standard
for Information Sciences—Permanence of
Paper for Printed Library Materials,
ANSI Z39.48-1984.

Library of Congress Cataloging-in-Publication Data

Black, Joel, 1950–
The aesthetics of murder : a study in romantic literature and contemporary
culture / Joel Black.
    p.   cm. — (Parallax: re-visions of culture and society)
Includes bibliographical references (p.   ) and index.
ISBN 0-8018-4180-1. — ISBN 0-8018-4181-X (pbk.)
1. Murder in literature. 2. Romanticism. 3. Fiction—History and criticism.
4. Detective and mystery stories—History and criticism. 5. Murder literature—History and criticism. 6. Murder in mass media. 7. Literature and society.   I. Title.
II. Series: Parallax (Baltimore, Md.)
PN56.M85B57   1991
809'.93355—dc20   91-8595

To my parents, Jan and John

CONTENTS

PREFACE

This study deals with an aspect of cultural history extending over the past two centuries; it is also quite specifically a book about, and inspired by, the 1980s. The project originated during an NEH fellowship in 1983–84 when I began thinking about Thomas De Quincey's "Murder" essays in relation to Kant's aesthetic philosophy. Over the following years I became increasingly aware of the degree to which both romantic and postmodern writers were preoccupied with aesthetic issues. Although the study is divided into two parts—the first treating romantic literature, and second dealing with contemporary culture—this division is not intended to separate literature from culture, or romanticism from postmodernism, but on the contrary, to reveal how readily these categories inform and interpenetrate one another.

Contemporary American and European culture consists of events and experiences that are virtually all aesthetically mediated in some way; and the most spectacular displays by the mass media are scenes of violence. Critics of the media who deplore such scenes overlook a crucial point: the graphic display of violence in both high and low art is not nearly so dangerous as the seductive power of fiction itself. How is it, I wondered in the aftermath of the slaying of John Lennon and the attempted assassination of President Reagan at the beginning of the decade, that artistic fictions like *The Catcher in the Rye* and the film *Taxi Driver* are able to provide such cogent and compelling models

for sociopathic behavior? Why are overtly fictional characters produced by the mass media able to engage impressionable and even crit-
ically sophisticated readers and viewers in ways that real-life human
beings cannot? What, in short, makes fiction even more powerful
than "reality" in shaping—and destroying—people's lives? Nagging
questions like these led me to extend my initial study of De Quincey
and Kant in order to explore such connections as those between De
Quincey's literary and Brian De Palma's cinematic aesthetic of terror,
between Pierre-François Lacenaire's and Jack Abbott's prison writings, between Jean Genet's and Yukio Mishima's ritualistic treatment
of murder and suicide, and between Mark David Chapman's and
John Hinckley, Jr.,'s media-mediated violence. A 1989 fellowship from
the University of Georgia Humanities Center and additional assistance from the Vice-President for Research enabled me to complete
the project.

A number of persons contributed to this book in ways they may or
may not recall. Among those who should be mentioned are Lidia
Berger, Tom Cerbu, Bernard Dauenhauer, Charles Eidsvik, Nancy
Felson-Rubin, Randall Hendrick, W. Wolfgang Holdheim, Charlie
Klein, Robert Leventhal, and Henk Vynckier. In preparing the final version of the manuscript, I benefited from Ann Waters's editorial exper-
tise; my thanks as well to Eric Halpern and the experienced staff at the
Johns Hopkins University Press for their encouragement and professional guidance. Karl Kroeber and Gerald Gillespie have my gratitude
for inspiring my interest in comparative literature; Lionel Trilling is
warmly remembered for having introduced me to cultural studies. For
her innumerable suggestions and kindnesses, Linda Brooks deserves a
very special word of appreciation. My greatest source of support has
assuredly been my parents, to whom this book is dedicated.

THE AESTHETICS
OF MURDER

INTRODUCTION

Doing It Beautifully

"Do it beautifully," says the heroine of Ibsen's 1890 play *Hedda Gabler* to Eilert Loevborg as she commands him to take his life. Years before, the youthful Eilert had dazzled Hedda with tales of his scandalous, drunken adventures in town, a world that was off limits to the well-bred, cloistered girl. She, in turn, had idealized Eilert as a kind of romantic poet or inspired prophet, wearing a crown of vine leaves in his hair. But when she found herself the object of his uncontrolled passion, she became terrified of losing her autonomy and respectability, and drove him off at gun point. Now, when Eilert has returned to town after a prolonged absence, supposedly rehabilitated by an adoring former schoolmate, Hedda provokes him to begin drinking again. Predictably, Eilert disgraces himself during a wild night on the town, and in his shame, he vows to Hedda "to put an end to it all." She responds simply by telling him to do it "beautifully." When Eilert questions what she means ("With a crown of vine leaves in my hair? The way you used to dream of me—in the old days?"), Hedda admits that she does not "believe in that crown any longer. But—do it beautifully, all the same. Just this once."[1] She then hands him one of two pistols that belonged to her dead father, the General.

That evening, Hedda exults when she first receives the news of Eilert's death. A few moments later, however, her joy becomes revul-

1

sion when she discovers the details of his wound. Eilert had not shot himself in the head as she had expected, or even in the breast, but in the groin—and it is not clear that he shot himself deliberately, or even that the shot fired was his own. "That too!" she cries. "Oh, why does everything I touch become mean and ludicrous? It's like a curse!" (p. 329). Once again, Eilert has let her down by failing to fulfill her command to "do it beautifully." The only character capable of a beautiful deed turns out to be Hedda, who minutes later takes her own life with the remaining duelling pistol—shooting herself in the head.

What is so beautiful, we ingenuous readers may ask, about blowing one's brains out? Any coroner can readily attest that, far from having any aesthetic appeal, such deaths are the bloodiest, the most gruesome, and the most violent. So why does Hedda find shooting oneself in the head so attractive? Clearly, the explanation can have nothing to do with the "aesthetic" experience of someone actually witnessing such a spectacle (the 1985 film *Wetherby* serves to illustrate this point), but must apply to the experience either of the person who takes his or her life in this way or of someone who empathizes and identifies with this person from afar. From their perspective, such a violent deed appears as a decisive, irrevocable, and therefore heroic act. Irresolute, bourgeois characters like Eilert (or like the protagonist of Goethe's *The Sorrows of Young Werther* [1774] who shoots himself in the head but botches the job, lingering on for hours before dying)[2] make a mockery of Hedda's aristocratic, aesthetic aspirations by becoming the passive victims of external forces and events beyond their control. Hedda, in contrast, is determined to make herself mistress of her fate in a definitive, existential act. What more compelling way to assert her will than to will her own destruction, and what more decisive means to destroy herself than to blast apart the brain, the seat of the will, where all executive decisions originate?

If the word *beautifully* seems a strange word to apply to suicide, what are we to think of Thomas De Quincey's use of the adverb *aesthetically* sixty-three years before Ibsen's play—and for the first time in the English language, no less—for the preposterous purpose of evaluating acts of murder? In his 1827 essay "On Murder Considered as One of the Fine Arts," De Quincey's speaker proposes that instead of treating murder in the customary manner from a moral perspective, it should rather "be treated *aesthetically*, as the Germans call it—that is, in relation to good taste."[3] This adaptation of a term from German philosophy (where it had been in use for a century, and where *aesthetics*, from the Greek *aistheta:* perceptible things, had come into its own as a full-fledged area of philosophical inquiry) to the context of criminality should not be taken lightly as mere gallows humor. Such an apparent misappropriation represents a deliberate attempt, I believe, to bring to light certain fundamental problems that De Quincey and other romantic writers familiar with German had detected in the relatively new philosophical field of aesthetics, especially as it had been formulated in the *Critique of Judgment* of Immanuel Kant. If the present study accomplishes nothing else, it may at least call attention to the duplicitous, macabre associations that attended aesthetics at the moment it was incorporated into the English language, that contributed to its delayed assimilation by Anglo-American philosophy,[4] and that continue to haunt Western culture today as never before.[5] For ours is a culture that has the unique distinction of being both hyper- and anaesthetic at the same time.

Once we recognize the peculiar inception of the word *aesthetic* in the English language, and begin to appreciate the problematic role that aesthetics has come to play in Western philosophy and culture in general, we may begin to sense—although not without resistance—the extent to which our customary experience of murder and other forms of violence is primarily aesthetic, rather than moral, physical, natural, or whatever term we choose as a synonym for the word *real*. Only the victim knows the brutal "reality" of murder; the rest of us view it at a distance, often as rapt onlookers who regard its "reality" as a peak aesthetic experience.

As early as 1757, Edmund Burke had implied as much in his *Philosophical Enquiry into the Origin of Our Ideas of the Sublime and Beautiful*. Ten years earlier, as an undergraduate at Trinity College, he had been struck by the eagerness with which the public clamored to watch the execution of Lord Lovat. What work of art could compete with the reality of such a spectacle? "Chuse a day," Burke wrote, on which to represent the most sublime and affecting tragedy we have; appoint the most favourite actors; spare no cost upon the scenes and decorations; unite the greatest efforts of poetry, painting and music; and when you have collected your audience, just at the moment when their minds are erect with expectation, let it be reported that a state criminal of high rank is on the point of being executed in the adjoining square; in a moment the emptiness of the theatre would demonstrate the comparative weakness of the imitative arts, and proclaim the triumph of the real sympathy.[6]

Burke's example enables him to make the case that sublimity in the arts pales next to sublime events in real life. But it could also be said that the reason the audience abandons the theater for the execution is because the latter is the more *theatrical* spectacle. It is not that art fails to match life, or that fiction can't compete with reality; in this particular instance, the public display of an actual killing simply has a greater aesthetic impact on its audience than the representation of violent death in a play.

(This explains why mime performances during the Roman Empire incorporated actual execution scenes in which convicted criminals took the place of actors. Before condemning such performances as barbaric, we might consider that they were actually an artistic refinement of the gladiatorial games. Jack Abbott reminds us that these games were themselves a highly developed form of the barbarian invention of staging violence between prisoners "as a way to make of punishment a spectator's sport."[7])

Burke's illustration of the public taste for actual scenes of violent death points up a basic truth that has less to do with art than with human nature: "We delight in seeing things, which so far from doing, our heartiest wishes would be to see redressed."[8] Because our aesthetic sensibility often conflicts with our moral sense, we are tempted to subordinate the former as deceit and illusion to the "truth" of the latter. By suppressing or denying our aesthetic experiences, we create a moral "reality" that is, in fact, our supreme fiction. This grand artifice or ideology of moral reason can only maintain itself as Truth at the continued expense of the individual's own subjective feelings, his or her aesthetic and erotic responses to the world. In societies governed by moral-rational values, these responses, and their objective embodiments as artifacts (or art-facts), are periodically stigmatized — either for being deceptive, as in Plato's attack on poetry, or for being decadent, as in the social realists' condemnation of abstract art, or as in the more recent criticism of brutality in Brian De Palma's films and of "sadomasochistic" imagery in Robert Mapplethorpe's photography. In either case, art is suspected of promoting violence, and of subverting the established moral order. Often, however, the violence depicted in works of art ultimately seems directed against the idea of art itself, and should be seen as art's suicidal attempt to pass beyond its culturally conditioned self-image of falsity, and to achieve some transcendent or nihilistic — but, in any case, pre-aesthetic — "reality."

While art may turn toward violence in a futile endeavor to make itself more authentic, actual instances of social violence are regularly presented to us artistically, and routinely experienced by us aesthetically. The very activity by which we represent or "picture" violence to ourselves is an aesthetic operation whereby we habitually transform brutal actions into art. We are greatly assisted in this by the mass media, which expose us, liminally and subliminally, to artistic representations of violence.

Murder in the Arts and the Media

If mediated lives, he figured, why not mediated deaths?
—Thomas Pynchon, *Vineland*

Typically, murder has been the province of three major disciplines: sociology (as studied in academic institutions), criminology (as the basis of the legal and penal systems), and pathology (as determined by the medical, and specifically the psychoanalytic, professions). Yet murder can be approached analytically from an entirely different angle. It can be subjected to the same kind of inquiry that literary historians and critics practice in the case of texts, or that art critics and historians bring to bear upon paintings or sculptures. For murder is as much a general cultural phenomenon as it is a specifically social, legal, or psychological problem. Besides being a daily

subject in the news media, it is a recurring, obsessive theme in a wide
variety of artistic fictions. In this form, murder can be studied in a relatively disinterested mode as a morally neutral phenomenon, in contrast to the approach taken by the sociologist, the criminologist, and
the pathologist, all of whom begin their investigations of actual murders with the assumption that murder is a moral problem and a social,
as opposed to a metaphysical, evil. "For specialists, magistrates, crim-
inologists, sociologists, there are no *evil* acts," writes Sartre in his
study of the writer-thief Jean Genet; "there are only punishable acts."
Sartre characterizes Genet's artistic endeavor as the rehabilitation of
evil in the anaesthetic world of the scientific specialist: "To rehabilitate
means, for Genet, to attribute poetically to a gratuitous and luxurious
will to do evil what sociologists and psychiatrists present as the result
of a determinism."[9]

Literary authors and other artists may succeed in revealing murder's undetermined, metaphysical dimension, but here too, many of
the greatest writers treat the act of taking another's life as a punishable
offense. Even when they do not overtly stigmatize murder, artists frequently imply a sense of its sinfulness or criminality. Poets who are
convinced of the high moral calling of their art may even try to specify
the precise sense in which murder is a sin or a crime. Thus, according
to Dante's elaborate classification of sins in the *Inferno,* murderers are
punished in the seventh of the nine circles of Hell, which is reserved
for those guilty of acts of violence,[10] and which consists of three sec-
tors or *gironi* ("rounds"). Murderers occupy the first *girone,* which is
reserved for those guilty of violence against their neighbors; they are
separated from suicides who are punished in the second *girone,* which
contains those guilty of violence against themselves, and from the sin-
ners of the third *girone,* who have committed acts of violence against
God (blasphemy), Nature (sodomy), and Art (usury).

The poet W. H. Auden secularized Dante's classification of sins.
"All crimes," he asserts, "are offenses against oneself." They are also
offenses against God, but in three different ways that correspond to
"three classes of crime: (A) offenses against God and one's neighbor
or neighbors; (B) offenses against God and society; (C) offenses
against God." Where Dante held murder to be a sin of violence against

one's neighbor, and suicide to be a sin of violence against oneself, Auden insists that murder belongs to class B, crimes against God and society (and is indeed the only kind of crime belonging to this class), while suicide belongs to class C as a crime against God. Auden gives the following explanation for his distinction between offenses committed against God and one's neighbors on the one hand, and offenses committed against God and society on the other: in the former case,

> it is possible, at least theoretically, either that restitution can be made to the injured party (e.g., stolen goods can be returned), or that the injured party can forgive the criminal (e.g., in the case of rape). Consequently, society as a whole is only indirectly involved; its representatives (the police, etc.) act in the interests of the injured party.
>
> Murder is unique in that it abolishes the party it injures, so that society has to take the place of the victim and on his behalf demand atonement or grant forgiveness; it is the one crime in which society has a direct interest.
>
> . . . Suicide is a crime belonging to Class C in which neither the criminal's neighbors nor society has any interest, direct or indirect. As long as a death is believed to be suicide, even private curiosity is improper; as soon as it is proved to be murder, public inquiry becomes a duty.[11]

The principal difference between the classificatory schemes of Dante and Auden consists in the distinction between the religious concept of sin and the secular concept of crime. Dante's concern in his poetic vision is to depict God's system for punishing human sins; Auden adopts a more humanistic perspective—he shifts his focus to human reparation for human crimes. He acknowledges that crimes are sins, and are therefore an affair between the criminal and God; but he adds that, except in the case of suicide, crimes are also "offenses" against other individuals, and, in the case of murder, an affront to the social order itself that compels society to respond by taking up the helpless victim's cause.[12]

As different as Dante's and Auden's perspectives are, they are alike in their conception of murder as a moral outrage, either as a sin or as a crime. In this respect, their "literary" classifications of murder— Dante's as a structural component in his poem, and Auden's as the basis for his analysis of the genre of the detective story—share the medical, legal, and sociological disciplines' assumption that murder is a violation of a system of moral order that consequently calls for some form of disciplinary action, whether it be that of God or man. Moral judgments are a way of establishing order, and the motivation to set up ordered systems is often rooted less in an artistic than in a moralizing impulse. The same ordering-moralizing impulse that informs the classificatory schemas of the poets Dante and Auden with respect to murder also informs the diagnostic distinctions in forensic medicine and criminal law that are used to determine the degree of a murderer's guilt, and therefore, the severity of his punishment.

Albert Camus makes a point of suspending moral judgments so that he can conduct his inquiry into murder on purely philosophical grounds. His study *L'Homme révolté* (1951) opens with a distinction between "crimes of passion" and "crimes of logic." Camus dismisses any act of murder that belongs to the former category so that he can devote his attention exclusively to cases that claim some kind of philosophical rationale.

> In the age of ideologies, we must examine our position in relation to murder. If murder has rational foundations, then our period and we ourselves are rationally consequent. If it has no rational foundations, then we are insane and there is no alternative but to find some justification or to avert our faces.[13]

But can the subject of murder be reduced to an either-or matter of premeditated versus unpremeditated murder, and can the former category then be further subdivided into murder premeditated on philosophical (moral, political, or ideological) grounds as opposed to premeditated murder committed for purely personal (emotional, idiosyncratic) reasons? What of dispassionate crimes that are not crimes of logic, but disinterested deeds? What about *actes gratuits*, murders committed with no apparent reason, that are not so much absurd as aesthetic? A philosophical approach to murder that tries to account for murder on purely rational grounds ultimately turns out to be as limited as attempts to systematize crime on moral grounds. Once again the aesthetic dimension of crime and violence is overlooked.

This study considers a variety of texts and films that present murder from an aesthetic rather than from a moral, psychological, or philosophical perspective, or even from the theoretical vantage of hermeneutics that W. Wolfgang Holdheim has detected in detective fiction.[14] Works of "criminal literature" have customarily been devalued as inferior or vulgar texts. They are not the stuff of great art, as modernist critics like Auden, Edmund Wilson, and most recently, Anthony Burgess have declared,[15] again in the specific case of detective fiction. This patronizing attitude toward criminal literature and film is especially evident in critics' responses—or lack of response—to works of the type that are my concern, works that do not constitute a (sub-)literary genre like the detective story, but that exemplify a particular aesthetic namely, that of murder. Much stands to be gained by attending to artifacts of this kind insofar as they invite us to suspend the disciplinary assumptions, moral judgments, and classificatory impulses that we typically make as ethical members of society when confronted with such a grim subject. By limiting ourselves initially to hypothetical or fictional representations of murder in nineteenth- and twentieth-century literary works, we may become accustomed to approach murder from an aesthetic-critical, rather than from a "moral-rational," perspective. Our reactions to these fictional representations of murder may range from horror to admiration, but whatever shock we experience will consist of aesthetic astonishment rather than of moral outrage. Later in the study, I will apply this aesthetic-critical approach to actual instances of suicide, assassination, and attempted assassination. In doing so, I hardly intend to justify these acts or to suggest that they lie beyond the limits of moral judgment. However, our understanding of these acts of violence may be enlarged through an aesthetic approach that offers a phenomenological description of these deeds in contrast to the more prescriptive assessments set forth by the legal and medical professions.

Some readers of this study may grant that while an extramoral, aesthetic approach may be appropriate for treatments of murder in literary and cinematic fictions, there are limits to our acceptance of artistic presentations of violence,[16] and especially to our application of aesthetic criteria to actual cases of cold-blooded killings. This is a valid objection, at least in principle. However, the particular real-life cases that I shall discuss in my final chapters—the Japanese writer Yukio Mishima's ritual suicide in 1970, the assassination of John Lennon in 1980, and the attempted assassination of President Reagan in 1981—all involve celebrated figures, and consequently have become sensational media events. And once an event is covered, or "mediated," by the press or by television, it essentially enters into the same quasi-fictional, hyperreal domain of all artistic representation and misrepresentation. This is precisely what has happened in the case of these violent episodes during the past two decades. If these occurrences have been subjected to endless public debate among legal, medical, and sociological experts, surely it is permissible to introduce a different approach derived from the methods of the human sciences.

A cultural, aesthetic-critical approach is particularly appropriate in cases of murder where the mass media have played a major role, not merely in reporting and commenting on the violent events in question, but in the circumstances leading up to these events. Besides lending themselves to media coverage, murders and suicides are frequently occasioned by the media. The most obvious example is the phenomenon of copycat killings in which a murderer or suicide victim imitates an incident that has been reported on the news, described in a novel, or portrayed in a film. The relative banality of such mimetic behavior stems from the fact that what is being imitated in most of these cases is not the motive of the murderer or suicide victim, which is often unknown and unreported, but merely the external manner and circumstances of the death—in short, its *style*. In cases of copycat violence, the media inadvertently assume Hedda's role; instead of murmuring "Do it beautifully" to the desperate reader or viewer, they simply hint "Do it sensationally, *like this*!" The arts have even been accused of literally voicing such messages: the sensational 1990 trial of CBS Records and the British heavy-metal group Judas Priest involved a multimillion-dollar lawsuit blaming the band for the deaths of two boys who shot themselves, apparently after listening to the album *Stained Class*. The boys' suicidal behavior, it was charged, had been provoked by a song on the album in which the subliminal command "Do it!" was allegedly repeated seven times.

Such instances of imitative violence are generally assumed to be a necessary evil of modern society where the mass media play such an unprecedented role. Yet the mass consumption of sensational poems, novels, and dramas was already under way in the eighteenth century. In *The Rise of the Novel*, Ian Watt refers to Samuel Richardson's "hostility to the epic," that prestigious genre which "afforded vicious models of individual behaviour."[17] A character in Richardson's novel *Sir Charles Grandison* (1753–54) asks, "would Alexander, madman as he was, have been so *much* a madman, had it not been for Homer? Of what violences, murders, depradations, have not the epic poets been the occasion, by propagating false honours, false glory, and false religion?"[18] But the sentimental genre of the novel was itself soon to prove an even more insidious behavioral model than the heroic genre of the epic. The suicide epidemic that followed the publication of Goethe's *The Sorrows of Young Werther* in 1774 is among the earliest, and one of the most well-documented, instances of this syndrome. Romantic writers of the first half of the nineteenth century have provided abundant evidence of their mimetic fascination with murder. Where authors like De Quincey, Stendhal, and Balzac based their criminal literature on actual murders, real-life murderers like Pierre-François Lacenaire and Jean-Baptiste Troppmann were inspired by their readings of popular romantic fiction, and they in turn provided fresh models for more of the same.[19]

More perplexing than the syndrome of murder modeled on the media (a special case of the general romantic tendency whereby life — *and* death — increasingly came to imitate art) is the characteristically postmodern phenomenon in which the mass media, by creating a "star," "idol," or "hero" for millions of adoring admirers, actually produce a potential victim for an alienated, anonymous individual. For such a person, the quest for identity may entail becoming an instant media-personality by taking a celebrity's life. The latter part of this study will explore some of the ways in which both fiction and the media impinge on actual instances of suicide, murder, and assassination. These cases are more readily understood — as opposed to being merely documented or diagnosed — in aesthetic terms as mimetic, imitative phenomena, rather than as socially, legally, or psychoanalytically defined aberrations.

The Aesthetics of Murder

You know how concerned people are about appearances—this is
attractive, that's not. Well, I've left that all behind me. I now do what
other people only dream. I make art until someone dies, see? I am
the world's first fully functioning homicidal artist.
                    —Jack Nicholson as the Joker in the 1989 film *Batman*

There are two ways that an object, idea, event, or act can achieve
artistic status. On the one hand, the object can be created, the idea
conceived, the event engineered, or the act performed by the artist
with the express intention of making it a work of art, whatever the
"artist" may mean or understand by "art." On the other hand, *any*
object or idea may be experienced or interpreted by a beholder (or witness, in the case of someone who is present at an event or an act) as
a work of art—again, according to whatever the beholder's definition
of "art" may be. The first alternative is *artistic,* and entails the artist's
production of an artifact. The second alternative is *aesthetic,* and refers
exclusively to the beholder's subjective experience, regardless of
whether or not the object of this experience was intended as a work of
art or designed for the beholder's aesthetic enjoyment. The object of
aesthetic contemplation need not be a work of art, or even a mere artifact. Indeed, what distinguishes eighteenth-century aesthetic theorists like Burke or Kant from their neoclassical predecessors is that
they virtually ignored man-made works of art, devoting their inquiries
instead to the experience of natural phenomena.

There is usually no discrepancy between the artistic and the aesthetic modes, which explains why these terms are commonly used
interchangeably. A painting created by an artist will generally be recognized and appreciated (or not appreciated) as a work of art (good or
bad). Painters, and especially photographers, routinely convert their
aesthetic experiences of nature into art objects that in turn elicit aesthetic responses in those who see them. Yet it is not difficult to imagine situations in which the artistic and aesthetic modes will be totally
at odds with one another. Children and self-proclaimed, would-be
artists impose their handiwork on us and demand that we accept it as
art; even if we acquiesce in their demand, we do so with a certain dis-

honesty, knowingly betraying our aesthetic judgment. Alternatively, it is not uncommon for us to experience objects and places aesthetically that were hardly intended to be regarded in this way; we may even be more likely to view something as beautiful when we feel there is no compelling reason to do so. When we experience a natural scene aesthetically, we respond to nature as if it were a work of art. We do this in spite (indeed, because) of our awareness that nature, by definition, is not art, and was not intended to be art—unless, of course, we stretch our definitions and consider God, as the creator of the natural world, to be an artist Himself. And if "natural" phenomena can be experienced as if they were art, it ought to be possible to experience certain "nonnatural" phenomena as art, since art by definition is itself unnatural.

The possibility of experiencing aspects of the world aesthetically, even (or especially) when they are not intended to be experienced this way, has important implications. Tranquil natural landscapes—sunlit fields and babbling brooks—can be experienced aesthetically and rendered artistically, to be sure, but so, for that matter, can turbulent, life-threatening natural cataclysms—hurricanes, earthquakes, fires, and floods—that overwhelm us with their magnitude and their devastating power. When the classical discipline of art theory began to give way in the late eighteenth century to the new philosophy of aesthetics, thinkers found it necessary to reconsider the experience of the sublime—a rhetorical and stylistic concept that dated back to Longinus in the first century A.D., which the neoclassical theorist Boileau had treated as a matter of artistic form rather than of formlessness, and of aesthetic pleasure rather than of aesthetic pain.[20] The new aesthetic theorists took painful as well as pleasurable perceptions into consideration. In the *Scienza nuova* (1725, rev. 1730, 1744), Vico presented the experience of sublimity as a formative cultural experience that was inseparably linked to the primitive feeling of fear: "it was fear which created gods in the world; not fear awakened in men by other men, but fear awakened in men by themselves."[21] Several decades later, Burke associated "the ideas of pain, and danger" with the sublime, which far exceeded the beautiful in its effect on the observer because "the ideas of pain are much more powerful than those which enter on the part of pleasure."[22] At a time when Enlightenment thinkers like the American authors of the "Declaration of Independence" were proclaiming "the pursuit of Happiness" to be man's natural right, Burke discerned what Ernst Cassirer has described as "a source of pure aesthetic enjoyment which is strictly distinguished from the mere desire for happiness, from the striving for enjoyment, and from the satisfaction of finite ends: 'a sort of delight full of horror, a sort of tranquillity tinged with terror.'"[23] As a source of aesthetic pleasure, the beautiful was conceived by Burke as a social, civilizing principle of unity, cohesion, and morality, while the sublime was rooted in a primal impulse of self-preservation that was intrinsically amoral and antisocial.

In the *Critique of Judgment*, Kant raised Burke's empirical and psychological account of the sublime and the beautiful to the level of speculative philosophy; henceforth, the critical distinction between the sublime and the beautiful would dominate discussions of aesthetics. Yet once natural violence was considered as a possible source of aesthetic experience, what was to prevent human violence, which inspired perhaps even greater terror, from making aesthetic claims as well? Why shouldn't the malevolence and the inscrutable purpose of the murderer—the heir of Cain, the transgressor of the sixth commandment—be capable of stirring us with awe? If any human act evokes the aesthetic experience of the sublime, certainly it is the act of murder. And if murder can be experienced aesthetically, the murderer can in turn be regarded as a kind of artist—a performance artist or antiartist whose specialty is not creation but destruction.

Burke had certainly been aware of this possibility, as shown by his example of the sensation caused by public executions. Kant's transcendental approach to aesthetics, in contrast, located the source of the sublime in humanity's moral-rational nature; violent upheavals in physical nature, and especially human acts of violence, are virtually left out of the discussion. Such acts do not illustrate the sublime, but rather the "monstrous": "An object is *monstrous* if, by its size [or "enormity"], it destroys the purpose which constitutes the concept of it";[24] ("*Ungeheuer* ist ein Gegenstand, wenn er durch seine Grösse den Zweck, der den Begriff desselben ausmacht, vernichtet"). Even war must be purified of violence and become gentlemanly—it must be "carried on with order and with a sacred respect for the rights of citizens"[25] —before it can be considered sublime. It is as if Kant could only sublimate aesthetics from Burke's empirical psychology to the domain of transcendental philosophy by limiting the occasion of sublime experience to encounters with "rude nature"[26] ("an der rohen Natur"), and by excluding from consideration human acts of premeditated violence such as executions and murders, or social upheavals such as the revolutionary reign of terror that was getting under way in France at the very time that the third critique appeared. Where Kant could argue that encounters with nature's power and magnitude could lead individuals to an awareness of their higher moral-rational being, acts of violence committed by man against man, or man against woman, or man against nature, would only reveal human nature to be intrinsically vicious and morally corrupt.

Of those philosophically inclined writers of the romantic era such as Schiller and Coleridge who tried to come to terms with Kant's moral-rational aesthetics, none exposed the contradictions inherent in this approach as compellingly as De Quincey. For it was he who brought Kant's concept of the natural sublime to its "logical" conclusion in the spectacle of murder. In his 1827 "Murder" essay, De Quincey jested that the most brutal killings can be appreciated as works of art if only they are viewed from an aesthetic, or disinterested, amoral perspective. De Quincey's outrageous idea that, under the appropriate conditions, cold-blooded murder can achieve artistic legitimacy has been viewed by most readers as a curious, but minor, example of rhetorical and artistic virtuosity. Taken together with its sequel of 1839, and "Postscript" of 1854, however, and viewed from a broader, cultural perspective, the essay "On Murder" has a far greater significance. It constitutes a sustained satiric critique of a philosophical tradition epitomized by Kant that consistently assumed a coherent, nonproblematic relation between ethics and aesthetics, and within the latter domain, between the experiential forms of the beautiful and the sublime. By treating murder as an art form, De Quincey demonstrated the aesthetic subversion of the beautiful by the sublime, and more generally, the philosophical subversion of ethics by aesthetics. Where De Quincey in the "Murder" essays set forth these disjunctions in an ironic mode, subsequent writers would not be so ambiguous. They would maintain with complete seriousness the incommensurability of ethics and aesthetics.[27] Insofar as he raised a host of aesthetic problems in the course of lampooning Kant's moral philosophy, De Quincey unwittingly (and, we must suppose, unwillingly) pointed the way toward Nietzsche's full-blown aesthetic critique of morality in general later in the century.

Fourteen years after De Quincey's first "Murder" essay, Poe developed in his tale "The Murders in the Rue Morgue" what Dennis Porter calls "the fine art of murder" into the "fine art of detection," thereby laying the foundations for the modern genre of detective fiction.[28] In Poe's "tales of ratiocination," the detective rather than the criminal emerges as the artist-hero. The tremendous popularity of this genre has had the unfortunate effect of overshadowing De Quincey's earlier experiment in criminal literature in which the murderer was portrayed as an artist and murder as an art form. It is understandable that this treatment of murder should fall by the wayside when we consider that literary works exemplifying such an aesthetic were bound to seem idiosyncratic and irrational in contrast to the rational, bourgeois ideology of detective fiction. Yet as absurd (or as daring) as the doctrine of the aesthetics of murder may appear in the writings of De Quincey, it has continued to be explored and exploited by an international tradition of modern writers and filmmakers. In their work, the classical idea of mimesis—the view that art is in some sense an imitation of nature or a representation of reality—is subverted to the point where being and appearance, ethics and aesthetics, are no longer distinguishable, but have become virtual simulacra of each other. Already in the 1930s, the critic Walter Benjamin reflected on the expansion of "mimetic activity" beyond specifically artistic endeavors to include every aspect of human behavior,[29] theorized about the violent origins of the law,[30] repudiated the fascist program to aestheticize politics, and called attention to the shift from an aesthetic of representation to one of reproduction in the new, "realistic" medium of film.[31] Indeed, as a medium that consists of a series of "shots," and whose technology is directly related to the development of automatic weaponry,[32] the cinema takes the mimetic duplicity and the aesthetic violence of the literary medium to its logical extreme.

Alfred Hitchcock's films provide the most obvious examples of the degree to which the cinematic medium exploits the specifically artistic dimension of murder.[33] His successors Martin Scorsese and Brian De Palma use the conventional doubling devices of film to simulate and expose the pathological fantasies of voyeurs, kidnappers, and murderers. In doing so, they call attention to the similarities between their "artistic" activity as filmmakers and the fantasy-lives of their sociopathic subjects. Moviemakers and murderers are often obsessed with the manipulation of fantasies via the mass media. The "psychopathic" murderer or hostage-taker who seems to have no control over his own actions may actually have absolute control over a situation he has set in motion and he alone understands; similarly, the film-director organizes the chaos of his own fantasy-life and the "group fantasies" of society— indeed, the two are ultimately indistinguishable[34]—through sheer artistic discipline. (With respect to the sexual fantasies and obsessions that deprive his characters of their self-control, De Palma has actually defined the artistic task of the film-director as "taking control" of this play of fantasy.)[35] Both the terrorist-killer and the film-director know how to manipulate the media and how to play on the fantasies and the fears of their mass audience, and they are profoundly aware of the effect their actions will have on their enthralled spectators. We are all too familiar with the process whereby murderers, assassins, and especially terrorists deliberately play up their actions for the press, often teasing a horrified population with speculations about their motives, intentions, and where they will strike next; is this much different from the way film-directors anticipate the reactions of their critics? At a time when "reality" is mediated to an unprecedented degree by the visual mass media, both the murderer and the film-director seize control of the arbitrary mechanism of fantasy, the differential principle governing the fundamental cultural distinction between the real and the nonreal.

The Politics of Murder

Politics in the midst of imaginative activity is like a pistol shot in the middle of a concert.

—Stendhal, *Red and Black*

It is a great shame we can forbid these bleedings in art but not in life.
    —Angela Carter, *The Sadeian Woman and the Ideology of Pornography*

From a cultural perspective, murder is interesting because it is so unsettling; it destroys any idealistic illusions we may cherish about the type of society in which we live. The Edenic myth of the "Great Good Place," of "an innocent society in a state of grace . . . where there is no need of the law, no contradiction between the aesthetic individual and ethical universal," is, as Auden has suggested, precisely what is shattered by the act of murder, the crime that originated with the first man to be born. For "murder is the act of disruption by which innocence is lost" and "the aesthetic and the ethical are [put] in opposition."[36] Murder drives a wedge into our comforting belief that things are what they seem, that the world is as it ought to be, that reality and appearance, ethics and aesthetics, are seamless, compatible realms.

The assassin Brutus's meditation in Shakespeare's *Julius Caesar*—"Between the acting of a dreadful thing / And the first motion, all the interim is / Like a hideous dream"—is even more true for society at large than it is for the individual. The "hideous dream" becomes most apparent whenever a radical attempt is made to transform a visionary ideal into a social reality. "Every act of rebellion," Camus observed, "expresses a nostalgia for innocence and an appeal to the essence of being. But one day nostalgia takes up arms and assumes the responsibility of total guilt; in other words, adopts murder and violence."[37] Even postrevolutionary societies, founded on the democratic ideals of the Enlightenment and officially condemning murder as uncivilized barbarism, unofficially rely on violence to implement many of their policies. As Sade and other social rebels have insisted, murder is regularly practiced by the most democratic states in a variety of "legal" forms—capital punishment, open warfare, covert and mercenary operations, military advice and assistance to allied nations and friendly rebel forces. Euthanasia and abortion are regarded by their opponents as legalized murder; yet American conservatives and fundamentalists, whose opposition to abortion is based on their belief in the "sanctity of life," find no contradiction in the fact that many of them support the death penalty, which is condemned by *its* opponents as legalized murder.[38]

What accounts for the fact that some forms of killing are regarded as socially acceptable, and even as morally sanctioned, while others are condemned as outrageous crimes? What determines the difference between the two?

The distinction between permissible and punishable killing is particularly problematic because it cannot be decided on strictly rational grounds. The most vicious and dangerous killers often act in an entirely logical, programmatic manner. "Not unlike its counterpart in organized political terrorism," write Jack Levin and James Alan Fox, "a mass slaying typically involves death and destruction as part of a killer's program of action."[39] But the authors contend that a similar "program of action" lay behind Truman's decision to drop "not one but two atomic bombs, causing instantaneous death or terminal illness for hundreds of thousands of Japanese. It ended the war, a war which we won; therefore, he was a hero. Had the bombings escalated the war instead, Truman might have been considered a lunatic." Levin and Fox conclude that "we judge the rationality of acts by their outcomes—their rewards and consequences."[40]

Such retrospective judgment of the rationality or irrationality— and therefore the legitimacy or illegitimacy—of mass killing is the province of the historian, a circumstance that prompted Michel Foucault to treat murder as the singular, decisive, but undecidable act that gives rise to cultural distinctions and to the historical narratives that organize cultural experience.

> When all is said and done, battles simply stamp the mark of history on nameless slaughters, while narrative makes the stuff of history from mere street brawls. The frontier between the two is perpetually crossed. It is crossed in the case of an event of prime interest— murder. Murder is where history and crime intersect. Murder it is that makes for the warrior's immortality (they kill, they order killings, they themselves accept the risk of death); murder it is that ensures criminals their dark renown (by shedding blood, they have accepted the risk of the scaffold). Murder establishes the ambiguity of the lawful and the unlawful.[41]

Where Auden regarded murder as the act that puts ethics and aesthetics in opposition to each other, Foucault claims that "murder" is the primal event that both compels and enables us to distinguish between "the historical and the everyday," between battles as the "stuff of history" and street brawls as the milieu of crime. Either in broadsheets or newsflashes, in histories or literary works, in courtroom transcripts or prison memoirs, murders are presented to the general public in the mediated form of "narratives of crime" which "magnify the two faces of murder"—the lawful and the unlawful, the heroic and the criminal, the historic and the quotidian. Foucault accounts for the public's ongoing fascination with narratives of crime, not on the grounds that such narratives provide a constant source of entertainment and escapist thrills, but on the premise that they impart some fundamental knowledge about human existence: "their universal success obviously shows the desire to know and narrate how men have been able to rise against power, traverse the law, and expose themselves to death through death."[42]

Since public executions are no longer staged as they were in Edmund Burke's time, modern audiences avail themselves of the essential knowledge that murder imparts through their exposure to simulations of violent death as performed in theaters or displayed in film. (The literal-minded can still gratify themselves with images of actual slayings depicted in "snuff" films.) Democratic societies continue to execute their worst offenders, but well out of the public eye. In 1989, however, the public broadcast of videotapes depicting secret executions emerged as an ethical and political issue. Romanian revolutionaries decided to allow a videotape of the Christmas execution of dictator Nicolae Ceausescu to be televised as a way of appeasing the vengeful populace. Earlier in the year, Lebanese terrorists sent U.S. officials a videotape of an American colonel whom they claimed to have just executed. The tape was carefully edited before being shown on television news programs. The unedited tape was accessible only to military experts who, in the manner of art historians, attempted to determine when the tape was made and whether the execution was real or fake. (They were able to confirm the victim's identity, and even that the execution was staged—"Just from the video, there's enough to tell the body didn't die from hanging," reported one State Department official[43]—but they failed to learn the really crucial information:

when the death had occurred.) The scrutiny of death was left, in any case, to the professionals; the general public was only permitted to glimpse individual frames of the tape on the evening news so that the faked hanging would appear even less "lifelike." Officially, the act of taking another person's life, either as a crime or a punishment, can be represented only as an artistic fiction or simulation. In this guise, murder is no longer a social reality; it has been neutralized and tamed as a supposedly harmless form of popular entertainment.

Although American society may be overexposed to what Lou Reed calls "video violence" in the form of popular, highly profitable, commercial entertainment, it is relatively sheltered from images of actual violence. It is especially kept in the dark about images that could compromise national policy initiatives, as in graphic depictions of the savagery committed in the 1980s by right-wing El Salvadoran death squads against innocent *campesinos*. Such "politically sensitive" video violence was documented by European filmmakers and aired on European television, but was unacceptable to the mainstream American media, which nevertheless have few scruples about representing depoliticized, fake violence for the purpose of boosting movie revenues and attracting television advertisers.

It is one thing to find the media's exploitation of simulated violence to be merely tasteless; it is something else when scientific studies conclude that violence shown on television leads to increased social mayhem. In the aftermath of a mass murder or some other sensational slaughter, restrictions on the media's portrayal of violence are as likely, if not more likely, to be demanded as measures for tougher gun control. But as the comedian George Carlin has quipped, it is absurd to deal with the problem of handguns by banning the sale of toy guns and keeping the real thing. Citizens who are truly concerned about the rise of violent crime would do better to lobby in support of gun control than to ban simulated representations of violence. No one has proposed eliminating the bloody image of the crucifix from Christian iconology because it might induce believers to enact this style of killing, although Jorge Luis Borges's story "The Gospel According to Mark" has suggested this very possibility.[44] The problem with claiming that violent representations promote actual outbreaks of violence was most dramatically illustrated by the Ayatollah Khomeini's call, several months before his own death in 1989, for the assassination of the novelist Salman Rushdie, author of *The Satanic Verses*—an allegedly blasphemous treatment of the Islamic religion. Where Western critics of the media condemn literary and cinematic fictions for promoting violence, the Ayatollah insisted upon violence as the only legitimate response to Rushdie's novel.

There is a curious logic in blaming the media for encouraging violent acts like murder. After all, the arts have been licensed as the domain where crime is representable and socially acceptable; any increase in social violence would suggest that the media and the arts have abused their privilege by setting a bad example for their viewers. Rather than go on debating whether the media actually promote violence, however, we ought to ask why the media are regularly *suspected* of promoting violence, a question that concerns the politics of representation. Blaming the arts and the media for violence in the streets provides an ideal diversion behind which unscrupulous state officials and corporate executives can practice their white-collar improprieties with impunity. During the Reagan administration, the nation's top law officer, Attorney General Edwin Meese III, waged a sweeping public campaign against pornography, based on allegations that explicit sexual representations in the media lead to an increase in violent crime.[45] Meese's interest in making a national, highly visible issue of a domestic problem like pornography is understandable when we recall his own involvement in a number of illegal, but largely invisible, activities both at home and abroad.[46] The war on pornography, the war on terrorism, the war on drugs—all these carefully planned "media wars" against sensational criminal activities have served government and business interests by diverting public attention from any "violations of the government ethics code," as white-collar crimes have come to be euphemized.

As was customary during Reagan's presidency, the regulation of representations—and hence of public perceptions—took precedence over the prior and tougher task of combating actual social problems. The decisions of the Supreme Court during the Bush administration have continued this tendency: while protecting such symbolic practices as pornography and flag-burning, they have worked to undo existing decisions on such substantive issues as civil rights and abortion. Executive and congressional policies such as those of the Meese Commission or the 1989 Helms amendment to bar federal spending on "obscene and indecent" art take a more direct approach. Assuming a link between images of explicit sexual activity and acts like molestation, rape, and murder, these policies blame the media for social violence, and seek to cleanse all images of their sexual content.[47] Right-wing iconoclasm of this sort is ultimately directed toward what Susan Stewart has called a pure "sexuality freed from representation":[48] besides limiting social violence, the suppression of sexual imagery would supposedly purify sex once and for all by rendering it altogether invisible. But we should bear in mind that such "visionary" policies always have a more immediate, diversionary purpose. In the 1990s, as Tom Mathews observes, "politicians who have found it hard to account for the HUD scandals and the S&L mess will strike heroic postures demanding accountability from artists and their small agency [the National Endowment for the Arts]."[49]

Political media strategists have made it unnecessary, however, for conservative interest groups to blame the liberal arts and the liberal (and libertine) media for the real or perceived rise of social violence. Although they cannot control the media as in authoritarian societies, democratic governments are capable of manipulating news broadcasts in ways that make state-sanctioned killings appear not only legal but heroic. The Vietnam war was brought to an end in large part because the American public was appalled by the bombings and atrocities televised evening after evening on the news. The problem posed by the media's negative coverage of U.S. military intervention abroad was solved in the 1980s under the administration of a president whose former experience as an actor in the movies and a salesman on television commercials gave him an intuitive understanding of the mass media. As president, Reagan's answer to Kennedy's Cuba and Johnson's Vietnam was Grenada—a tiny Caribbean resort island that was invaded in October 1983, ostensibly in order to "rescue" a group of American medical students who were alleged to be in imminent danger of being taken hostage in the aftermath of a left-wing coup.

What otherwise had the appearance of a grade-B Hollywood screen-play—the cavalry galloping to the rescue in the nick of time—was different in one key respect: no reporters or cameramen were on hand to record the invasion, which was already over by the time it became "news." Any way it is seen, Grenada was less a military victory than a media success. It was a piece of cosmetic violence that was staged largely for the purpose of downplaying the truly devastating violence that had occurred two days earlier in Beirut when 230 U.S. Marines were killed in a terrorist attack. The media triumph of Grenada was followed by the surprise air attack on Libya and the downing of Libyan jet fighters in the Mediterranean. Such hit-and-run encounters became media coups precisely because of the media's absence. The possibility of negative press coverage was eliminated because the strikes were virtually over before they began. Repeatedly during the Reagan administration, the role of the news media was limited from investigative or even eye-witness journalism to the dutiful transmission of official government versions of world events.[50] (By the time of the 1991 war in the Persian Gulf, unprecedented restrictions were imposed on the news media's access to combat sites—with the approval of most Americans. The officially sanctioned images of the war were provided by the U.S. military in the form of aerial videos of Iraqi targets being approached by camera-guided "smart" weapons. In contrast, pictures taken by Western news reporters on the ground of civilian casualties resulting from American air raids were denounced by media critics as enemy propaganda.)

Reagan's Achilles' heel as a media-celebrity, however, became evident only three months into his presidency, when he was the victim of an assassination attempt that was not politically motivated (as in the case of the Kennedy killings of the 1960s), but media-motivated. The most dramatic instances of media-related crimes are those in which a lone individual—a John Hinckley, Jr., or a Mark David Chapman—becomes obsessed with a movie he has seen or a book he has read, and proceeds to commit a sensational act of violence such as an assassination or a multiple murder. It would be absurd to hold *Taxi Driver* and *The Catcher in the Rye* responsible for their key role in Hinckley's and Chapman's actions. Both the film and the novel have a legitimate artistic value that cannot be discounted by a single individual's aberrant reaction. That reaction needs to be studied and accounted for, however, so that we may learn what specific cultural conditions help to bring about such media-related killings. Is the individual in these cases really a psycho- or sociopath who mistakes fantasy for reality, fiction for fact, art for action? Or should we regard him rather as an artistic illiterate who is unable to recognize the figural and fictive suspension from the real that art entails? Might such an individual even be a rigorous realist or supreme literalist who detects a deeper reality hidden beneath the veil of art, and who responds by iconoclastically tearing away those media-mediated appearances that bear no relation to the real? In the postindustrial, postmodern society of the late twentieth century, where violence is routinely sublimated into art and where almost every aspect of reality has been thoroughly aestheticized by advertising and the mass media, the criminal sociopath may be the individual who desperately tries to see the world as it "really" is, in all its unsublimated, sublime violence. Artistic representations of slayings provide fictional displacements or simulacra of the act of murder for everyone except the artistically illiterate. Such persons are unable to recognize art as art, not simply because they live in a private world of make-believe fantasy, or because they have not received the proper "aesthetic education," but because they are absolute Realists who find no truth or meaning whatsoever either in their own private fantasies (the Imaginary) or in the collective fantasies of art and the media (the Symbolic). Having been deprived access to, or having simply denied, the aesthetics of violence that socially adjusted individuals routinely employ and enjoy but hardly ever acknowledge, the Realist only has access to an ethics of murder—murder as a code or principle of action.

The analysis in the second half of this study of John Lennon's assassination by Chapman in December 1980, and its relation to Hinckley's attempted assassination of President Reagan three months later, is an attempt to understand these murderous acts as culturally conditioned, media-related events. The role of Martin Scorsese and Paul Schrader's 1976 film *Taxi Driver* in Hinckley's assassination attempt has been well-documented. But the subsequent films of Scorsese and Schrader suggest that both filmmakers were themselves responding in their respective ways to Hinckley's "crime": Scorsese's *King of Comedy* (1982) explores the phenomenon of mimetic doubling at length, while Schrader's *Mishima* (1985) employs a complex interplay of the literary and cinematic media to reconstruct the celebrated Japanese author's suicidal enterprise to transform his life into a work of art.

The mimetic interplay between life and art, between actual violence and images of violence, is pertinent to the experience of a particular sort of murderer—the voyeur who "likes to watch" from his or her own private vantage. Book-readers and movie-goers who turn to the artistic media in order to escape what they experience as a vapid, meaningless existence tend to be white, middle-class youths who may then turn against the media's heroes in a desperate attempt to create an identity and a sense of reality for themselves. In contrast to these relatively passive killers, black gang-members in the ghetto, mass murderers, and artists like Mishima who "stage" their own suicide are typically active, demonstrative exhibitionists whose "work" can be regarded as an extreme form of performance art. Such acts are cathartic rituals of purification and martyrdom whereby the artist seeks to leave the world behind, not by escaping into some media-fiction, but by transcending a world that is itself perceived to be trapped in the mimetic, media-mediated play of simulacra. From Hedda to Mishima, the artistic endeavor to "do it beautifully" takes the form of an act of violence no longer directed outwardly toward others as murder, but inwardly toward the self—the supreme Illusion upon which all other illusions are founded.

P   A   R   T

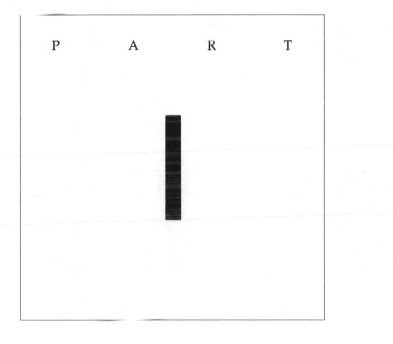

ONE

MURDER AS (FINE) ART

Once that you've decided on a killing
First you make a stone of your heart
And if you can find that your hands are still willing
Then you can turn a murder into art.
—The Police, "Murder by Numbers"

A Portrait of the Criminal as Artist

Murder is as fashionable a crime as a man can be guilty of.
—Peachum, in John Gay's The Beggar's Opera (1728)

There is no essential incongruity between crime and culture.
—Oscar Wilde, "Pen, Pencil, and Poison" (1889)

From its beginnings, literature has been concerned with crime. The founding texts of both Judeo-Christian and Greco-Roman culture deal with violations of the law. The Old Testament begins with the stories of Adam and Eve, eating the forbidden fruit in Eden, and of their sons who became the first murderer and murder victim. The Homeric epics weave together such legends associated with the Trojan War as the abduction of Helen, the occupation of Odysseus' home by the suitors, and the murder of Agamemnon by his wife. The greatest crime story in the classical world may well be the legend of Oedipus; however, his tragedy consists less in his role as criminal—after all, his crimes of incest and patricide were ordained by fate and were committed unknowingly—than in his role as detective.

All these characters, engaged in their various legendary crimes, have a common quality: they appear to the reader as figures who are larger than life. Dennis Porter has observed that the violent crimes

29

described in ancient literature tend to "occur in a context defined by the sacred" where they "have the unexpungeable character of sins or of transgressions against a superhuman order."[1] This kind of "mythic crime" committed by demonic, superhuman characters at first seems to be of a very different order than the secularized transgressions that we begin to find in works of literature from the eighteenth century onward; such "profane crime" involves more or less average men and women, and "is quasi-political in character."[2] Nevertheless, some of these later figures retain traces of the awesome power of their literary ancestors. In Laurence Senelick's words, "the romantics seized upon the criminal as one of the few legendary types who could be related to nineteenth-century life. Satan, Faust, Ahasuerus were all very well as mythical prototypes, but their discrepancy with modern society led to effects that were more often grotesque or comic than sublime."[3] The figure of the criminal is all that remains in the modern age of the sacred and demonic characters of the age of myth.

Cultural historians agree about dating the modern phenomenon of crime from the late eighteenth century and finding its first literary appearance during the romantic era. "To speak of crime in our modern generic sense before the eighteenth century is in itself to be guilty of an anachronism," writes Porter.[4] And what Albert Camus has called "metaphysical rebellion," or crimes committed as deliberate acts of protest against the human condition, "does not appear, in coherent form, in the history of ideas until the end of the eighteenth century—when modern times begin to the accompaniment of the crash of falling ramparts."[5] The eighteenth-century connection between literature and crime is particularly significant when we consider that the modern concept of "literature" itself—of literature as *art*—also dates from this period. This coincidence hints at what may be modern art's own inherently criminal mode of existence.

The romantics introduced the modern idea of literature as an autonomous art form.[6] No longer feeling himself bound to formal conventions or literary traditions, the romantic poet could indulge in artistic license as a way of declaring his uniqueness and his exemption from conventional morality as encoded in human law. As Shelley's "unacknowledged legislators of the world," poets were the spokespersons of divine and eternal truths in contrast to merely profane and temporal law, which they felt at liberty to scorn in their art and sometimes spurn in their acts.

This recognition of literature's artistic autonomy—the romantic author's self-image as someone whose detachment from human laws and conventions gave him privileged access to supermundane realms—dialectically coincided with society's recognition of the author as a mundane, social being. The introduction of copyright laws in the late eighteenth century established the legal identity of individual literary works as well as the institutional identity of literature itself. Michel Foucault has drawn attention to the emergence of these laws that ostensibly protected the author by authorizing him as the owner of his literary "property." The law cuts both ways, however, and the new copyright regulations not only protected the author, but also marked him as a potential criminal who was himself liable not only for plagiarism, but for any other crimes that could be attributed to his work. The emergence of literature as an institution and of writing as a profession has prompted Foucault's claim that it was toward the end of the eighteenth century that "the transgressive properties always intrinsic to the act of writing became the forceful imperative of literature."[7] When literature came into its own as a transgressive medium—as a system of language ownership, and as the fully self-reflective use of language to test the limits of human self-expression—it is not surprising that a recurring theme in this new art form should prove to be crime. The romantic apotheosis of the criminal in literature was symptomatic of literature's own emergence in the romantic period as a social institution and as a professional vocation that was perceived as being inherently transgressive and potentially insurrectionary.

Actually, the modern literary figure of the criminal was less the creation of individual authors endowed with an inflated sense of their own identity, or of new legislation that accorded literature unprecedented social prestige and legal liability, than it was a product of the popular media. As early as the fifteenth century, the deeds of murderers, their confessions, and accounts of their executions had been sung by itinerant bards as newspaper songs. The eventual rise of literacy among the masses and the development of cheaper printing techniques made it possible to broadcast news about crimes in flyers and pamphlets. As the traditional medium in which sensational crimes, trials, and executions were reported to the populace, the broadsheets belonged to a lyrical genre that Foucault has called the "song of murder." "In these strange poems the guilty man was depicted coming forward to rehearse his deed to his hearers; he gave a brief outline of his life, drew the lessons of his adventure, expressed his remorse, and at the very moment of dying invoked pity and terror." The songs of crime were "intended to travel from singer to singer; everyone is presumed able to sing it as his own crime, by a lyrical fiction." In this manner, a new kind of subject was constituted, "a subject who both speaks and is murderous." Foucault emphasizes that the murderer's song which was heard and echoed by the general public hardly consisted of the guilty individual's own words. Rather, the "lyrical position of the murderous subject" was "defined from outside it by those responsible for composing the fly sheets."[8]

Once the popular media had constituted the criminal as a subliterary, lyrical subject through their accounts of actual crimes, writers could develop this figure into a full-fledged literary subject. The ballads about infamous outlaws sung at German fairs, and the confessions made by criminals to the prison chaplains at Newgate who then turned these chronicles or "calendars" to their own profit, were succeeded by collections of famous criminal trials like the *Causes célèbres et intéressantes* of François Gayot de Pitaval—"that Enlightenment police gazette," as Theodore Ziolkowski calls it, which began to appear in 1734 and which, in its later expanded versions, inspired generations of writers with a penchant for crime.[9] The early pamphlets of prison confessions were subsequently bound in deluxe editions like *The Newgate Calendar* and *The Tyburn Chronicle*, which in turn were refashioned into the nineteenth-century Newgate novel.[10] John Gay's *The Beggar's Opera* (1728) and Henry Fielding's *Jonathan Wild, The Great* (1743) were both based on the deeds of the most notorious criminal of the time.[11] Wild (1683–1724) brilliantly manipulated London's corrupt criminal justice system in which official posts were bought and sold, virtually any theft was a capital offense, and (after 1706) informers were not only pardoned but offered a forty pound reward. As "Thief-

Taker General of Great Britain and Ireland," Wild made a fortune by blackmailing and "peaching" thieves, as well as running a "Lost Property Office" out of the Old Bailey itself![12]

At least since the 1730s, reports of criminal trials were diligently recorded and avidly read by general audiences without any legal training.[13] A century later such reports, interspersed with sensational fiction, filled the new Sunday newspapers in England, a feature that increased their circulation beyond that of the daily papers.[14] Criminal reporting came into its own as a legitimate literary genre in the nineteenth century in response to "a more refined public taste for crime."[15] But journalistic and literary treatments of crime did not always lend themselves readily to each other. Thomas De Quincey's taste proved to be less than refined during his brief term as editor of the *Westmorland Gazette*; his policy of filling this journal with reports of sex cases and murder trials taken from the assize court news led to his dismissal in 1819, but served him well in his subsequent "Murder" essays. Where readers found the *Westmorland Gazette* too sensational under De Quincey's direction, Stendhal found fault with the *Gazette des Tribinaux*, a journal founded in the 1820s that reported notable law cases in France, for its stylistic banality. It was in this journal that Stendhal came upon the case in 1827 of a young peasant named Antoine Berthet who became a tutor and then a seminarian, and who later shot his employer's wife; this story became the basis for *Le Rouge et le Noir* (1831).

So refined had the public taste for crime become by the mid-nineteenth century that it was the subject of "long cosy talks together over the fire" between the Puritan zoologist Philip Gosse and his eight-year-old son Edmund at Devonshire during the winter of 1857-58. "Our favourite subject was murders," the younger Gosse was to remember, wondering whether it was usual for boys his age, "soon to go upstairs alone at night," to "discuss violent crime with a widower-papa."[16] The fact that a pious Creationist like the elder Gosse regularly engaged in fireside chats with his son on such sensational matters suggests that murder may actually have been a much more prevalent topic of domestic discussion than Edmund imagined.

From a man of the people whose public execution was announced to the uneducated masses in pamphlets and broadsheets much as playbills announce a forthcoming theatrical spectacle, the criminal was endowed with "heroic stature" in "fiction with pretenses to art, fiction aimed at an educated readership."[17] As a vestige of the mythical past in the profane present, the criminal became an elite member of the privileged class. His subtle exploits and eventual apprehension by an equally subtle detective gave birth to what Foucault called "a whole new literature of crime":

> a literature in which crime is glorified, because it is one of the fine arts, because it can be the work only of exceptional natures, because it reveals the monstrousness of the strong and powerful, because villainy is yet another mode of privilege: from the adventure story to de Quincey [sic], or from the *Castle of Otranto* to Baudelaire, there is a whole aesthetic rewriting of crime, which is also the appropriation of the criminal in acceptable forms. In appearance, it is the discovery of the beauty and greatness of crime; in fact, it is the affirmation that greatness too has a right to crime and that it even becomes the exclusive privilege of those who are really great.[18]

Foucault's references to "the discovery of the beauty and greatness of crime" and to greatness's "right to crime" echo Georges Bataille's insight into the close relation between transgression and the sacred, which itself harks back to Sade's extreme valorization of the romantic recognition of the criminal's poetic power. But it was De Quincey who, in his 1827 essay "On Murder Considered as One of the Fine Arts," provided a quasi-philosophical rationale for homicide, suggesting in a half-serious vein that this crime may evoke a feeling of sublimity so long as it is a disinterested, malevolent act. Murder loses its claim on the aesthetic judgment if the assailant acts out of petty self-interest, as in the case of robbery, or if the victim turns out to be a thief or a killer himself instead of a helpless innocent.

> I could mention some people (I name no names) who have been murdered by other people in a dark lane; and so far all seemed correct enough; but, on looking further into the matter, the public have become aware that the murdered party was himself, at the moment, planning to rob his murderer, at the least, and possibly to murder him, if he had been strong enough. Whenever that is the case, or

may be thought to be the case, farewell to all the genuine effects of the art. (13:47)

De Quincey was not the first to advance the daring idea that murder could be considered a legitimate art form. He could have come across the idea in an essay by Friedrich Schiller—one of his favorite authors—entitled "Gedanken über den Gebrauch des Gemeinen und Niedrigen in der Kunst" ("Reflections on the Use of the Vulgar and the Lowly in Works of Art," 1802), in which theft is judged aesthetically to be a more base act than murder:

> Ein Mensch, der stiehlt, würde demnach für jede poetische Darstellung von ernsthaftem Inhalt ein höchst verwerfliches Object seyn. Wird aber dieser Mensch zugleich *Mörder* so ist er zwar *moralisch* noch viel verwerflicher; aber *aesthetisch* wird er dadurch wieder um einen Grad brauchbarer. Derjenige der sich (ich rede hier immer nur von der ästhetischen Beurtheilungsweise) durch eine *Infamie* erniedrigt, kann durch ein *Verbrechen* wieder in etwas erhöht und in unsre *ästhetische* Achtung restituirt werden.

> A man who robs would always be an object to be rejected by the poet who wishes to present serious pictures. But suppose this man is at the same time a murderer, he is even more to be condemned than before by the *moral* law. But in the aesthetic judgment he is raised one degree higher and made better adapted to figure in a work of art. Continuing to judge him from an aesthetic point of view, it may be added that he who abased himself by a *vile* action can to a certain extent be raised by a *crime,* and can be thus reinstated in our *aesthetic* estimation.[19]

Shortly before this essay appeared, a friend of Schiller's on a visit to St. Petersburg came into possession of a copy of the manuscript of Diderot's *Le Neveu de Rameau* (composed around 1761, but as yet unpublished) in the Hermitage. The copy was delivered to Schiller, and translated by Goethe as *Rameaus Neffe* (1805). At one point in Diderot's dialogue the nephew remarks:

> S'il importe d'être sublime en quelque genre, c'est surtout en mal. On crache sur un petit filou; mais on ne peut refuser une sorte de considération à un grand criminel. Son courage vous étonne. Son atrocité vous fait frémir.

> If it is important to be sublime in anything, it is especially so in evil. You spit on a petty thief, but you can't withhold a sort of respect from a great criminal. His courage bowls you over. His brutality makes you shudder.[20]

To which the appalled narrator reacts by observing that

> Je commençais à supporter avec peine la présence d'un homme qui discutait une action horrible, un exécrable forfait, comme un connaisseur en peinture ou en poésie, examine les beautés d'un ouvrage de goût; ou comme un moraliste ou un historien relève et fait éclater les circonstances d'une action héroïque.

> I was beginning to find irksome the presence of a man who discussed a horrible act, an execrable crime, like a connoisseur of painting or poetry examining the beauties of a work of art, or a moralist or historian picking out and illuminating the circumstances of a heroic deed.[21]

From Diderot to Schiller to De Quincey, we can trace the traditions of the aesthetic evaluation of crime and of the literary presentation of the criminal in the privileged role of the artist. And from De Quincey to Norman Mailer, writers have portrayed real-life criminals in their own artistic self-images.

Here, however, an important distinction needs to be made between the criminal-as-artist and the artist-as-criminal. The latter situation is illustrated by E. T. A. Hoffmann's tale "Das Fräulein von Scuderi" (1820), in which the assassin who is terrorizing Paris turns out to be the goldsmith Cardillac. (As the result of a trauma experienced by his mother during her pregnancy, Cardillac becomes demonically attached to his creations, and is driven to slay their owners to get them back.) But the romantic artist himself may even be a murderer. This was the case with Thomas Griffiths Wainewright, whom De Quincey was to recall meeting in 1821 at a dinner given by Charles Lamb, and whom Oscar Wilde was to celebrate in "Pen, Pencil, and Poison" (1889) for "being not merely a poet and a painter, an art-critic, an antiquarian, and a writer of prose, an amateur of beautiful things and a dilettante of things delightful, but also a forger of no mean or ordinary capabilities, and as a subtle and secret poisoner almost without rival in this or any age."[22] (Where Wilde commemorated this artist-murderer, it was an artist-victim that Gérard de Nerval had taken as the subject of his play *Léo Burckart* [1839], a collaboration with Alexandre Dumas based on the death of the German dramatist August von Kotzebue, whom a radical student assassinated in 1819 as an alleged spy.)[23] A more recent artist-victim is the filmmaker Pasolini.

If the romantics raised assassination—or at least its description—to an art form, they were by no means the first artists to commit murder; one thinks of such temperamental spirits as Caravaggio (who killed a man in a gambling dispute), or Cellini (who killed a rival goldsmith). Charles Le Brun is believed to have poisoned fellow-painter Eustache le Sueur in an episode of artistic rivalry, and this diabolical motive has given rise to the sensational speculation of Antonio Salieri's poisoning of Mozart. To return to the romantics, the painter Richard Dadd in 1843 killed his father in a fit of madness, and there is the story of the youthful Berlioz who in 1831, upon learning that his fiancée had become engaged to a piano-manufacturer, armed himself with pistols, strychnine, and a made-to-order dress. He hastened from Rome, en route to Paris, where, disguised as a lady's maid, he planned to slay his faithless mistress, her lover, and her mother, and, as a finale to this "petite *comédie* que j'allais jouer," to kill himself. In Nice, however, he was distracted from his revenge plot by the charms of the Riviera, and composed the overture to *King Lear* during what he described as "les vingt plus beaux jours de ma vie."[24]

Writing to his artist-patron William Hayley in 1804, William Blake deplored the murderous competition between artisans in London where "every calumny and falsehood utter'd against another of the same trade is thought fair play. Engravers, Painters, Statutaries, Painters, Poets, we are not in a field of battle, but in a City of Assassinations."[25] This statement need not be taken metaphorically; artists may indeed kill off their professional and sexual rivals, and have even been accused of dispatching their sexual partner for being a professional rival.[26] Such instances are admittedly rare; more prevalent are cases of homicide, and even genocide, committed by frustrated artists, or artists manqués. Where practicing artists often present themselves in their work in the guise of criminals, the artist manqué may actually commit a crime, either "as a response, or partial response, to rejection as an artist" (e.g., John Wilkes Booth's lack of success as an actor, and

Hitler's failure to pass the entrance examination at the Vienna Academy of Fine Arts), or in response to some work of art that provides a "motivation to crime" (e.g., Booth's enactment of Shakespearean tyrannicide, and Hitler's enthusiasm for Wagner).[27]

Of course, we need not take the formula of the artist-as-criminal literally. Most of the time it is used to designate the modern literary phenomenon that Ziolkowski describes of a criminal character presented in a work of art "as a projection of the artist's own subjectivity."[28] For the author to project his qualities as an artist onto his criminal subject implies his identification with the criminal, his self-glorification as a transgressor. Sartre's celebration of Jean Genet and Mailer's adulation of Jack Abbott are perhaps the most publicized examples of the artist-as-criminal phenomenon; a chapter of Sartre's *Saint Genet* is called "On the Fine Arts Considered as Murder."

This formulation of the artist-as-criminal theme has been echoed by other writers on the subject, and constitutes a modernist inversion (and obfuscation) of the exemplary romantic statement of the criminal-as-artist phenomenon found in De Quincey's essay "On Murder Considered as One of the Fine Arts."[29] In his murder narratives, the "Postscript" to the "Murder" essays and the story "The Avenger," De Quincey presents the killer as an artist in his own right; through his narrator, the author acknowledges his *difference* as a would-be artist from the criminal-artist he portrays. We do not sense the author's identification with the murderer as much as we are made aware of his acute sense of separateness from a deed that is at once horrific and fascinating, monstrous and sublime. Unlike the murderer whose deed he describes, the narrator is not an active artist but an aesthetic spectator. Confronted with a spectacle of destruction, the author can no longer create, and his narrator can no longer narrate; they can only bear witness to a mystery of unnatural violence beyond good and evil, beyond the customary limits of human experience.

Murderers are even less likely to be artists than artists are to be murderers. Typically, the murderer only *appears* as an artist from the perspective of the reader or his intermediary, the narrator. It may be the case that the murderer is made to appear as an artist through the conceit of the author who heightens his own artistry by projecting it upon his awe-inspiring subject. But in this case we are again dealing with the artist-as-criminal phenomenon. And although this has been proposed as De Quincey's motive for presenting the real-life murderer John Williams as an artist in the "Postscript,"[30] it obscures a simpler explanation of why writers portray criminals as artists. Violent acts compel an aesthetic response in the beholder of awe, admiration, or bafflement. If an action evokes an aesthetic response, then it is logical to assume that this action—even if it is murder—must have been the work of an artist.

In the "Postscript," a text I will discuss in greater detail, the murderer is presented as a demon who, besides terrorizing his victims, threatens to reduce the narrator to impotent passivity. This produces a narrative crisis that repeats the life-and-death crisis being described: the killer's deed is so awful and awesome that it seems to challenge the narrator's own abilities, and to call his own identity as an artist into question. The narrator is forced to admit his inadequacy; he is a mere con-artist who has been exposed by the far greater powers of the subject he describes. The murderer is the true artist who threatens to expose as an impostor the writer who records his deeds. This uncanny phenomenon of the criminal-as-artist is evoked in the work of other writers in the romantic tradition such as Hoffmann ("Der Sandmann" [1816], *Die Elixiere des Teufels* [1815–16]), Poe (in the case of his supernatural tales, in contrast to his "tales of ratiocination"), and later Marcel Schwob. These writers present themselves to their readers as artists manqués, as individuals who are themselves undergoing—and simultaneously attempting to communicate—an aesthetic experience staged by someone *else* who is the *real* artist: namely, the murderer. Altogether different is the artist-as-criminal phenomenon prevalent among modernist writers such as Dostoyevsky and Gide, in which the author actively creates murderous characters as a kind of mask whereby he alternately disguises or dramatizes his own real or imagined vices.

Oscar Wilde's *The Picture of Dorian Gray* (1890) is a good example of a transitional work that bridges the romantic criminal-as-artist and the modernist artist-as-criminal traditions. While Dorian can certainly be viewed as an imaginative projection of Wilde's transgressive artistry, it is significant that he brings about the deaths of the actress Sibyl Vane and the painter Basil Hallward by exposing the limitations of their respective crafts. As artists, Sibyl and Basil are no match for Dorian who, instead of merely performing or producing art, transforms himself into a masterpiece. That is to say, he becomes a killer whose victims are false artists—a true artist assassin. It is fitting that his portrait should be the agency of his own death.

Literary narratives or films that describe murder in a manner that evokes an aesthetic response in the reader or viewer are actually metafictions—works of art about art. Through his narrator or his camera, the author or film-director presents the murderer's violence as an artistic mystery in its own right that is fundamentally inexplicable and foreign. Whatever meaning might be concealed in the killer's deed, it is simply too problematic to be fully understood by the author/*auteur* or communicated to his reader/viewer. Like the "message" of any art work, the significance of murder can only be suggested in vague hints and approximations. As a work of art, the act of murder will always appear more profound than the work of art that merely describes it. The criminal-artist is the mute, semisacred vanishing-point of a chain of scribes of decreasing artistic prestige but increasing volubility. Sade's crimes presumably did not include murder, yet murderers are the true artists in his voluminous writings. Sartre writes at interminable length about the criminal Genet, who is himself not a murderer but a thief; Genet in turn assumes the role of writer-spectator vis-à-vis the actual murderers, many of them illiterate, whom he glorifies in his work. In contrast to the hybristic modernist fiction implied by Sartre and Mailer that the writer's artistic powers exceed those of the criminal ("The criminal kills," writes Sartre; "he *is* a poem; the poet *writes* the crime; he constructs a wild object that infects all minds with criminality; since it is the spectre of the murder, even more than the murder itself, that horrifies people and unlooses base instincts"),[31] the romantic artist acknowledges himself with a good deal more modesty to be the murderer's apostle and evangelist who stands in awe of the criminal whose deeds he records.

Criminal Literature and Detective Fiction

"The criminal is the creative artist; the detective only the critic."
—The French sleuth-who-soon-turns-slayer Valentin in
G. K. Chesterton's "The Blue Cross" (1910)

Criminality came into its own as a literary subject in the late eighteenth century. By romanticism's height in the early years of the nineteenth century, the criminal had emerged, to use Ziolkowski's phrase, "from the marketplace to the salon," or in the words of Ernest Mandel, "from the streets to the drawing room."[32] He was celebrated in literature as a hero of the people, as a socially acceptable monster, a kind of elephant man. The criminal's reign as fashionable hero, however, was short-lived. Literature was soon to return the criminal, as Mandel puts it, "back to the streets." Ziolkowski calls attention to this "transformation of the criminal from a titanic hero into a guilty man," without which "the criminal would be useless as a metaphor and symbol in much modern literature." He dates the turning point of the criminal's literary fortunes at 1828, the year of Eugène-François Vidocq's alleged *Mémoires* documenting the former thief's work as informer and agent for the Paris police. (With respect to England this date is also noteworthy, as it is a year after the appearance of De Quincey's first "Murder" essay, and a year before the Metropolitan Police Act whereby Sir Robert Peel consolidated law enforcement in London.) Not only did Dumas, Hugo, Gaboriau, Dickens, and Poe draw on what Ian Ousby has called the "unredeemably fictional . . . form and spirit"[33] of the *Mémoires* in their writing, but Vidocq's dramatic career-change from convict to head of the Sûreté (which he founded during Napoleon's rule) was itself the stuff of fiction, and found its way into such eminent literary works as Balzac's *Splendeurs et misères des courtisanes* (1845). Balzac knew Vidocq personally, and used him as the model for his character Vautrin, the arch-criminal who appears in several novels of the *Comédie humaine*.[34]

In 1833 Vidocq founded the *Bureau des Renseignements*, the first modern detective agency. Thus his life exemplifies the transformation of the traditional romantic roles of rebel hero and despotic villain, and the corresponding shift in the average reader's sympathies "from the criminal to the 'detective.'"[35] As liberal-democratic institutions and judicial-penal systems began to develop in the new, relatively stable social orders, the literary figure of the romantic rebel or "noble bandit" came to be perceived and represented as a threat to bourgeois society. The detective answers what Mandel calls "the rising need of the bourgeoisie to defend instead of attack the social order,"[36] to discipline the criminal subculture. Sensational criminal literature evolved into the more sedate, bourgeois, rationalist genre of detective fiction in which the sleuth's artful ingenuity comes to match and even surpass that of the criminal whom he pursues. Poe's "tales of ratiocination" that inaugurated this genre in the 1840s roughly coincided with the actual appearance of professional investigators on the police forces in London who, in response to the growing class of professional criminals, replaced paid informants like the Bow Street Runners. (The Runners had served as an adjunct to the police since 1749 when they were founded by the author Henry Fielding; he and his half-brother Sir John Fielding were major reformers of the police system.) "The Murders in the Rue Morgue" of 1841, generally regarded as the first detective story, appeared a year before the creation of a Detective Department to assist the Metropolitan Police until the 1870s when the modern Criminal Investigation Department was formed. The term *detective* itself only became widely used in English with the nearly simultaneous publication of a work of "low" and a work of "high" literature: William Russell's fictional *Recollections of a Detective Police-Officer* (serialized from 1849 to 1853 under the name Thomas Waters), and Dickens's *Bleak House* (1852).[37] The detective can thus truly be said to be a literary invention.

Although the sleuth seems to have supplanted the criminal as the "hero" of criminal literature, and the "'deeds and ruses' of the pursuer began to supersede those of the pursued,"[38] the focus of the new detective genre actually remained much the same as it had been in works with the romantic rebel or noble bandit as hero—namely, the extraordinary abilities, and often extralegal activities, of the protagonist, *whether he was criminal or detective*. From amateur detectives like Dupin and Holmes to the spate of professional private investigators and agency operatives who are their twentieth-century successors, it has become a convention of the genre to portray the sleuth at odds with the established police force. In fact, the literary figure of the detective typically was and continues to be an extraordinary, marginal figure who frequently bears a closer resemblance to the criminal he pursues than to the police officers with whom he supposedly collaborates. Ziolkowski is right to see the detective as the criminal's double, as a transgressor in his own right "whose methods in themselves were often scarcely preferable to those of the men [he] hunted."[39] Given the interchangeability in many instances between real-life thieves and thief-takers, Ian Ousby has even claimed that the detective "entered fiction not as a hero, but as, at worst, a villain and, at best, a suspect and ambiguous character."[40] We should not forget that the precursor of the professional detective was the professional informer— men like Wild in the eighteenth century and Vidocq in the nineteenth who had been outlaws themselves, who knew how to exploit their criminal connections (Vidocq boasted that during "the twenty years I spent at the head of the Sûreté I hardly employed any but ex-convicts, often even escaped prisoners"[41]), and whose eventful lives passed directly into literature.

Rather than supplant the romantic hero of the criminal, the realist figure of the detective continued to be something of a scofflaw—if not an outlaw—himself, albeit in a rational guise. One wonders whether the popularity of the literary figure of the detective is more a result of readers' interest in his analytic, puzzle-solving abilities or of their fascination with his bizarre personality which barely disguises his criminal tendencies. It is essential that such tendencies remain disguised if the work of detective fiction is to succeed; neither the criminal nor the detective's own eccentricities can become the focus of the reader's interest. Joseph Roth's *Beichte eines Mörders* of 1936 and Jim Thompson's 1952 novel *The Killer Inside Me* are classic examples of nondetective works in which a law officer narrates his own exploits as a murderer rather than as an investigator. Detection is also irrelevant in the 1989 film *Batman*, in which Jack Nicholson's "homicidal artistry" as the villainous Joker easily allows him to upstage the "hero" with all his hi-tech surveillance wizardry. And the endlessly deferred ending to Mark Frost and David Lynch's hit 1990 TV serial *Twin Peaks* ought to have clued even the most diehard detective-story fan into realizing that the answer to the question "Who killed Laura Palmer?" was beside the point. In the true detective story, the sleuth's abilities as sleuth—rather than his tics and foibles, or even his intuitions and visions—must be the focus of the reader's attention. The criminal's role must be limited to that of the guilty suspect whose identity (or secret) it is the detective's task to discover. For all their similarities as superior intellects, Dupin and the treacherous minister in "The Purloined Letter" cannot be confused.[42] If, as one recent aficionado of the genre has admitted, "the recognition that the sleuth and the culprit are more alike than different" is the "most subversive thing that can happen in a detective novel,"[43] then the writer's need to conceal, and the reader's need to deny, the detective's inborn criminality makes the enterprise of detection an exercise of mutual self-deception.

The apparent replacement of the criminal-hero by the detective-hero is a relatively superficial literary manifestation of the more significant sociocultural shift from the criminal-as-artist mode of representation to the artist-as-criminal mode. After the mid-nineteenth century, when the criminal is marginalized in literature and his heroic stature vastly diminished, one is less likely to find works in which the criminal is himself presented as an artist than one is bound to find works either in which the detective appears as artist, or in which the author qua artist actually projects himself in the role of criminal. The principal texts in which the criminal remains the focus of aesthetic interest after the romantic era, and even appears as an artist in his own right, are the quasi-literary courtroom transcripts of actual criminal trials. "The interest here," as Mary Hottinger has noted, "is always in the accused, while in the detective novel the criminal is seldom interesting and almost never appealing."[44]

This explains why a critic as perceptive as Jacques Barzun has promoted the tradition of detective literature initiated by Poe at the expense of the earlier tradition inspired by De Quincey which treats murder rather than detection as a subject of aesthetic interest: "since Poe's great feat, we need no longer depend on . . . De Quincey, nor on the four or five disciples of the last-named who have reshaped for us the incidents of actual crime. We have for our solace and edification the literary genre . . . abundant, variegated, illustrious, classical—[of] the detective story."[45] From the standpoint of an investigation into the aesthetics of murder as an artistic genre in its own right (a genre that Barzun curiously dismisses without referring to it by name, and a genre to which some of Poe's own mysteries like "William Wilson" would seem to belong), the tradition of detective fiction—the focus of most studies of criminal literature—would itself have to be dismissed as a red herring. For detective fiction distracts our attention from the issue of criminality in three ways: first and most obviously, by reducing the significance of the criminal in the work; second, by disguising the detective's own criminal tendencies behind a veneer of harmless indulgences and eccentricities; and third, by concealing the author's own social identity as a transgressing artist behind the veneer of his "art." Against Barzun's defense of detective fiction and his curt dismissal of De Quincey's "Murder" essays, we may cite De Quincey's own criticism of the hero of William Godwin's *Caleb Williams*—a figure who has been identified as "the first important detective in the English novel"[46]—for being a thoroughly reprehensible rogue, consumed by a "vile eavesdropping inquisitiveness" (11:330).[47]

The impact of detective fiction has been to direct the interest in criminal literature away from the criminal, and to shift it instead toward the rational, epistemological and hermeneutic problem of detection, on the one hand, and toward the artistic "game" of ingenious plot construction, on the other. The detective plot strips narrative down to its bare essentials: it displays the Logos-as-Law working itself out in the person of the detective as logical lawman. Not only does the detective plot expose and excoriate the criminal's moral transgressions, but in the process it reveals all the false leads and red herrings that throw the reader off the criminal's trail as extraneous digressions, as secondary subplots that obstruct the primary investigation, the unfolding of the Law. This is precisely why the antidetective narratives of Alain Robbe-Grillet, Dennis Potter, David Lynch, and Paul Auster foreground secondary, "atmospheric" elements while revealing the irrelevance of the detective plot.

Detective fiction is the most inauthentic and artificial of all the varieties of crime literature. It deals neither with the criminal-as-artist nor with the artist-as-criminal alternatives, but with the artist-as-detective: its "art" consists in the author's showing off his clever construction of the story.[48] A subtler, and therefore relatively unappreciated, class of crime literature focuses less on the author or detective's logical artistry than on the uncanny, otherworldly, avowedly amoral, and artistically superior (anti-)art of the criminal himself.[49] Borges's tale "Death and the Compass" and Umberto Eco's novel *The Name of the Rose* are narratives of detective failures in which the criminal waits for the super-rational sleuth to "discover" a pattern in an arbitrary sequence of murders. The detective mistakenly attributes this ingenious design to his adversary, who simply plays along with the imagined scenario, manipulating and eventually trapping his pursuer. Confronted with the duped detective, the reader may learn to distrust his own moral-rational categories of judgment; might not such evaluative criteria themselves be based on mistaken perceptual and aesthetic *pre*-judgments?

The widely recognized shift from the criminal to the detective as protagonist in nineteenth-century literature turns out to be merely a secondary phenomenon that should not distract us from what is of primary importance: the criminality of the literary subject both before and after the romantic "turning point." Where romanticism had glorified the outlaw or outcast as a social rebel, the age of realism rationalized the criminal subject of literature *as Reason* in the figure of the detective; this is what Foucault called "the appropriation of the criminal in acceptable forms." After all, the first detective in literature—Oedipus—was not only the very taboo-breaker whom he struggled to unmask, but he was also the king, the authorized head of state, the incarnation of the Law.

Murder under the Influence

> I was always haunted by the idea of a murder which would cut me
> off irremediably from your world.
>
> —Jean Genet, *Journal du Voleur*

In 1822, only two months after his sensational *Confessions of an English Opium-Eater* appeared in book form, De Quincey entertained the idea of writing a sequel. This was to be another confessional work, dealing this time with the theme of murder: "One night in high summer, when I lay tossing and sleepless for want of opium,—I amused myself with composing the imaginary *Confessions of a Murderer;* which, I think, might be made a true German bit of horror, the subject being exquisitely diabolical."[50]

Unfortunately, De Quincey never pursued this project, and we are forced to speculate about what the "imaginary" sequel to the *Confessions* would have been. We may assume its criminal narrator would have gone beyond the early romantic paradox of the "reasonable murderer" or "scrupulous homicide" explored by William Godwin in *Caleb Williams* (1794) or Coleridge in *Remorse* (1797).[51] A possible hint concerning the nature of De Quincey's "exquisitely diabolical" subject is contained in an observation of 1847, in which he jestingly conjectures about the possibility of murdering a double:

> Any of us would be jealous of his own duplicate; and, if I had a *doppel-ganger* who went about personating me, copying me, and pirating me, philosopher as I am I might (if the Court of Chancery would not grant an injunction against him) be so far carried away by jealousy as to attempt the crime of murder upon his carcase; and no great matter as regards HIM. But it would be a sad thing for *me* to find myself hanged; and for what, I beseech you? for murdering a sham, that was either nobody at all, or oneself repeated once too often. (11:460–61)

Whether or not De Quincey had actually considered incorporating the idea of killing off one's double in his projected *Confessions of a Murderer,* the idea informs some of his other writings and has been treated by authors as different as the Scotsman James Hogg in *The Private Memoirs and Confessions of a Justified Sinner* (1824) and the Austrian Joseph Roth, whose 1936 novel is explicitly called *Beichte eines Mörders (Confession of a Murderer).*[52] Whatever idea De Quincey may have had in mind, the composition of his sequel would have made the close connection in his imagination between opium-eating and murder far more obvious than it presently is.

"Murder committed under the influence of drugs: surely this would appeal to De Quincey's fancy," observes one commentator.[53] As De Quincey reminds the readers of his first "Murder" essay (13:21),

his two favorite subjects of opium-eating and murder are etymologi-
cally linked: the word "assassination" is derived from the Arabic word
hashshashin, or "hashish-eaters," a sect of fanatic Moslems in the time
of the Crusades who primed themselves with hashish before setting
out on their murderous missions. As an opium-eater, De Quincey was
himself a literary descendant of these hashish-eaters—ingesting
opium before indulging in the *character*-assassination of such figures
as Kant and Coleridge. Later masterworks in the genre of detective
fiction such as Wilkie Collins's *The Moonstone* (1868) and Dashiell
Hammett's *Red Harvest* (1929), as well as nonfictional studies like Joe
McGinniss's "true-crime novel" *Fatal Vision* (1983), would take up the
De Quinceyean theme of a crime that may or may not have been committed by an individual under the influence of drugs. In such works,
the question is raised whether the "criminal" can be considered to
have been himself at the moment of his "crime," or whether he was
someone else—his demonic double.

Of course, it is perfectly possible to experience a murderous
trance without the use of drugs. In the 1880s, the internist Hippolyte
Bernheim discovered that he could induce his subjects to commit
crimes such as murder under hypnosis. Bernheim reports that he
showed one subject

> an imaginary person at the door and told him that he had been
> insulted by him. I gave him an imaginary dagger and ordered him to
> kill the man. He hastened forward and ran the dagger resolutely into
> the door.[54]

While his rival Jean Martin Charcot linked hypnosis to hysteria,
Bernheim maintained that his large pool of subjects were healthy individuals who were merely "suggestible." This interpretation had apoc-
alyptic implications: if ordinary men and women could be so easily
manipulated, then wasn't civilization threatened by epidemic outbreaks of murderous violence? Such was the physician Paul Aubrey's
warning in *La Contagion du Meurtre* (1894); he blamed this grim prospect on the atrophied nervous systems of individuals in modern industrialized society.

Long before clinical experimentation with hypnotism and homicide, and well before De Quincey formulated an aesthetics of murder, we find a noteworthy analysis of the criminal's psychological condition in purely aesthetic terms. In his *Philosophical Enquiry into the Origin of Our Ideas of the Sublime and Beautiful,* Edmund Burke cites Pope's translation of Homer's description of the state of mind of a killer who has managed to escape his pursuers:

> As when a wretch, who conscious of his crime,
> Pursued for murder from his native clime,
> Just gains some frontier, breathless, pale, amaz'd;
> All gaze, all wonder!

Burke comments that "this striking appearance of the man whom Homer supposes to have just escaped an imminent danger, the sort of mixt passion of terror and surprize, with which he affects the spectators, paints very strongly the manner in which we find ourselves affected upon occasions any way similar." This statement implies that the "mixt passion" with which the "spectator" or reader reacts to the description of the murderer approximates the killer's own emotional state. The experience of murderers and nonmurderers alike "upon escaping some imminent danger, or on being released from the severity of some cruel pain" is a very different matter in Burke's view from that associated with "positive pleasure." Where the latter sensation "quickly satisfies" and lets us "fall into a soft tranquillity," the "removal of pain or danger" gives rise to a state of "sobriety" in which the mind is "impressed with a sense of awe, in a sort of tranquillity shadowed with horror."[55] The murderer's "delightful horror, a sort of tranquillity tinged with terror,"[56] is here an aesthetic experience of sublime sobriety or clarity that has nothing to do with sadistic pleasure or with a drug-induced state of intoxication; rather, such delight is associated with the relief from pain, fear, or guilt afforded by an anodyne.[57]

The murderers portrayed in De Quincey's writings were themselves not under the influence of drugs when they committed their deeds. Opium dreams merely provide an objective correlative for the murderer's profound, subjective experience at the instant of his crime, when he finds himself sealed off from normal existence, inhabiting his own private world. In such a state, the murderer might well be in a

ice. The classic description of this condition appears
the Knocking at the Gate in Macbeth" (1823). In the
speare's play discussed in this essay—Macbeth's slay-
in in his own castle—it is the act of murder itself that
th into a dreamlike state that bears a close resemblance to the passive state of the opium-eater:

> The murderers and the murder must be insulated—cut off by an
> immeasurable gulf from the ordinary tide and succession of human
> affairs—locked up and sequestered in some deep recess; we must be
> made sensible that the world of ordinary life is suddenly arrested,
> laid asleep, tranced, racked into a dread armistice; time must be
> annihilated, relation to things without abolished; and all must pass
> self-withdrawn into a deep syncope and suspension of earthly pas-
> sion. (10:393)

This description of Macbeth's state of mind following his crime
not only resembles De Quincey's passages from the previous year in
the *Confessions* describing the effects of opium, but it is also similar to
eighteenth-century philosophical accounts of aesthetic experience.[58]
The murderer's violent deed "suspends" him from the world in a state
of rapture that resembles the killer's experience of "delight" as described in Burke's *Enquiry*. And just as Burke's comment on Homer's
simile, in Thomas Weiskel's words, "appears to imply an empathetic
identification on the part of the spectators"—who "have committed no
crime"—with the murderer,[59] Macbeth's slaughter of the King transforms him, in De Quincey's account, into a kind of aesthetic spectator
in his own right, and creates a profound sense of communion
between the audience and the murderous protagonist of Shakespeare's
play.

De Quincey's descriptions of a quasi-aesthetic experience in both
the "Macbeth" and the "Murder" essays are closer to Burke's than to
Kant's account of the sublime in that these extraordinary states of
mind are not occasioned by natural phenomena, but by violent acts of
murder. Macbeth's subjective, dreamlike rapture as an aesthetic spectator is the result of a decisive rupture whereby he severs all connections with human existence. Where Kant had posited a continuity
between ethics and aesthetics—even in the case of the sublime which,

by revealing the inadequacy of the imaginative faculty, made the subject aware of its "higher" moral provenance—De Quincey drew a radical opposition in the "Macbeth" and in the "Murder" essays between the world of ethical action and the world of aesthetic experience, between the dull domain of everyday reality and a supermundane realm of heightened intuition. His "aesthetic experiences" are visionary dream-states associated with the transgressions of opium-eating and murder which entail a suspension of moral-rational law: "Hence it is that, when the deed is done, when the work of darkness is perfect, then the world of darkness passes away like a pageantry in the clouds" (10:393).

De Quincey's acute insight into the psycho-aesthetic experience of a killer was matched more than a century later by Jean Genet in his reconstruction of the state of mind of his black cellmate Clément Village after his accidental slaying of his Dutch girlfriend in their Montmartre apartment.

> Par un effort puissant de volonté, il échappa à la banalité,—maintenant son esprit dans une région surhumaine, où il était dieu, créant d'un coup un univers singulier où ses actes échappaient au contrôle moral. Il se sublimisa. Il se fit général, prêtre, sacrificateur, officiant. Il avait ordonné, vengé, sacrifié, offert, il n'avait pas tué Sonia. Il usa avec un instinct déroutant de cet artifice pour justifier son acte. Les hommes doués d'une folle imagination doivent avoir un retour cette grand faculté poétique: nier notre univers et ses valeurs, afin d'agir sur lui avec une aisance souveraine.

> By a powerful effort of will, he escaped banality—maintaining his mind in a superhuman region, where he was a god, creating at one stroke a private universe where his acts escaped moral control. He sublimated himself. He made himself general, priest, sacrificer, officiant. He had commanded, avenged, sacrificed, offered. He had not killed Sonia. With a baffling instinct, he made use of this artifice to justify his act. Men endowed with a wild imagination should have, in addition, the great poetic faculty of denying our universe and its values so that they may act upon it with sovereign ease.

Genet imagines Clément sealing himself off from the ethical world in a private, sovereign sphere that allowed him to dispose of Sonia's body with a clear conscience by sealing *her* off from the world of the living—entombing her inside a brick bench. For someone of a poetic temperament, such a gruesome undertaking could only be performed through a supreme imaginative act of aesthetic detachment: "He sanctified his acts with a grace that owed nothing to a God Who condemns murder. He stopped up the eyes of his spirit. For a whole day, as if automatically, his body was at the mercy of orders that did not come from here below." ("Il sanctifia ses actes d'une grâce, qui ne devait rien à un Dieu qui condamne le meurtre. Il se boucha les yeux de l'esprit. Pendant une journée entière, comme automatiquement, son corps fut à la merci d'ordres qui ne venaient pas d'ici-bas.")[60]

For De Quincey as for Genet, murder ushers in an extraordinary aesthetic experience that is not of this world, and that cannot coexist with any world familiar to ethical beings. This sort of aesthetic experience presupposes a radical break with the world. Clément's killing of his girlfriend may have been an accident, but having committed the deed, he willfully severs any connection with moral values. In Macbeth's case, the slaying of Duncan was itself willed. Beyond his resentment at being denied what he feels to be his right to be king, Macbeth must bear the additional insult of the King's presence under his own roof. His slaughter of the King temporarily puts the world in "suspension," and calms his soul which is "raging," in De Quincey's words, with "some great storm of passion" (10:392). This swift emotional progression from "righteous rage" to an act of "sacrificial violence" to a sublime experience of "transcendence" is not a poetic fiction devised by Shakespeare and De Quincey. These terms are taken from Jack Katz's phenomenological description of a "common" killer's experience at the instant of his crime: "Like the promise of an erotic drive, rage moves toward the experience of time suspended; it blows up the present moment so the situation becomes a portentous, potentially an endless present, possibly the occasion for a destruction that will become an eternally significant creativity. This is the spiritual beauty of rage."[61]

We begin to suspect that De Quincey's introduction of the word "aesthetics" into English in the context of his 1827 "Murder" essay was no accident. The quiescent aesthetic experience of the beautiful is not separate, as in Kant, from the experiential terror of the sublime, but is necessarily related to it. By the same token, aesthetic experience in general as described by De Quincey is not, as in Kant, a heightened or purer form of ordinary experience, but entails a violent rupture with reality.

The point is vividly rendered in René Magritte's painting *The Menaced Assassin* (*L'assassin menacé*, 1926–27). The painting was inspired by a scene from one of Louis Feuillade's films about the character Fantômas, the hero of a spate of thriller novels and films popular during the 1920s, who, as Suzi Gablik notes, differed from the detective-heroes of "more conventional thrillers" in being "a diabolical criminal," a Maldoror-figure who "revelled in the delights of cruelty and human treachery."[62] In Magritte's painting, the central figure's rapt absorption in the music playing on the gramophone[63] has struck commentators like Albert Cook as schizophrenic behavior, considering that he must be assumed to have just slain the woman lying nude on the divan behind him. Cook dismisses the suggestion that the killer's absorption in the phonograph is a way of "calming his nerves"; this "would be to revise the permanence of this painting into an episode."[64] There seems no solution to Magritte's "mystery." In light of the "Macbeth" essay, however, we have no difficulty in reconciling the central figure's receptive serenity with his savagery only minutes before. It is precisely the act of murder that occasions the killer's aesthetic state of suspension.

But if the murderer's aesthetic suspension is achieved by a decisive break with the ethical world, the eventual resumption of worldly affairs entails nothing less than a corresponding act of violence. Surrounding the oblivious killer in the painting are men who watch his every move, and who are about to accost him violently and put an end to his reverie. Whether or not the killer will be apprehended is unclear. Viewers of the painting in the 1920s who were familiar with Fantômas knew that he "was the perfect criminal who never got caught." He was admired by the Surrealists "because he could outwit the forces of the law"; even "if the police managed to seize him and get him convicted, he always escaped at the last moment, substituting

some imbecile who would take his place on the guillotine."[65] Yet even
if the blasé murderer in Magritte's painting, menaced as he is,
manages incredibly to escape his many pursuers, the fact remains
that, for the moment at least, he is beseiged by "the forces of the law."
The large figures at either side of the canvas—one of whom wields a
club while the other is equipped with a net—are the visual equivalent
of the knocking at the gate in the "Macbeth" essay. This symbolic
stage device signals the reassertion of the Law; its brusque interruption of the murderer Macbeth's free-floating reverie recalls him to himself (and us to ourselves) and to a realization of what he has done:

> the knocking at the gate is heard, and it makes known audibly that
> the reaction has commenced; the human has made its reflux upon
> the fiendish; the pulses of life are beginning to beat again; and the re-
> establishment of the goings-on of the world in which we live first
> makes us profoundly sensible of the awful parenthesis that had sus-
> pended them. (10:393)

Like the shattering burst of the assault rifles that rouses Tony Montana
from his cocaine binge in his cocoon-like lair in Brian De Palma's 1983
remake of the film *Scarface*, Macduff's knocking at the gate of Macbeth's
castle disrupts the assassin's trance, thereby making both him and the
audience watching him conscious both of the levity (and brevity) of
that suspended moment and of the gravity of the deed that had occasioned it.

In the final stanza of Keats's "Ode to a Nightingale," the poet
awakens from the reverie he has slipped into while listening to the
bird. Like Macbeth, the poet is not under the influence of drugs, but
he may as well be: he feels as if he has "emptied some dull opiate to
the drains." What awakens him from his trance is the last word of the
penultimate stanza, repeated as the first word of the final stanza:

> Forlorn! the very word is like a bell
> To toll me back from thee to my sole self!

The tolling bell with which the ominous word "Forlorn" is associated
(a word whose appearance in the poem Paul de Man once jokingly lik-
ened to a foghorn)[66] has a very similar function to the knocking at the
gate described by De Quincey. Both sounds recall the suspended

dreamer to an awareness of his own mortal (in Keats's case) or guilty (in Macbeth's case) condition. The poet seems to hear the bird's song most intensely after it flies off; he awakens from his reverie wondering

> Was it a vision, or a waking dream?
> Fled is that music: — do I wake or sleep?

Similarly, Macbeth's trance as described by De Quincey becomes all the more palpable and powerful when it is disrupted — "at no moment was his sense of the complete suspension and pause in ordinary human concerns so full and affecting as at that moment when the suspension ceases and the goings-on of human life are suddenly resumed." The violence of Macduff's knocking at the gate is, of course, all in Macbeth's mind; such apparent violence suggests to the audience the profundity of the trance which the knocking has disrupted, and reminds both the audience and Macbeth of the actual violence that has only just occurred. If the poet's return to (self-)consciousness in Keats's ode at the imagined sound of the word "forlorn" is so unsettling, how much more jarring must Macduff's knocking sound, and how much further removed from reality must Macbeth be when the knocking shatters his trance.

To summarize, De Quincey employs not one, but a series of three objective correlatives in his writing to describe the disparity between ethical and aesthetic experience: the act of murder is the correlate of the violence with which the artist breaks with the conventional world, the opium trance is the correlate of the artist-assassin's state of aesthetic suspension from the world, and the knocking at the gate is the correlate of the re-entry from aesthetic hyperreality back into mundane reality, and of the reassertion of moral-rational Law. (From a psychoanalytic perspective, this last movement entailing the resumption of the Law is bound up with the return of the Father.)[67] We shall now see how De Quincey's revision of Kant's aesthetics of the beautiful and the sublime — namely, his insight into the inherent violence of aesthetic experience — is pertinent to his own pioneering presentation of the criminal-as-artist phenomenon, as well as to later works in the romantic tradition.

The Sublimity of Sheer Terror: De Quincey and De Palma

Anybody who has had any first-hand experience in any kind of violent situation knows there is absolutely no relationship between theatrical violence and real violence. The use of murders in movies is aesthetic stuff. Motion. Form. Shapes.
> —Susan Dworkin, referring to Brian De Palma's films

It looks like one of Bill's paintings.
> —Patricia (Sarah Miles) in Antonioni's film *Blow-up*, comparing a greatly enlarged photograph of a murdered man with her husband's abstract canvases of colored dots.

Of all the romantics, De Quincey was the most keenly aware of the artistic and aesthetic implications of murder. He was well-prepared to write his essay "On Murder Considered as One of the Fine Arts" and its sequels, thanks to his short, controversial career as editor of the *Westmorland Gazette* from July 1818 to November 1819. For De Quincey and his successors, murder could not simply be explained away or condemned as an immoral, criminal act. The most violent, abhorrent, and unpardonable of crimes—transgression in its most glaring guise, terror in its starkest form—could be presented artistically and experienced aesthetically. Summing up the achievement of the "Murder" essays, Dennis Porter writes that "De Quincey legitimates the idea that discriminating pleasure may be obtained not from the sight of inflicted pain—he is no Sade—but from the spectacle of an artist at work in a medium that includes the human body. The shock of murder is no longer in the act but in its aesthetic treatment."[68] What precisely was this "aesthetic treatment" of murder? Taking our cue from the "Macbeth" essay, we begin to suspect that murder fascinated the romantic sensibility because it revealed new and totally unexpected insights into the nature of everyday ethical existence by offering a premonition of an aesthetic hyperreality that was altogether removed from natural and human law. Even the physical law of gravity was temporarily suspended as the murderer—and his witnesses— were borne aloft and "pass[ed] self-withdrawn into a deep syncope and suspension of earthly passion."

The original essay "On Murder" of 1827 consisted of a Swiftian address extolling murder as an art form that was delivered by a lecturer to a dissolute club called "The Society of Connoisseurs in Murder." In a "Supplementary Paper" of 1839, the narrator offers an uproarious account of a dinner party given by the Society to celebrate the sensational Williams murders of 1811. In 1854 De Quincey added a "Postscript" to the "Murder" essays when they were reprinted in his collected writings. Nearly as long as both the "Murder" papers combined, the "Postscript" differs markedly from those earlier essays. In contrast to their gallows humor about murder in general, the "Postscript" gives a detailed account of the Williams killings themselves. De Quincey's technique in describing these murders consists neither in relating the gruesome events as they objectively happened, nor in fictionalizing these events (although a certain amount of invention may be expected in a narrative published forty-three years after the actual murders occurred).[69] Instead, the killings are described as they might have been experienced by selected witnesses who were known to have been at the murder scenes, witnesses whose lives were momentarily endangered, but who managed to escape unharmed. Such a technique enables De Quincey to present the murders in their aesthetic aspect. The "Postscript" is therefore an actual demonstration of the outrageous thesis that is merely asserted in the earlier burlesques—namely, that murder can indeed be considered a form of art.

In his imaginative reconstruction of John Williams's slaughter of the Marr family, De Quincey breaks off his narrative at the crucial moment of the murder in order to follow the Marr's servant-girl Mary who, off on an errand to buy oysters, has left the house toward midnight, only seconds before Williams has slipped inside and latched the front door.

> Meantime, at this point, let us leave the murderer alone with his victims. For fifty minutes let him work his pleasure. The front-door, as we know, is now fastened against all help. Help there is none. Let us, therefore, in vision, attach ourselves to Mary; and, when all is over, let us come back with *her*, again raise the curtain, and read the dreadful record of all that has passed in her absence. (13:85)

Elsewhere in his writings, we find De Quincey digressing as a means of deferring a traumatic experience, thereby offering relief both to the character and the reader;[70] here, digression is used not to postpone horror but to heighten terror. The narrative describing the carnage inside the Marr household is interrupted by a digressive passage that recounts Mary's experience of growing unease as she pursues her search for oysters away from the house. Despite her foreboding after she catches a glimpse in the shadows of a stranger loitering outside the premises, Mary hurries on to complete her errand. She anxiously searches in the falling darkness for a shop that is still open. When this proves futile she starts to return home, but loses her way in the darkness and the unfamiliar neighborhood. It is late, and she is already distraught when she finally arrives back at the house, only to find that no one answers her repeated knocking.

> Yet how is this? To her astonishment,—but with the astonishment came creeping over her an icy horror,—no stir nor murmur was heard ascending from the kitchen. At this moment came back upon her, with shuddering anguish, the indistinct image of the stranger in the loose dark coat whom she had seen stealing along under the shadowy lamplight, and too certainly watching her master's motions. (13:87)

Recalling the stranger, and hearing no response to her summons, Mary is overcome with "something like hysterical horror," and rings the bell "with the violence that belongs to sickening terror." Instead of arousing her master, however, she only succeeds in alerting the murderer who is still inside the house. Terrified, Mary hears his creaking steps on the stairs and his footsteps in the hallway. At last "there is but a door between him and Mary. What is he doing on the other side of the door?" (13:88).

This remarkable scene, in which Mary becomes aware of the murderer Williams's presence on the other side of the front door, is echoed later in the "Postscript," in the account of Williams's slaughter of a second family, the Williamsons. The assault on the ground floor of the victims' home is here presented from the perspective of a terrified journeyman lodging in the house who has secretly descended from his second-floor room to observe the murderer's activities, and who then returns upstairs to make his escape and raise an alarm.

Sixteen years before the publication of the "Postscript," De Quincey had already employed the technique of describing murders from the perspective of a surviving witness in his tale "The Avenger" (1838).[71] But the most significant parallel to the suspenseful doorway scene in the "Postscript" is the "Macbeth" essay published thirty-one years earlier in which De Quincey had analyzed his own profound response to the primal murder scene in Shakespeare's play.

> My understanding could furnish no reason why the knocking at the gate in Macbeth should produce any effect, direct or reflected. In fact, my understanding said positively that it could *not* produce any effect. But I knew better; I felt that it did; and I waited and clung to the problem until further knowledge should enable me to solve it. At length, in 1812, Mr. Williams made his *début* on the stage of Ratcliffe Highway, and executed those unparalleled murders which have procured for him such a brilliant and undying reputation. On which murders, by the way, I must observe that in one respect they have had an ill effect, by making the connoisseur in murder very fastidious in his taste, and dissatisfied by anything that has been since done in that line. All other murders look pale by the deep crimson of his; and, as an amateur once said to me in a querulous tone, "There has been absolutely nothing *doing* since his time, or nothing that's worth speaking of." But this is wrong; for it is unreasonable to expect all men to be great artists, and born with the genius of Mr. Williams. Now, it will be remembered that in the first of these murders (that of the Marrs) the same incident (of a knocking at the door soon after the work of extermination was complete) did actually occur which the genius of Shakspere has invented; and all good judges, and the most eminent dilettanti, acknowledged the felicity of Shakspere's suggestion as soon as it was actually realized. (10:390–91)

Several years before the first "Murder" essay, De Quincey had already noted in a wry vein that the actual event of the Marr family's slaughter had given him the key to his otherwise inexplicable aesthetic response to Shakespeare's scene. The artistic genius of the gate scene remained unnoticed by Shakespeare's admirers, De Quincey included, until "the genius of Mr. Williams" disclosed by means of his brutal "hammer murders" the profundity of the Bard's technique. This ironic conception of the murderer as a kind of artist provided the germ that was to flower over the next three decades into the series of papers dealing with the subject of murder. The lecture in the original essay is delivered in honor of John Williams who, the speaker declares, has exalted the ideal of murder to all of us, and to me, therefore, in particular, has deepened the arduousness of my task. Like Aeschylus or Milton in poetry, like Michael Angelo in painting, he has carried his art to a point of colossal sublimity, and, as Mr. Wordsworth observes, has in a manner "created the taste by which he is to be enjoyed." (13:12)

What, then, is the source of the sublimity that De Quincey discerned in the gate scene in *Macbeth*, and that he tried to express in his own account of Mary's frantic knocking at the door of the Marr residence? According to his own analysis in the "Macbeth" essay, the "solution" to the artistic mystery of the play concerns the realization that most descriptions of murder are presented from the perspective of the helpless victim. Such a perspective produces a "coarse and vulgar horror" because

> it flings the interest exclusively upon the natural but ignoble instinct by which we cleave to life: an instinct which, as being indispensable to the primal law of self-preservation, is the same in kind (though different in degree) amongst all living creatures. This instinct, therefore, because it annihilates all distinctions, and degrades the greatest of men to the level of "the poor beetle that we tread on," exhibits human nature in its most abject and humiliating attitude. Such an attitude would little suit the purposes of the poet. What then must he do? He must throw the interest on the murderer. Our sympathy must be with *him*. (10:391)

Descriptions of murder, in other words, achieve artistic merit—that is, they become aesthetically interesting—when the reader's focus is shifted from the point of view of the victim to that of the murderer.

Auden makes a similar point in "The Guilty Vicarage" when he argues that "detective stories have nothing to do with works of art" because the reader identifies, not with the criminal, but with the sleuth who solves the mystery and restores order. Where "the interest in the study of a murderer is the observation, by the innocent many, of the sufferings of the guilty one, . . . the interest in the detective story is the dialectic of innocence and guilt."[72] Auden echoes De Quincey in his insistence on the need of the artist (in contrast to the author of detective fiction) to focus attention on the murderer's state of mind, rather than that of the detective or the victim. He cites the example of *Crime and Punishment* as a work of art whose "effect on the reader is to compel an identification with the murderer which he would prefer not to recognize."[73] Auden learned from Dostoyevsky's characteriza-tion of Raskolnikov what Burke thought he had learned from Homer's simile of the murderer,[74] and what De Quincey claimed to have learned from Shakespeare's treatment of Macbeth—namely, the artis-tic effectiveness of presenting murder from the murderer's point of view. De Quincey's recognition of this device led him to contemplate writing the *Confessions of a Murderer* as a sequel to his *Confessions of an English Opium-Eater*. Although never written, this project anticipated such psychological studies of homicide in nineteenth- and twentieth-century literature as that of Raskolnikov in *Crime and Punishment*, Laf-cadio in Gide's *Les Caves du Vatican*, Meursault in Camus's *L'Étranger*, the terrorist Chen in Malraux's *La Condition humaine*, and most recent-ly, of the drifter Freddie in John Banville's *The Book of Evidence* (1990). In a variation of this technique, contemporary authors have applied their talents to fictional reconstructions of historical murderers as in the case of Jorge Luis Borges's tale *El Asesino desinteresado Bill Harrigan* ("The Disinterested Killer Bill Harrigan" [1935]) about Billy the Kid, Angela Carter's portrait of Lizzy Borden in the story "The Fall River Axe Murders" (1985), Don DeLillo's novel *Libra* (1988) about Lee Har-vey Oswald, and E. L. Doctorow's portrayal of the gangster Dutch Schultz in *Billy Bathgate* (1989).

Based on De Quincey's recognition of the artistic possibilities in-volved in portraying homicide from the murderer's point of view, we would expect the description of the murderer Williams's psychological condition to be the focus of the account of the Marr family's slaughter in the "Postscript." After all, the "Macbeth" essay had been expressly inspired by De Quincey's insight that the circumstances of the Wil-liams murders bore a certain resemblance to Shakespeare's presenta-tion of Macbeth's murder of Duncan: "Now, it will be remembered that in the first of [the Williams] murders (that of the Marrs) the same incident (of a knocking at the door soon after the work of extermina-tion was complete) did actually occur which the genius of Shake-speare has invented." We have seen, however, that De Quincey de-

liberately refrained from exploiting this similarity and from following Shakespeare's technique in his own description of the murder of
the Marr family. Whereas Dostoyevsky was to come very close to the
Shakespearean model in *Crime and Punishment*—presenting the
murder scene and its aftermath from the killer Raskolnikov's point of
view, and describing his terrified reaction to Koch's banging on the
door of the apartment in which he is alone with the two women he
has just slain—De Quincey chooses to leave Williams's reaction to the
servant-girl's knocking a mystery, and instead presents the climactic
doorway scene from the perspective of the terrified servant-girl outside the house.[75]

This technique of depicting a gruesome murder from the point of
view of an endangered girl who manages to escape the carnage may
be a far cry from Shakespeare, but it is a familiar sight for aficionados
of modern horror movies, and in particular, of slasher films. Carol J.
Clover has described the hero of this genre as the "Final Girl"—a
female victim who "is abject terror personified," and yet who emerges
as the sole survivor of the male killer's malevolence.[76] De Quincey's
character Mary appears to be a precursor of this popular modern heroine. In many of these films, however, the Final Girl does not merely
survive, but actually succeeds in bringing about the killer's death.
Mary fails to appropriate the killer's role in De Quincey's narrative;
more significantly, it is not clear that she can even be considered a victim. In contrast to many "post-1974 slashers," which typically feature
a "penetration scene" in which the action is presented from the point
of view of a female victim who finds herself locked in an enclosed
space and waiting "with pounding heart as the killer slashes, hacks,
or drills his way in,"[77] in the "Postscript" it is the killer who is inside
the house and the "victim" who is safely outside. Mary is less a victim
than a witness; it is from this perspective that De Quincey constructs
an aesthetic of murder.

We can appreciate how De Quincey's treatment of the doorway
scene in the "Postscript" differs from the "high" artistry of Shakespeare and Dostoyevsky on the one hand, and from the "low" drama
of the contemporary slasher film on the other, by considering a

sequence of shots from Brian De Palma's 1980 film *Dressed to Kill*. Despite Clover's assertion that the "idea of a female [victim-hero] who outsmarts, much less outfights—or outgazes—her assailant is unthinkable in the films of De Palma,"[78] *Dressed to Kill* features a female hero, a streetwise hooker named Liz Blake (played by Nancy Allen) who, like Mary, is less a victim than a witness. When Liz and her date call an elevator after an assignation, they are appalled to find, as the doors open, a brutally knifed but still conscious woman (Angie Dickinson in the role of Kate Miller). Kate—whose violent struggle inside the claustrophobic enclosure of the elevator with her assailant, a sex maniac in drag, has already been shown—pleads for help as Liz looks on in horror (her date has fled in fright). She is just about to assist Kate when, in a mirror-fixture inside the elevator, she glimpses the distorted reflection of the razor-wielding attacker who has concealed himself in a blind corner of the elevator, prepared to strike Liz the instant she reaches the threshold to offer help to the dying victim. In a strikingly similar scene, the servant-girl Mary in De Quincey's account of the Williams murders realizes that the person whom she hears but cannot see on the other side of the door—and who in turn is listening intently to *her* and trying to make out who *she* is and what she is doing—is a murderer, "and upon the least indication of unlocking or unlatching she would have recoiled into the asylum of general darkness" (13:88–89). As De Quincey presents this scene from Mary's point of view, so De Palma's camera assumes Liz's point of view at the instant she discovers Kate's slashed body and senses the presence of the killer in the elevator.[79]

De Palma's elevator scene in *Dressed to Kill* and De Quincey's doorway scene in his "Postscript" both differ from Shakespeare's gate scene in that they do not present the murder from the killer's point of view. Nor, for that matter, do they present their respective murder scenes exclusively from the point of view of the victim in the manner of contemporary slasher films.[80] Neither the prostitute at the elevator door nor the servant-girl in the doorway of the Marr residence are examples of helpless murder-victims in whom, as De Quincey puts it in the "Macbeth" essay, "all strife of thought, all flux and reflux of passion and of purpose, are crushed by one overwhelming panic"

(10:392). On the contrary, De Palma's prostitute handily escapes the murderer's clutches, and then actually participates in the scheme to identify and apprehend him.[81] Mary may be terrified of the murderer's presence behind the door, but her awareness of his presence and her intuition that he *is* a murderer protect her from his savagery despite his proximity to her. De Quincey and De Palma, in short, fail to conform to the genre of the great psychological dramas of Shakespeare and Dostoyevsky where murder is presented from the killer's point of view, and where the primary interest lies, according to Auden, in "the observation, by the innocent many, of the guilty one." Nor do De Quincey's and De Palma's artistic treatments of murder belong to the genres of the "pure suspense story" or the slasher film in which the hero is neither a detective nor a murderer, but a victim, or rather, a potential victim.[82] Nor can these representations of murder be described as detective fictions with the sleuth as the protagonist and with the interest in what Auden calls "the dialectic of innocence and guilt."

De Quincey's writings are difficult to classify because his literary career is marked by a series of generic shifts and breaks. In the early "Macbeth" essay of 1823 and in the unfulfilled project of the *Confessions of a Murderer* which he planned to write at about this time, he seems to have contemplated writing an ambitious psychological tragedy or confessional work featuring a murderer-hero. Such a work could hardly have been considered a suspense thriller; the key word in the "Macbeth" essay is not "suspense" but "suspension," the dreamlike state of suspended animation that Macbeth experiences immediately upon killing the King.[83] We will never know if it was De Quincey's intention to develop this insight concerning the murderer's quasi-aesthetic condition in his projected *Confessions of a Murderer*. In some of the finest passages from his *Suspiria de Profundis*, however, he did give eloquent expression to such suspended visionary states[84] — apart from the context of murder, to be sure, but with respect to the one transgression that obsessed him even more than murder, opium-eating.

Unlike Poe, De Quincey never tried his hand at the rationalist

genre of detective fiction. But in the two "Murder" essays of 1827 and
1839, he turned aside from psychological and visionary modes of writing to take up the rationalist mode of satire. In these essays De Quincey puts satire to the ultimate test: his startling thesis that murder is
a valid art form is put forward for the serious purpose of critiquing reason itself as set forth in Kant's philosophy, and more specifically, of
critiquing Kant's aesthetic precept that the beautiful is a symbol of
morality. (In "Lord Arthur Savile's Crime" [1891], Wilde continued
this satiric project, going so far as to present murder as a moral obligation!)[85] Then, in the 1854 "Postscript" added to the "Murder"
essays, De Quincey abandoned both the visionary-confessional as
well as the rational-satiric modes in order to turn his talents in an altogether different direction. The "Postscript" presents neither the
ethical-psychological world of confession with its visionary moments
of suspension from the moral realm, nor the rhetorical-critical world
of ironic satire which challenges the innate moral sense of the reader.
The project undertaken in the "Postscript" is rather to conjure up a
nonrational, amoral, purely aesthetic world of sublime, inescapable
terror. In doing so, De Quincey avoids descending to the level of the
suspense thriller by presenting the action, not from the point of view
of any of the actual murder victims inside the Marr household, but
from the point of view of the servant Mary, a murder-witness safely situated outside the Marr home. Mary's "sickening terror" in the murderer's presence transports her momentarily into another world, much
as Macbeth's murder of Duncan (as De Quincey had described decades
earlier) opened "an immeasurable gulf" that separated Macbeth and
his witnesses—namely, the audience—from "the ordinary tide and succession of human affairs."

Mapping the Aesthetic

We have shaping before us the outline of a general typology of the
aesthetics of murder as depicted in the following diagram:

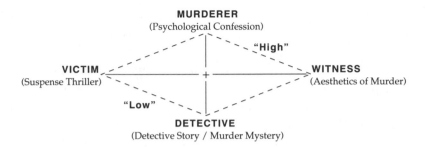

MURDERER
(Psychological Confession)

"High"

VICTIM   WITNESS
(Suspense Thriller)   (Aesthetics of Murder)

"Low"

DETECTIVE
(Detective Story / Murder Mystery)

On the one hand, we have the popular subliterary genres of question-able artistic status, the detective story and the suspense thriller, which focus the reader's (or, in the case of film, the viewer's) interest on the sleuth's deductive brilliance and the helpless victim's terror, respec-tively. On the other hand, we have the "high" artistic literary forms of the psychological drama (Shakespeare) or novel (Dostoyevsky, Gide) which focus the reader's or viewer's interest primarily on the mur-derer's point of view. The remaining alternative is the quasi-artistic form exploited both by De Quincey in the medium of literature and by De Palma in the medium of film, in which murder is presented neither from the detective's, nor from the victim's, nor from the killer's point of view, but from the perspective of a fourth party—the by-stander, who is at once vulnerable and immune to the murderer whose devastation he or she witnesses.[86]

Often, as in the examples from De Quincey and De Palma under discussion, the murder witness is a girl or young woman who, for once, is allowed to gaze rather than be gazed at.[87] Her gaze, however, is altogether different from the conventional masculine gaze which is voyeuristically directed at an arousing spectacle or desirable object. In contrast, the object of the feminine gaze is typically a scene of vio-lence. "Abject terror," maintains Clover, "is gendered feminine"; this accounts for "the femaleness of the victim" in the modern horror film, and even for the "incorporati[on]" of the "feminine" in the spectators who are collectively violated "in ways otherwise imaginable, for males, only in nightmare."[88] But the female victim's look of terror is not the only expression of the feminine gaze; there is also the female witness's look of anguish as she reacts to a tragic scene of suffering and violence with the classical responses of pity and fear. In the passive role of spectator, the reader of a text or the viewer of a film hardly becomes a victim, but rather assumes the role of (feminine) witness or (masculine) voyeur. The device of having the reader-viewer identify with the witness (in a murder story) or with the voyeur (in an erotic narrative) serves to thematize the reader-viewer's own experience *as* observer. That experience will be erotic when it is mediated by a voyeuristic persona who takes pleasure in what he sees and describes; it will be an aesthetic experience of the sublime when it is mediated by a witness to a murder or some other terrifying, arresting spectacle. (As I show in Chapter 3, however, the two sorts of experience at their most intense are often indistinguishable.)

The reader-viewer's identification with the murder witness produces a multifaceted aesthetic that combines the technique of the thriller (in which identification with the unrelieved terror of the murder-victim creates a sensation of suspense) with that of the confession (in which identification with the detached perspective of the murderer creates a vertiginous psychological state of suspension). Identification with the murder witness rather than exclusively with the murder victim allows the reader or spectator to experience terror-at-a-distance, so to speak, terror without the lurid torment of suspense. The spectator's terror is sublimated by the experience of the murder witness, which is itself mediated by her distance from the victim and the assailant. In their capacity as beholders, both the reader-viewer and the murder witness experience the victim's terror indirectly, *as if* they themselves were in mortal danger. (If martyrs, as the Greek meaning of the word suggests, were "witnesses" as well as victims, readers and moviegoers offer themselves up as victims as well as witnesses.) But if the relative safety of the reader-viewer and murder witness allows them to pass beyond the victim's terror, it initiates them into the mysterious experience of the murderer himself and invites them to participate in his otherworldly "suspension of earthly passion." Identification with the murder witness rather than exclusively or primarily with the murderer allows the reader-viewer to experience the rapture of suspension without having committed a crime and without having to face a penalty—like experiencing an opium "high" without having to face the prospect of a "crash." Georges Bataille claimed that transgression "suspends a taboo without suppressing it" ("elle lève l'interdit sans le supprimer");[89] De Quincey devised a means of using the innocent murder witness to suspend the moral opprobrium associated with the murderer's transgression while at the same time retaining a full sense of the thrilling horror of being in the presence of a transgressor who "had kicked himself loose of the earth" and for whom "nothing [was] either above or below."[90] The witness is physically safe from the killer's fury at the same time she is morally safe from the punishment and torment the killer will eventually bring upon himself.

De Quincey's technique of describing murder in the "Postscript" is, in short, subjective and sublime. Subjective, because even if the crucial doorway scene is not presented from the murderer's haunted perspective as in *Macbeth,* its terror is conveyed through the experience of a person present at the scene of the crime. And sublime, because even if we are not shown the psychology of a murderer like Macbeth in whom there is "raging some great storm of passion—jealousy, ambition, vengeance, hatred—which will create a hell within him" (10:392), we are presented with the stark terror of an innocent witness who is nevertheless safe from physical injury, and free from that "natural but ignoble instinct by which we cleave to life"—that "most abject and humiliating attitude" of self-preservation. In these two respects, De Quincey's artistic representation of murder conforms precisely to Kant's "Analytic of the Sublime" in the *Critique of Judgment.* Kant repeatedly affirms that the sublime is not an external object or event, but a subjective experience: "it is the state of mind produced by a certain representation with which the reflective judgment is occupied, and not the object, that is to be called sublime" ([sec. 25] "Mithin ist die Geistesstimmung durch eine gewisse die reflectirende Urtheilskraft beschäftigende Vorstellung, nicht aber das Object erhaben zu nennen.")[91] As a subjective experience rather than an objective event, the sublime would seem to lend itself better in literary form to the free-association of digression than to the linear logic of narrative. The digression on Mary's terror evokes a sense of the sublime more readily than the straightforward narration of the outward, "objective" facts concerning the murder itself.

But is murder really an appropriate subject with respect to an aesthetic of the sublime, or, in De Quincey's own terminology, a "literature of power"? Kant does not say as much, to be sure, and murder must have been farthest from his mind while he was writing the third critique. Murder was beyond the pale of aesthetics where it would appear, not as an instance of the sublime, but of the "monstrous"; for Kant, murder was essentially a moral issue. Yet De Quincey saw that murder furnished an excellent opportunity for exploring the troubling moral issues underlying aesthetics in general, and the aesthetic phenomenon of the sublime in particular. He exploited this opportunity by describing scenes that evoked the threat of violent death in the "Postscript" to the "Murder" essays, as well as in his tale "The Avenger" and in the section on "The Vision of Sudden Death" in *The English Mail-Coach*. S. K. Proctor has remarked that the "originality of De Quincey's conception of the sublime would appear to consist in his notion of the dark sublime, and, in particular, in his emphasis on the element of mystery in that species."[92] Insofar as it produces feelings of mystery, dread, and the sinister—feelings, Proctor notes, that are absent from Coleridge's and Kant's theories of the sublime—De Quincey's "dark sublime" is particularly suited for representations of murder.

Dark as De Quincey's personal sense of the sublime may be, it is only able to accommodate such a violent and scandalous subject as murder by following the Kantian principle that scenes of imminent destruction *cannot be presented from the perspective of the subject as victim.* Kant defines the sublime as that experience of natural grandeur or power which seems to be "zweckwidrig für unsere Urtheilskraft" ("to violate purpose in respect of the judgment"), and "gewaltthätig für die Einbildungskraft" ([sec. 23, 5:245] "to do violence to the imagination" [p. 83]). In contrast to the beautiful which "directly brings with it a feeling of the furtherance of life" ("directe ein Gefühl der Beförderung des Lebens bei sich führt"), the feeling of the sublime "is produced by the feeling of a momentary checking of the vital powers and a stronger outflow of them, so that it seems to be regarded as emotion—not play, but earnest in the exercise of the imagination" ([sec. 23, p. 83] "so daß sie durch das Gefühl einer augenblicklichen

Hemmung der Lebenskräfte und darauf sogleich folgenden desto stärkern Ergießung derselben erzeugt wird, mithin als Rührung kein Spiel, sondern Ernst in der Beschäftigung der Einbildungskraft zu sein scheint" [5:244–45]).[93] Kant insists that terror, while an aspect of the experience of the sublime, must not overwhelm the beholder. We may experience the sublime in the presence of terrible calamities and awesome spectacles "provided only that we are in security" ([sec. 28, p. 100] "wenn wir uns nur in Sicherheit befinden" [5:261]).

This is why Mary's "sickening terror" and "killing fear" at finding herself only inches away from Williams—"The unknown murderer and she have both their lips upon the door, listening, breathing hard"—is "sublimated" by the protective presence of the door which, as a barrier, affords the serving-girl a tenuous but effective form of security: "but luckily they are on different sides of the door; and upon the least indication of unlocking or unlatching she would have recoiled into the asylum of general darkness" (13:88–89). The sublimity of Mary's experience in the doorway results from the fact that although she is exposed to Williams's terrifying presence, her fate is not in his hands. Her presence of mind is not reduced to what De Quincey calls "the natural but ignoble instinct by which we cleave to life"; she does not exhibit "human nature in its most abject and humiliating attitude," nor is she "abject terror personified," as Clover describes the Final Girl in the slasher film. Rather, Mary's turmoil in Williams's presence is an exemplary instance of Kant's account of the sublime as it is experienced in the presence of overpowering natural phenomena:

> so giebt auch die Unwiderstehlichkeit ihrer Macht uns, als Naturwesen betrachtet, zwar unsere physische Ohnmacht zu erkennen, aber entdeckt zu gleich ein Vermögen, uns als von ihr unabhängig zu beurtheilen, und eine Überlegenheit über die Natur, worauf sich eine Selbsterhaltung von ganz andrer Art gründet, als diejenige ist, die von der Natur außer uns angefochten und in Gefahr gebracht werden kann, wobei die Menschheit in unserer Person unerniedrigt bleibt, obgleich der Mensch jener Gewalt unterliegen müßte. (sec. 28; 5:261–62)

> And so also the irresistibility of its might, while making us recognize our own physical impotence, considered as beings of nature, discloses to us a faculty of judging independently of and a superiority

over nature, on which is based a kind of self-preservation entirely different from that which can be attacked and brought into danger by external nature. Thus humanity in our person remains unhumiliated, though the individual might have to submit to this dominion. (p. 101)

We have seen in the "Macbeth" essay that the experience of an opium-trance provided De Quincey with a good analogy for the murderer's experience at the time of his deed. It appears that opium may actually have provided De Quincey himself with the precise sensations of fear and security which, according to Kant, are necessary conditions for the aesthetic experience of the sublime. De Quincey's daughter Florence reports of her father that "It was an accepted fact among us that he was able when saturated with opium to persuade himself and delighted to persuade himself (the excitement of terror was a real delight to him) that he was dogged by dark and mysterious foes."[94] Opium, in other words, permitted De Quincey to experience a sense of nonthreatening pseudo-terror in accordance with Kant's description of the sublime. Similarly, Mary's experience of the sublime in the "Postscript," in which fear seems to outweigh security, is complemented by the reader's feeling of the sublime in which security outweighs fear. Indeed, the reader of the description of Mary's turmoil, rather than Mary herself, is in a better position to experience the "*Astonishment* that borders upon terror" ("Die *Verwunderung,* die an Schreck gränzt") that, Kant writes, "in the safety in which we know ourselves to be, is not actual fear but only an attempt to feel fear by the aid of the imagination" ([sec. 29, p. 109] "bei der Sicherheit, worin er sich weiß, nicht wirklich Furcht, sondern nur ein Versuch, uns mit der Einbildungskraft darauf einzulassen" [5:269]). Through the intermediary figure of the servant Mary, De Quincey evokes in his reader the otherworldly experience of sublime suspension associated with murder that (as he recognized thirty-one years earlier) Shakespeare had evoked in him without any mediators in the more direct medium of the drama.

As closely as De Quincey in his "Postscript" conforms to Kant's requirements for producing the artistic effect of the sublime, he appears elsewhere to have either totally ignored or fundamentally misread Kant's remarks on the sublime in the *Critique of Judgment.* He lambasted Kant in 1836 for portraying man as "an abject animal" (2: 89)[95]—the same reason for which he had reviled those cheap attempts at horror which show "human nature in its most abject and humiliating attitude" (10:391) in the earlier "Macbeth" essay. Yet man is hardly a pathetic, abject creature desperately clinging to life in Kant's account of the sublime; on the contrary, Kant declares that in sublime encounters with nature "die Menschheit [bleibt] in unserer Person unerniedrigt" ("humanity in our person remains unhumiliated"). Only through a very haphazard reading or through a willfully "perverse interpretation," as René Wellek has claimed in another context,[96] could De Quincey have failed to note the striking correspondence between his own aesthetic of murder and Kant's aesthetic of the sublime. With minor revisions, the "Analytic of the Sublime" could serve an entirely unsuspected and unintended purpose as a philosophical rationale for a literature and cinema of crime.

Nevertheless, the transgressive sublime, the aesthetics of crime, went virtually unsuspected by the Enlightenment philosopher. Four decades later, their literary possibilities were vividly recognized by De Quincey. Through an imaginative literary-philosophical synthesis of Shakespeare and Kant that he worked out over a thirty-year period, De Quincey developed a technique for portraying the criminal-as-artist, devising a means of transferring a visionary state of sublime suspension from the guilt-tinged conscience of the murderer to the pure, aesthetic experience of the innocent murder witness.[97] However ironic De Quincey's idea of considering murder as a fine art may have been as expressed in the early "Murder" essays, Kant's aesthetic philosophy provided an unexpected impulse for an innovative art form cum aesthetic that came to fruition in the 1854 "Postscript," and that pointed the way toward the work of Poe and Baudelaire, of Wilde and Borges, of Robbe-Grillet and Eco, of Hitchcock and De Palma.

T W O

MURDER AS (PURE) ACTION

Acts must be carried through to their completion. Whatever their point of departure, the end will be beautiful. It is because an action has not been completed that it is vile.

—Genet, *Journal du Voleur*

A work of art is a dream of murder which is realized by an act.

—Sartre, *Saint Genet*

Murder for Art's Sake

De Quincey's chief discovery in the "Postscript" to his "Murder" essays was how to aestheticize the brutality of murder by presenting sensational mass killings from the point of view of a terrified witness at the scene of the crime who has the good fortune to be just beyond the murderer's reach. The terror of the servant-girl Mary as she stands outside the door behind which the Marr family has just been slaughtered, and the panic of the lodger who glimpses Williams's butchery of the Williamson household before fleeing to safety through the second-floor window, evoke in the reader a vivid aesthetic experience of the sublime. This experience entails a sense of suspense, to be sure (will the witness succeed in getting away in time?), but more significantly, it consists of an otherworldly state of suspension which, for a timeless interval, binds the murderer, the witness, and the reader together in a sealed, private space until the ethical world of human reality intervenes.

Such is the aesthetic experience of murder—life-threatening violence as perceived by an involved, but secure, observer. But what of the experience of the murderer himself, the actual perpetrator of these atrocious acts? This is a more difficult matter since, unlike Shakespeare's Macbeth, De Quincey's Ratcliffe Highway murderer is presented at a distance. John Williams embodies the romantic view of the artist: he is a mystery whose dark intentions remain inscrutable. The aesthetic experience of both narrator and reader is one of awe; they are the murderer-artist's captive audience. In order to free themselves from this thralldom, they are called upon to exercise their own imagination, to penetrate the mind of the murderer as he sets about his deed. What emotions does he feel while committing his crimes? What prompted him to commit them in the first place?

In his portrayal of the Ratcliffe Highway murderer, De Quincey was able to give free rein to his fancy because almost nothing was known about the actual assailant whose name itself was most likely an alias. The historical "John Williams" hanged himself in his jail cell after he was arrested on purely circumstantial evidence, and further inquiries into his case were not pursued.[1] The apparent motive in both the Marr and the Williamson slaughters was robbery; in both cases, a substantial sum of cash was on the premises. De Quincey significantly alters the facts by presenting the victim Marr as being on the verge of bankruptcy. Instead of accepting robbery as the motive, De Quincey invents a tale of a past rivalry between Marr and Williams over "a very pretty young woman" who subsequently became Marr's wife and who aroused Williams's jealousy. There is no evidence, however, of any such prior familiarity between the real-life Williams and his victims, and De Quincey's narrator himself admits that

> it has sometimes happened, on occasion of a murder not sufficiently accounted for, that, from pure goodness of heart intolerant of a mere sordid motive for striking murder, some person has forged, and the public has accredited, a story representing the murderer as having moved under some loftier excitement: and in this case the public, too much shocked at the idea of Williams having on the single motive of gain consummated so complex a tragedy, welcomed the tale which represented him as governed by deadly malice, growing out of the more impassioned and noble rivalry for the favor of a woman.

"The case remains in some degree doubtful," the narrator concedes, but then illogically concludes that "certainly, the probability is that Mrs. Marr had been the true cause, the *causa teterrima*, of the feud between the men" (13:80). By attributing a romantic motive to Williams's assault against the Marr household, the narrator suggests that the murders were a crime of passion. But this explanation is based only on rumor and on the public's "intoleran[ce] of a mere sordid motive for striking murder," and cannot be given much credence. The romantic motive simply doesn't suit the artistic nature of the killings. While jealousy is certainly a motive for murder, it is hardly an *artistic* motive—even when, as in the 1988 trial of New York City sculptor Carl Andre, the suspect was accused of killing his wife out of professional, rather than sexual, jealousy as a rival artist.[2] An artistic murder cannot be a hot-blooded crime of passion, but must be a cold-blooded act in which jealousy and revenge play no part.

Thus, we return in the case of Williams's slaughter of the Marrs to the robbery motive. Diderot, Schiller, Genet, and De Quincey himself in the first "Murder" essay thought theft to be a far baser act than homicide when judged from an aesthetic perspective.[3] But was robbery aesthetically acceptable as a motive for murder? Perhaps, when the victim put up no resistance, and when the cash involved was a paltry sum, as De Quincey made out to be the case in the Marr slayings. Jack Katz has observed that "robberies in which nonresisting victims are murdered seem especially 'senseless'";[4] in such instances, the murders themselves appear to be the criminal's primary intention, while the robberies appear gratuitous. As abhorrent as murders committed for profit may be, they pale beside killings carried out by robber-murderers like Gary Gilmore in which, as Katz suggests, a token robbery provides the "cold-blooded" killer with a rationale to disguise the "madness" of his deed. In such cases, the robbery is not really senseless or gratuitous, but serves as a blind behind which the killer can act out a scenario of evil or deviance in which he is scrupulously attentive to the artistic and strategic aspects of his "work." "Cold-blooded, 'senseless' robber-killers . . . set up the scene of violence to make a point, often remaining longer than the robbery requires to ensure that their design has been properly executed."[5]

By altering the facts of the Ratcliffe Highway murders in order to present the Marrs as virtually destitute, De Quincey intensifies the cold-blooded character of Williams's deed. The narrator is unable to accept petty theft as a credible motive for such a monstrous act. So he invents a story of romantic jealousy out of whole cloth in order to make the murders more intelligible. But even this motive, for all its value as an efficient cause, is inadequate as a formal and final cause because it fails to explain the excessive and "complex" nature of Williams's killings, his apparent intention to cut the throats of every member of the Marr and Williamson households. It is this excess that shocks the reader. We are terrified and baffled by Williams's frustration during his carnage of the Marrs when the servant Mary escapes him, and again during his slaughter of the Williamsons when he is prevented from slaying the sleeping grandchild by the escaped lodger's call for help. What motive can possibly account for such savage bloodlust?

There can be only one explanation: the killer is motivated by a purely artistic impulse, or as Katz would say, he is "executing a design." In the case of the Marrs:

> What was the murderer's meaning in coming along the passage to the front-door? The meaning was this:—Separately, as an individual, Mary was worth nothing at all to him. But, considered as a member of the household, she had this value, viz. that she, if caught and murdered, perfected and rounded the desolation of the house. (13:89)

And in the case of the Williamson murders, regarding Williams's inexplicable loitering at the scene of the crime before the alarm is raised, we are told that

> the reason which governed him is striking; because at once it records that murder was not pursued by him simply as a means to an end, but also as an end for itself. . . . As to plunder, he has already bagged the whole. And it was next to impossible that any arrear, the most trivial, should still remain for a gleaner. But the throats—the throats—there it was that arrears and gleanings might perhaps be counted on. And thus it appeared that, in his wolfish thirst for blood, Mr. Williams put to hazard the whole fruits of his night's work, and his life into the bargain. (13:108)

Instead of flying with his booty, Williams heads upstairs where the Williamsons' granddaughter—a child of nine in De Quincey's version, but actually a girl of fourteen[6]—lies sleeping. The narrator stresses the ironic circumstance that the child is saved, not by the murderer's moral conscience, but by his artistic conscientiousness: his compulsion to kill every member of the household gives the upstairs lodger time to escape.

> The logic of the case, in short, all rested upon the *ultra* fiendishness of Williams. Were he likely to be content with the mere fact of the child's death, apart from the process and leisurely expansion of its mental agony—in that case there would be no hope. But, because our present murderer is fastidiously finical in his exactions—a sort of martinet in the scenical grouping and draping of the circumstances in his murders—therefore it is that hope becomes reasonable, since all such refinements of preparation demand time. Murders of mere necessity Williams was obliged to hurry: but in a murder of pure voluptuousness, entirely disinterested, where no hostile witness was to be removed, no extra booty to be gained, and no revenge to be gratified, it is clear that to hurry would be altogether to ruin. If this child, therefore, is to be saved, it will be on pure aesthetical considerations. (13:110)

In a note, De Quincey emphasizes that Williams had no reason to want to kill the sleeping child apart from purely artistic concerns; the child had seen nothing of the murders and could not have testified against him. This excessive brutality—killing individuals for no other reason than that they "belong" to the ill-fated house, delaying the killings for maximum pleasure—makes it clear that motives such as robbery, or even jealousy, are not primary factors. Such gross disproportion between motive and murder, end and means, suggests that the murders have no motive at all, and supports the narrator's statement about Williams that "murder was not pursued by him simply as a means to an end, but also as an end for itself." It is this apparent lack of motive that gives Williams's crimes their specifically gratuitous and aesthetic character. The killer's "art" is judged quite differently from the work of the conventional artist: De Quincey applauds Williams for his gratuitous acts of violence, but he himself avoids gratuitous descriptions of such acts that would be deemed tasteless. In describing what from the murderer's point of view is "a murder of pure voluptuousness, entirely disinterested," De Quincey portrays a condition of artistic disinterestedness on the part of the murderer that evokes and corresponds to a condition of aesthetic disinterestedness in the reader.

From Aesthetics to Pragmatics:
Nietzsche's Critique of Disinterestedness

As one contemplates or looks back upon *any* action at all, it is and remains impenetrable; . . . our opinions about "good" and "noble" and "great" can never be *proved true* by our actions because every action is unknowable.

—Friedrich Nietzsche, *The Gay Science*

De Quincey's literary subversion in the "Murder" essays of Kant's morally governed aesthetics anticipated philosophy's ultimate reformulation of the arts as an extramoral discourse by Nietzsche and his successors later in the nineteenth century. In the course of subjecting the classical humanistic and artistic tradition to the rigorous treatment of philosophical analysis, Nietzsche succeeded in aestheticizing philosophy itself once and for all, purging it of the moral presuppositions that had doggedly dominated it since Plato.[7] Kant and Hegel, according to Nietzsche, had extended the "dominion of morality" ("die Herrschaft der Moral") in philosophy to its limit. Kant had posited "a realm of moral values, withdrawn from us, invisible, real" ("ein Reich der moralischen Werthe, uns entzogen, unsichtbar, wirklich"). At best, this moral absolute might be dimly manifest in nature and art as the beautiful; Hegel's dialectical idealism merely provided a means for further developing the "becoming-visible of the moral realm" ("Sichtbarwerdung des moralischen Reichs"). But, declared Nietzsche, "Let us not be deceived either in the Kantian or in the Hegelian manner: — we no longer *believe* in morality, as they did, and consequently we have no need to found a philosophy with the aim of justifying morality" ([sec. 415, p. 223]; "Wir wollen uns weder auf die Kantische noch Hegel'sche Manier betrügen lassen: — wir *glauben* nicht mehr, wie sie, an die Moral und haben folglich auch keine Philosophien zu gründen, *damit* die Moral Recht behält" [18:289]). "Anyone who still judges 'in this case everybody would have to act like this'" — anyone, that is, who accepts Kant's categorical imperative — has failed to progress towards self-knowledge for the reason that "our opinions about 'good' and 'noble' and 'great' can never be *proved true* by our actions because every action is unknowable" ("Unsere Meinungen von 'gut,' 'edel,' 'gross' durch unsere Handlungen nie *beweisen* werden können, weil jede Handlung unerkennbar ist" [12:246]).[8] The philosophical project undertaken by Nietzsche entailed nothing less than the dissolution of the established metaphysical categories operative in both ethics (good versus evil) and in epistemology (truth versus lie), and the exposure of such "absolute" values as merely provisional, functionally related determinations that are actually motivated by the ceaseless interplay of various competing manifestations of the will to power. "Let us therefore *limit* ourselves to the purification of our opinions and valuations and to the *creation of our own new tables of what is good*, and let us stop brooding about the 'moral value of our actions'!" (*"Beschränken* wir uns also auf die Reinigung unserer Meinungen und Werthschätzungen und auf die *Schöpfung neuer eigener Gütertafeln:—* über den 'moralischen Werth unserer Handlungen' aber wollen wir nicht mehr grübeln!" [12:246]).[9]

In the process of liberating art and philosophy from the dominion of morality, Nietzsche cleared the way for a radical reformulation of the Kantian idea of disinterestedness in the arts. Kant had established aesthetic contemplation as a purely disinterested activity on the part of the beholder. No strings were attached in aesthetic experience; the beholder was assumed to be free from any interest in, or from any desire to possess or to master, the object of beauty before him. In the nineteenth century, aesthetic disinterestedness became a central doctrine, the rationale behind the art-for-art's-sake movement, which some critics believe De Quincey to have influenced through such intermediaries as Baudelaire and Gautier.[10] It is highly unlikely, however, that De Quincey—given what S. K. Proctor calls his "instinctive religious mysticism"[11]—would himself have tolerated a final rupture between (interested) ethics and (disinterested) aesthetics leading ultimately to art-for-art's-sake and Decadence. But he clearly ridicules Kant in his 1827 essay "On Murder" and its 1839 sequel as a moralist trapped in his own rigid system by an inflexible commitment to the truth, who could neither entertain nor envision the possibility of a darkly sublime aesthetics of murder.

Nietzsche was even more direct than De Quincey in his assault on Kant's principle of aesthetic disinterestedness, making explicit what is left implicit in the description of the Ratcliffe Highway murders in the 1854 "Postscript." Citing Kant's claim in the *Critique of Judgment* that "that is beautiful which gives us pleasure *without interest*" ("Schön ist . . . was *ohne interesse* gefällt"), Nietzsche derisively comments:

> Without interest! Compare with this definition one framed by a genuine "spectator" and artist—Stendhal, who once called the beautiful *une promesse de bonheur*. At any rate he *rejected* and repudiated the one point about the aesthetic condition which Kant had stressed: *le désintéressement*. Who is right, Kant or Stendhal?[12]

Keeping in mind that Stendhal, like De Quincey, was a writer fascinated by actual murder cases who adapted such incidents in his own fiction (*Le Rouge et le Noir* and the unfinished *Lamiel*), we can better appreciate Nietzsche's antithesis between the passionless condition of aesthetic disinterestedness theorized by Kant, and Stendhal's portrayal of murder as a *crime passionel*. The problem with the idea of disinterestedness, Nietzsche was quick to recognize, was "that Kant, like all philosophers, instead of envisaging the aesthetic problem from the point of view of the artist (the creator), considered art and the beautiful purely from that of the 'spectator,' and unconsciously introduced the 'spectator' into the concept 'beautiful.'"[13]

This one-sided emphasis on the aesthetic experience of the spectator—the spectator as "view-master"—could not last. During the nineteenth century, the idea of disinterestedness began to acquire a profoundly demonic resonance as it was shifted from the relatively passive experience of aesthetic perception elaborated by Kant to the act of artistic creation itself. It is not surprising in this respect that Kant treated the subject of aesthetics as fundamentally a matter of *judgment*—an "act of mind" midway between the passive, almost automatic activity of perception and the voluntarism of moral action.[14] It was one thing for the connoisseur to regard an object, and even an act such as murder, with aesthetic disinterest; it is quite a different matter for the artist to produce a work—and, ultimately, to commit a criminal act—in a spirit of what Nietzsche called "disinterested malice" ("uninteressirte Bosheit" [15:329]),[15] in a state of cool detachment without any demonstrable motive and with no regard for the moral and emotional consequences that his act must bring about. The fact that the artist produces his work while in such a detached state of disinterestedness gives his creation a criminal appearance when viewed from a moral perspective.

By the second half of the nineteenth century, then, we have come a long way both from Kant's Enlightenment view of aesthetic perception as disinterested, unprejudiced judgment, and from the high romantic view of perception as a creative artistic activity where, in Wordsworth's words, the world is something that the senses "half create" and half "perceive." No topic so readily exposed the inherent contradictions in the ideas of aesthetic disinterestedness and of artistic creativity as that of criminality, and especially that of murder, as demonstrated by De Quincey's essays on the subject. Kant's principle of disinterestedness had inadvertently provided a rationale whereby murder could become palatable to aesthetic taste and acceptable as an art form. Not only was murderous violence a logical subject for later romantics in search of sublime effects, but the psychology of the murderer—his passionate spirit of rebellion, his unfulfilled fantasies and desires, his overworked imagination—was a superb object for aesthetic (dispassionate, disinterested, value-free) contemplation. Theodore Ziolkowski's insight that the "criminal mind rather than the criminal act" came to be recognized "as a worthy object of aesthetic contemplation" in "works of romanticism . . . concerned with crime,"[16] is exemplified in De Quincey's essay on *Macbeth* and in the spate of psychological studies of the criminal in nineteenth-century literature. In these works, however, we detect a transformation in the concept of disinterestedness itself: from the witness or beholder's passive, awe-struck state of aesthetic contemplation of sublime violence, to the hyperactive, quasi-demonic state of mind of the criminal-as-artist. Toward the end of the century, modernist artists appropriated the murderer's disinterested state of mind for themselves in what I've called the artist-as-criminal phenomenon. The criminal in literature came to be regarded less, in Ziolkowski's words, as an "object of aesthetic contemplation" than as "a projection of the artist's own subjectivity."[17] In the course of writing with increasing obsessiveness about the criminal, the late-romantic artist discovered that he was actually writing about himself. From literary fictions centered on the writer's own projection of himself in the role of assassin, to actual autobiographical accounts composed by real-life killers like Pierre-François Lacenaire, De Quincey's unwritten *Confessions of a Murderer* would finally materialize, not as an individual text or even as a literary genre, but as a pervasive aesthetic that defied classification.

This chapter explores the subtle but significant transition from the aesthetic disinterestedness associated with high romantic idealism (corresponding roughly to what Foucault calls the "aesthetic rewriting of crime") to the program of artistic disinterestedness that typifies certain forms of modernism (corresponding to Foucault's reference to "the appropriation of criminality in acceptable forms," and to "the affirmation that greatness too has a right to crime"[18]) — and in particular, fascism, with its program, memorably described by Walter Benjamin, to aestheticize politics.[19] As Kant's philosophy provided a logical rationale (though Kant himself would have balked at the prospect) for an aesthetics of murder of the type set forth by De Quincey, so Nietzsche is the figure in whose name the crime of murder has been rationalized and raised from merely passive aesthetic experience to outright epistemological pursuits, and ultimately, to pure, often outrageous, spontaneous action — a path that De Quincey, in turn, would have feared to tread.[20] Small wonder then that, in Sander Gilman's words, Nietzsche has been repeatedly designated as "a 'dangerous' thinker — not merely [because] he espoused dangerous thoughts, but [because] he caused dangerous acts."[21] Acts, that is, such as murder.

Gratuitous Acts: Schwob, Hitchcock, Gide, Robbe-Grillet

> This story is one I have been retelling, with small variations, ever since. It is the tale of the motiveless, or disinterested, duel — of courage for its own sake.
>
> — Jorge Luis Borges, "An Autobiographical Essay"

A year after the appearance of De Quincey's first "Murder" essay, two Irishmen named William Burke and William Hare committed a series of killings in Edinburgh. Their method was to lure indigents from the street to their lodgings, where they would smother them;

then they would dispose of the corpses by selling them to the renowned anatomist Robert Knox. So great was the sensation surrounding their trial in 1829 that it gave rise to a new word for murder, "to burke." A decade later in the second "Murder" paper, De Quincey was to refer sardonically to the "Burke-and-Hare revolution in the art" (13:60). But De Quincey says no more about the murderous duo, reserving his literary talent for his account of the 1811 Ratcliffe Highway murders in the 1854 "Postscript."

In fact, no author of note touched the Burke and Hare case in the years immediately following its occurrence; it was regarded as too tasteless and abhorrent a subject for literary treatment. Sir Walter Scott was approached by "Dr. Knox's jackal for buying murdered bodies," who offered to supply colorful anecdotes concerning the case for the writer to work into literary form; Scott rejected the proposal with disgust.[22] Later in the century, however, after the journalistic approach to murder first practiced by De Quincey in the "Postscript" caught on, and after the technique of creating a forbidding criminal character based on newspaper reports, police records, and trial transcripts of actual homicides had become standard literary procedure, a number of writers turned to the case of Burke and Hare for their subject. Laurence Senelick mentions such examples as Robert Louis Stevenson's "The Body-Snatcher," James Bridie's *The Anatomist*, and Dylan Thomas's *The Doctor and the Devils*,[23] but he neglects what is perhaps the most interesting and influential treatment of all: the French writer Marcel Schwob's tale "MM. Burke et Hare, Assassins" from the collection *Vies imaginaires* (1896). Schwob's story was admired by Jorge Luis Borges, who translated it into Spanish,[24] as did his mentor Rafael Cansinos-Assens, who also translated De Quincey's *Confessions of an English Opium-Eater*.[25] In "Burke and Hare," Schwob brilliantly realizes the thesis of his precursor De Quincey that murder can aspire to the distinction of fine art.

In order to present the historical figures of Burke and Hare as artists, Schwob needed to transform his subject even more than De Quincey did in the case of John Williams. For the two Irishmen were actually little more than "low-life butchers"[26] who lived in the seediest of circumstances and dispatched their helpless victims merely for the money they could get from the sale of their corpses. In his colorful account of the killers, William Bolitho characterizes Burke as "a dog, an ill-bred country mongrel that on sight any shepherd would shoot," while his accomplice "Hare's appearance had somewhat of the devilry or the insane levity of the wolf."[27] Bolitho does all he can to debunk the criminal-as-artist conceit. He makes a point of stating that Burke and Hare—and, indeed, all multiple murderers—are anything but creative individuals:

> The mass-murderer repeats himself, blindly, because he has no imagination. If he had imagination it would breed sympathy and pity. The complete lack of these feelings is necessary before a man can kill. He repeats the details of his first crime, because he is afraid the least innovation would endanger a recurrence of his immunity.[28]

Yet it is just such unimaginative sociopaths who are afraid of novelty and of taking risks whom Schwob presents as consummate artists in his tale. Following De Quincey's reference to the "Burke-and-Hare revolution in the art," Schwob prophesies that these names will "remain as inseparable in the art as are those of Beaumont and Fletcher" (p. 165).

Of the two characters in Schwob's tale, "Mr. Burke" (as this ne'er-do-well is dignified) is clearly the mastermind while "Mr. Hare" is merely the accomplice. Such was the latter's "complete disinterest" ("complet désintéressement")[29] that he "never contested the popular favour that attached itself to the name of Burke" (p. 165). Hare's disinterestedness with respect to his reputation parallels that of Burke with respect to his actual "work." This disinterestedness appears in several ways. First, the choice of a murder victim was haphazard and almost arbitrary. Burke would make nightly forays through Edinburgh: "He would roam the street to scan the faces that aroused his curiosity. Sometimes he chose at random" (p. 166). The arbitrary selection of the murder victim underscored the gratuitous nature of the killings. There was nothing personal about the choice of the stranger, nothing that could be construed as a motive. Such disinterestedness enhanced the artistic effect of the crime.

A second form of artistic disinterestedness came into play after Burke, with a show of impeccable civility, struck up an acquaintance with the evening's stranger, and—in a scene altogether of Schwob's invention—invited him up to an unassuming garret leased by Hare.

> They would surrender the settee to him; they would offer him Scotch whisky to drink; and Mr. Burke would question him regarding the most unusual incidents in his life. Mr. Burke was a perfectly insatiable listener. The narrative was always interrupted before daybreak by Mr. Hare. The form Mr. Hare's interruption took was always the same, and was most imperative. To cut short the recital, it was Mr. Hare's custom to slip behind the settee and apply both his hands to the mouth of the storyteller. At the very same moment Mr. Burke would seat himself on the man's chest. The pair would remain in this position motionless, dreaming of the end of the story which they never heard. In this way Messrs. Burke and Hare finished a great number of tales the world will never know. (p. 166)

In an ironic inversion of the Scheherazade story, in which the wily storyteller saves her life by breaking off her narrative before dawn, Burke and Hare take it upon themselves to cut short their guest's narrative of his life by cutting short his life itself. The stranger's story is left hanging on his dying gasp, an open-ended narrative that Burke and Hare—indifferent to the actual conclusion that the stranger was about to relate—complete with their own unspoken imaginings. The two killers would then strip the corpse, not for the purpose of robbery, but in order to inspect the stranger's jewelry, count his money, and read his correspondence—some of which "was not without interest" (p. 166; "ne furent pas sans intérêt" [p. 189])—all with a view toward assisting them in their reconstruction of the stranger's narrative.

Insofar as they kill the storyteller and take over his narrative function, Burke and Hare improve on the story in *The Thousand and One Nights* in which Scheherazade's life is spared each morning because the caliph cannot suppress his *interest* in finding out what happens next. Burke and Hare are truly disinterested in this regard, as shown by their habit of murdering their victims in mid-story, an act that suspends the victims' narratives indefinitely and leaves their listeners in interminable suspense. But the most telling proof of the killers' disinterestedness comes to light after the murder. Here Schwob depicts Burke's artistic gifts as being far superior to those of the caliph of the *Arabian Nights*:

There is in what he did, as it were, a distant breath of the *Thousand-and-One-Nights*. Like a caliph wandering in the nocturnal gardens of Baghdad, he desired mysterious adventures, intrigued as he was by tales of the unknown and of men from foreign parts. Like a great black slave armed with a scimitar, for him there was no end more proper to his enjoyment than the death of others. But his Anglo-Saxon originality consisted in his being able to draw the greatest advantage from the play of his Celtic imagination. When his artistic pleasure was at an end, what, pray, did the black slave do with those whose head he had cut off? With a wholly Arabian barbarism, he carved them into quarters so as to preserve them, salted, in a cellar. What profit did he obtain of this? None. Mr. Burke was infinitely superior. (p. 165)

Burke's solution regarding the artistic disposal of the corpses consisted in an arrangement with Dr. Knox, whom he agreed to furnish with an ample supply of fresh specimens for dissection—ordinarily impossible to come by. In this way, the genteel "Mr." Burke, as Schwob refers to him, managed to avoid the unseemly Arabian barbarism of carving up corpses and preserving them. By pairing his own disinterestedness as an artist with a medical professor's interest in the human anatomy, Burke received a handsome sum for letting someone else do the dirty work of cutting up and disposing of his own victims.

Eventually, Burke's genius led him, in Schwob's account, to abandon the traditional artistic trappings of Hare's "garret," and the lengthy sessions listening to his victims' narratives which turned out to be "endlessly similar" (p. 167). Human lives and their narrative representations are essentially invariable and repetitious; Burke discovered that only the unspeakable instant of death itself was truly unique: "He came to be interested only in the real aspect, for him always different, of death" (p. 167; "Il en vint à ne s'intéresser qu'à l'aspect réel, toujours varié pour lui, de la mort" [p. 190]). Life, like art (which, after all, is only life re- or foretold), was uninteresting and banal. Death alone was able to captivate Burke and to sustain his interest; it was the act of murder itself that provided the aesthetic sensation of pure suspense. Thus, Burke induced his associate Hare to take their act from the garret to the streets, where they performed their killings with sudden swiftness, without any preambles and without any props except for a linen mask filled with pitch which they used to stifle the first stranger who happened to pass by. In this fashion, Burke succeeded in paring his artistic technique down to the bare essentials, perfecting a minimal style whereby art (the imitation of living action, according to Aristotle) was converted into the pure act of murder itself.

Of the subsequent events in the lives of Messrs. Burke and Hare— their capture, trial, and punishment—we learn next to nothing. Schwob's narrator, himself a critic of some sophistication, considers "the end of their life . . . commonplace, and like so many others" (p. 167; "la fin de leur vie fut vulgaire et semblable à tant d'autres" [p. 191]). The narrator's attitude in this respect resembles that of Burke whose imagination soon tired "of the endlessly similar narratives of human experience" (p. 167; "des récits éternellement semblables de l'expérience humaine" [p. 190]) reported by his victims. As Burke and Hare killed their victims before they could conclude their confessions, preferring to dream "of the end of the story which they never heard," so Schwob's narrator leaves his protagonists' end, their inglorious retribution to society, to the reader's imagination. What other biographers would find sensational, Schwob's narrator finds commonplace. He departs from customary biographical procedure by breaking off his narrative while Burke and Hare are

> haloed in their glory. Why destroy so fine an artistic effect [un si bel effet d'art] by leading them languishingly to the end of their career, by exposing their failures and their disappointments. There is no call to see them otherwise than on foggy nights, their mask at the ready. (p. 167)

On purely artistic grounds, the narrator refrains from recounting the details of the murderous pair's downfall and appeasing society's moral demand for justice. Instead, he breaks off his account of the "imaginary lives" of Burke and Hare much as they suspended their victims' narratives, freezing all action and discourse in a motionless tableau consisting of Mr. Hare in the act of gagging the storyteller from behind the settee while Mr. Burke straddled the victim's chest.

Schwob's "Burke and Hare" invites comparison with Alfred Hitchcock's early film *Rope* (1948), based on the play *Rope's End* by

Patrick Hamilton, itself inspired by the sensational Leopold and Loeb murder case of 1924. That case had involved the slaying of a fourteen-year-old boy by two youths of prominent Chicago families who "wanted the excitement of committing a perfect detection-defying crime."[30] Where the actual murderers Leopold and Loeb were apparently motivated by the desire to commit a *perfect* murder (that is, an undetected crime), their fictional counterparts in Hitchcock's *Rope*, as well as in Schwob's "Burke and Hare," are bent upon committing a *pure* murder— a motiveless crime, murder for its own sake, murder as art.[31]

In Hitchcock's film, as in Schwob's story, two men invite a guest up to their chambers on a social pretext, and then proceed to strangle him. But the situation in *Rope* differs from that in "Burke and Hare" in two significant ways. First, the victim is not a stranger. As in the Leopold and Loeb affair, in which the victim, Bobby Franks, was a neighbor and distant cousin of Richard Loeb, the murder victim and his assailants in Hitchcock's film are acquaintances. The counterpart to Burke in the film, a conniving student named Brandon (played by John Dall), has persuaded his companion Phillip (Farley Granger) to kill their former classmate David Kentley for no other reason than to prove the bizarre thesis of Brandon's teacher Rupert Cadell (played by James Stewart) that "murder is an art and as such should remain the privilege of superior beings"—presumably beings of a superior moral and aesthetic sensibility.[32]

The second way in which Hitchcock's film differs from Schwob's tale (and, in this respect, also from the Leopold and Loeb affair) has to do with the circumstance that Brandon really isn't interested in committing a perfect murder, a crime that escapes detection. As a would-be artist, Brandon has an urgent need to exhibit his handiwork before an audience. For this purpose, he has invited a number of friends— including Cadell, the victim David's parents, David's girlfriend, and even David himself—to a cocktail party in the apartment where the murder has taken place only hours before. Brandon has prevailed on Phillip to help him conceal the body in a chest that serves as a buffet off of which the guests take their hors d'oeuvres. David's failure to appear at the party, or even to call, makes the guests increasingly uneasy, and Cadell's suspicions are aroused when Brandon repeatedly baits him about his theory of murder as the privilege of exceptionally gifted individuals. Phillip begins to panic as he realizes that Brandon has half-intentionally contrived the means by which their deed will be discovered—and, Brandon deludes himself, approved—by his mentor, Cadell. Brandon is prepared to let himself be caught, and to forfeit his achievement of the perfect murder, just to have his deed appreciated as an act of pure murder.

Perhaps the best-known novelistic treatment of murder as a pure act is André Gide's novel, *Les Caves du Vatican* (1914). Lafcadio's sudden impulse to push a stranger sitting across from him (who, unbeknownst to him, is his brother-in-law, Amédée Fleurissoire) out the door of the speeding train appears entirely unpremeditated and unmotivated. No one witnesses the crime except, possibly, for Lafcadio's former schoolmate Protos, who has put Fleurissoire up to a mad quest to rescue the supposedly imprisoned Pope, and who thus has his own interest in tailing Lafcadio's bumbling brother-in-law. The scene in the railway compartment is presented not from the point of view of a disinterested observer, but from the murderer Lafcadio's own perspective as a disinterested agent. It is hardly Gide's purpose to elicit from his reader an aesthetic response of awe or terror to Lafcadio's act as De Quincey had done in his description of the Williams murders. Gide's concern is rather to depict the psychology of a murderer acting without a motive—to depict murder itself as a disinterested *acte gratuit*. Or as another character in the novel—Lafcadio's half-brother Julius de Baraglioul, who is himself a novelist—meditates about the book he yearns to write, "I don't want a motive for the crime—all I want is an explanation of the criminal" ("Je ne veux pas de motif au crime; il me suffit de motiver le criminel").[33]

Julius elaborates a psychology of the man who acts without motives, a character he intends to use as the protagonist of his new novel. He explains his idea to his brother-in-law Amédée, who a few pages later will become his other brother-in-law Lafcadio's victim. "The important point," says Julius, "is that what makes him act should not be a matter of interest, or, as the usual phrase is, that he should not be merely actuated by interested motives" (p. 166; "l'important c'est que ce qui le fasse agir, ce ne soit plus une simple raison d'intérêt ou, comme vous dites ordinairement: qu'il n'obéisse plus à des motifs intéressés" [p. 311]). Echoing the view of Dostoyevsky's underground man concerning the nonrational nature of human behavior ("whoever he might be, [man] has always and everywhere preferred to act according to his own wishes rather than according to the dictates of reason and advantage. And his wishes may well be contrary to his advantage; indeed, sometimes they *positively should be* . . ."),[34] Gide has Julius theorize "that self-advantage is *not* man's guiding principle—that there *are* such things as disinterested actions" (p. 171; "M'est avis que . . . le profit n'est pas toujours ce qui mène l'homme; qu'il y a des actions désintéressées" [p. 316]). Julius explains that he has in mind gratuitous actions that have nothing to do with conventional ethical standards of behavior, and that are as likely to be considered evil as they are to be judged good by an "objective" observer. When Amédée naively asks why anyone would commit such gratuitous acts, Julius replies, "Out of sheer wantonness—or from love of sport" (p. 171; "par luxe, par besoin de dépense, par jeu" [p. 317]). Later, after Amédée's mishap, Julius explains to his murderer-brother Lafcadio that the character he envisions for his novel "acts almost entirely in play, and as a matter of course prefers his pleasure to his interest" (p. 197; "je veux . . . qu'il agisse surtout par jeu, et qu'à son intérêt il préfère couramment son plaisir" [p. 350]). Such capriciousness is suggested by Julius, in all seriousness, as a plausible "motive" for murder as well as for art.

Or rather: for murder *as* art. Julius's theory collapses when he is forced to apply it to the actual murder of Amédée. Confronted with the reality of this murder, and with the possibility—in keeping with his own theory—that the unknown assailant may indeed have had no motive for his action, Julius promptly falls back upon the traditional view that "there's no such thing as a crime without a motive" (p. 203; "il n'y a pas de crime sans motif" [p. 356]). Because of his failure to be consistent in his views about literature and life, Julius is exposed in *Les Caves du Vatican* as a false, or counterfeit, novelist, presumably in contrast to Gide himself, whose own novel at least shows an awareness of the contradiction.[35]

Some of Gide's commentators have tried to resolve the inconsistencies that inevitably arise whenever the idea of the *acte gratuit* is invoked by questioning the idea's validity. "Lafcadio's action is not truly motiveless," writes one such critic; "it is an intensely theoretical action, done in order to test a philosophy of motivelessness; which is a very different thing."[36] According to this view, Julius's intellectual about-face results not from his inability to accept the possibility of motiveless action in real life, but on the contrary, from his initial credulity regarding such hypothetical actions. The same argument could be used to account for the flagrant discrepancies between Rupert Cadell's aesthetic and moral views in Hitchcock's *Rope*. Cadell is caught in the contradiction of his own murder-as-art philosophy, and he is forced to reject his own teachings when his overeager student translates his clever ideas into appalling action. Cadell's fault consists not in his failure to remain committed to his thesis—he seems only to have been playing the devil's advocate—but in his having so strenuously argued that (hypo)thesis before his impressionable students that he himself lost sight of its practical implications.

Cadell's student Brandon is caught in a different kind of double bind: not being a truly disinterested agent in the manner of Lafcadio, his satisfaction as an artist-criminal, as a practitioner of pure murder, remains incomplete until an observer like Cadell is on hand to appreciate his work aesthetically. Brandon resembles Julius in this regard, the novelist who continues to rely on the presence of a reader or beholder to validate the artistic integrity of his work. But Cadell is also like Julius who, after all, is only able to maintain that murder is disinterested and gratuitous so long as it is presented hypothetically by the novelist as fiction, or as the artistic object of a reader's aesthetic experience.

Whether or not one accepts Lafcadio's "crime" as an *acte gratuit* is finally beside the point. The significance of his deed is that it exemplifies an ideal of pure murder—the idea that murder can only be an art form when it is committed by the artistic agent as a purely disinterested, gratuitous act[37]—that characters like Julius, Cadell, and Brandon all fail in their own ways to live up to. Because of their failure to maintain to the end a purely disinterested *ethos*, Julius, Cadell, and Brandon are bound to strike the reader or viewer as more interesting and credible as characters than Lafcadio, whose perfect detachment from conventional moral values sets him apart from the human community ("taken out of the region of human things, human purposes, human desires," as De Quincey described the murderer's state of "suspension"), and makes him non- as well as inhuman. And indeed, that appears to be the (artistic) function of Lafcadio's character in Gide's novel—to provide a foil for the human, to expose the foibles and *mauvaise foi* of the other characters and thereby render them all the more vital. A similar role is played by Wilde's character Dorian with respect to Sibyl Vane and Basil Hallward, the conventional artists who perish because of their lack of disinterestedness. But Dorian himself can't approach the disinterestedness of Lord Henry Wotton, let alone Lafcadio, and in the end becomes a victim of his own narcissism. Situated midway between romanticism and modernism, *The Picture of Dorian Gray* features a protagonist who exposes (by arousing) the interestedness of other artists, but who can't escape his own self-interest. Dorian, too, is a more interesting and human character than Lafcadio in Gide's modernist fiction, a figure whose radical disinterestedness renders him unbelievable and uninteresting. Ultimately, Lafcadio becomes a kind of scapegoat whose disappearance in the novel reaffirms the human community and its moral values.

Pure murder is a thoroughly unmotivated, disinterested act, a supreme fiction that is only possible in the realm of art, and that sets off by contrast all the impurities and contradictions associated with human existence. The pure murder takes place in an enclosed, theatrical setting—a railway compartment or a "secret room," as one of Alain Robbe-Grillet's early short narratives is called—before a voyeuristic spectator/witness. Robbe-Grillet's text consists quite simply of a detached narrator's impersonal description of a woman's murder. No reason is given for the slaying, which appears to be some kind of sacrifice—the woman lies naked and enchained in what could be "a dungeon, a sunken room, or a cathedral"[38] while the killer flees up a staircase. What little action there is narrated in reverse, beginning with a dispassionate description of the corpse and the fleeing assailant, and progressing backwards toward the actual stabbing of the victim. Only with the last word of the text—"la toile" ("canvas")—does it become clear that the description is not of an actual murder, but of a painting executed in the manner of Gustave Moreau, to whom the story is dedicated. The narrator's detachment is explained by the fact that he is an aesthetic spectator who is imaginatively attempting to reconstruct the instant of the murder, which (as in Magritte's *The Menaced Assassin*, the painting that figures so prominently in Robbe-Grillet's novel *La Belle Captive*)[39] would have taken place a minute or so before the painted scene depicting the killer's flight from the corpse. Despite his detachment, the narrator's gaze is not exactly disinterested or pure, as we learn from his erotic lingering over details of the naked corpse. But the murder depicted in the painting must be considered pure since the killer's motive, or his relation to his victim, is a secret that will never be known.

In marked contrast to Robbe-Grillet's postmodernist image-text in which reality is so thoroughly interpenetrated by art and vice versa, modernist representations of murder typically reinforce the sense of a clear-cut difference between art and life. Murder is presented in the great modernist works of literature (Gide, Musil, Eliot) and surrealist painting (Magritte) in a formalized, de-realized guise,[40] its brutal aspect is relegated to what modernist critics dismissed as the subartistic forms of the hard-boiled detective story and the spy thriller. Once murder was aestheticized in modernist works of art, actual murder in all its brutality was free to flare up on an unprecedented scale in the form of fascist genocide. One of the most tragic aspects of the mass killings of the 1930s and 1940s was that, thanks in part to the aestheticizing of violence by the futurists, surrealists, and other modernists, the brutal reality of murder went unnoticed for far too long by all but the victims.

Paranoiac Aesthetics: The Romantic Critique of *l'Acte Gratuit*

The idea of a motiveless crime—or, more accurately, of an act that is regarded as a crime precisely because it lacks a motive, and that, by violating the fundamental law of cause-and-effect relations, becomes a crime against reason itself—is a modernist discovery. Traditional Christian teachings about the will preclude the possibility of gratuitous crime. "When there is an inquiry to discover why a crime has been committed," wrote Saint Augustine, "normally no one is satisfied until it has been shown that the motive might have been either the desire of gaining, or the fear of losing. . . . Surely no one would believe that [a man] would commit murder for no reason but the sheer delight of killing." Augustine rejects Sallust's implication that Catiline was "cruel and vicious without apparent reason"; his ultimate objective was to seize control of the government. "So even Catiline did not love crime for crime's sake. He loved something quite different, for the sake of which he committed his crimes."[41]

Most romantic writers remained committed to the idea of motivation as the basis for human action. Some kind of inner, intensely personal animus was essential to romantic doctrines of individual free will. De Quincey himself, who in his "Murder" essays seems to presage the modernist obsession with the *acte gratuit*, elsewhere vigorously denied such purely capricious action:

> Any reason which has reference to action, we call a motive. To act without a motive – i.e. without a reason – is (otherwise expressed) to act irrationally. Now all action in obedience to a motive the Necessarians call necessity: and to establish liberty, as against them, it would be required of us to establish a case of action without (or against) motives. The true liberty however . . . lies in this, that we by our own internal acts [i.e., feelings] create our own motives: those considerations, which to you or me are motives, to another are not so: and why? Because my reflexions upon the tendency of particular acts, or because my feelings connected with them, have given to certain considerations a weight which raises them into the strength and power of motives. Here lies our liberty. And to an obedience to motives thus created it is an easy artifice to give the name of necessity: but that creates no real necessity. The autonomy of Man is still secure.[42]

De Quincey reasoned that certain acts committed by individuals may seem unmotivated to outside observers because the motive responsible for the act in question is a personal "creation" of the agent himself, and thus remains invisible to philosophical or psychological analysis. As we have seen, De Quincey's narrator was careful to assign John Williams a more plausible motive than robbery to account for "so complex a tragedy" as his savagery toward the Marrs; and even when the romantic motive of jealousy proved inadequate, Williams's artistic scruples were invoked as a motivating factor in themselves.

Is it possible for murder to be truly motiveless, or are such apparently gratuitous acts actually the product of complex circumstantial chains of cause-and-effect relations that elude all attempts at detection or reconstruction? De Quincey believed in the latter alternative. As a romantic, he was struck by the overwhelming effects brought about by apparently insignificant or unseen phenomena. Such "involutes of human sensibility," as he called them, entail complex "combinations in which the materials of future thought or feeling are carried as imperceptibly into the mind as vegetable seeds are carried variously combined through the atmosphere, or by means of rivers, by birds, by winds, by waters, into remote countries" (2:147).[43] One can imagine De Quincey's reaction to the efforts of today's meteorologists to trace weather patterns using sophisticated computer models. Such complex combinations of physical (and possibly even nonphysical) occurrences elude the most advanced scientific monitoring techniques. The weather continues to seem fortuitous and unpredictable, not because it is, but because human beings are simply unable to discern all the links connecting the myriad, apparently unrelated and insignificant events that work together to bring about the specific set of conditions in which disasters like hurricanes or tornados can occur.[44]

What is true of such sublime cataclysms in nature is even more striking in the human mystery of murder. Laurence Senelick observes "that the murders that charmed De Quincey always contained an element of existential absurdity—there was no good reason on the surface why a particular person should fall beneath the assassin's blade. The more unknown the motives and dark the suppositions, the greater the interest De Quincey took."[45] And he later adds that an "unseen network of causes and effects, eventuating in bloodshed, remains for De Quincey the perfect crime."[46] There are no pure murders for De Quincey, only perfect ones. What appears to be pure or motiveless crime is only a special instance of the perfect or unsolved crime in which the criminal's motive, rather than the criminal himself, goes undetected.

There is nothing particularly uncanny or strange in Lafcadio's gratuitous murder of his brother-in-law by throwing him off a train. Given Fleurissoire's ingenuous nature, his absurd mission, and Lafcadio's mistaking him for a stranger, the effect is almost comic, and Gide himself referred to the work as a *sotie*.[47] Quite a different effect is achieved in a late romantic work like Schwob's fin de siècle tale "L'Homme voilé" ("The Veiled Man") from the collection, *Coeur double* (1891). This tale also involves a murder committed aboard a train, but here the narrator is not placed outside the events in the story as in Gide's novel or Schwob's own "Burke and Hare." Instead, the narrator claims to have been the sole witness to a bizarre murder. He confesses to having sat by helplessly, robbed of all capacity to act or resist, while a mysterious fellow-traveler, who embodies all the narrator's deepest fears, inexplicably slashes the throat of a third passenger dozing in the same compartment. The murderer, whose face is concealed by a flesh-colored silken veil, proceeds to daub the paralyzed narrator's face and hands with the dead man's blood. Then he flees, leaving the narrator to take the rap for the crime.

Schwob's tale harks back to the romantic scenario represented early in the century by works like Hoffmann's *Die Elixiere des Teufels* and Hogg's *Confessions of a Justified Sinner* in which the protagonist is blamed for crimes committed by his double. But Schwob works a subtle variation on this theme by presenting his narrating subject less as the victim of supernatural powers than as the witness of an otherworldly vision. His narrator is an aesthetic martyr. As he awaits his execution, he composes his tale which opens with an expression of wonder: the murder which he has had the fatal misfortune to have witnessed, and for which he is about to pay with his life, inspires the same sort of awe one feels before a portentous work of art.

> Of the combination of circumstances that have been my undoing I can say nothing; certain accidents of human life are as artistically contrived by chance or by the laws of nature as by the most demoniacal invention: one cries out in wonder before them as before a painting by an impressionist who has captured a singular and momentary truth. (p. 31)

Instead of experiencing outrage or despair over what from a modernist perspective would be his "absurd" predicament, the narrator can only marvel at the astounding "combination of circumstances" ("concours de circonstances")[48] that has made him a chosen witness/victim.

As a victim of circumstance who claims to have witnessed a murder and to have been framed for it, the narrator is able to appreciate the aesthetics of victimage in a manner that would have been impossible for the actual murder victim. The narrator in "The Veiled Man" has been vouchsafed a visionary insight into the artful interconnectedness of circumstances behind what must appear to everyone else as mere "accidents of human life." This point at which aesthetic insight and paranoiac fantasy converge, where it is revealed to a select individual that apparently chance events are actually designed "by the most demoniacal invention," is both romantic and postmodern, De Quinceyan and Pynchonesque—paranoia in Thomas Pynchon's definition referring to those moments of heightened perception when it is revealed that *everything is connected*."⁴⁹

Gravitation and Murder: The Problem of Action at a Distance

To hinder another is not an act it is the contrary it is a restraint on action both in ourselves & in the person hinderd. for he who hinders another omits his own duty. at the time
    Murder is Hindering Another
            —William Blake, annotations to Lavater's *Aphorisms on Man*

Early in the "Postscript," De Quincey compares sensational crimes like "the immortal Williams murders" of 1811 to spectacular conflagrations like the Drury Lane fire of 1809, arguing that "the tendency to a critical or aesthetic valuation of fires and murders is universal" (13:72). He later compares violent murders to earthquakes, observing that all "perils, specially malignant, are recurrent" (13:96). Fires, earthquakes and murders—all are instances of the sublime, although murder has the distinction of being the chief form of the man-made, in contrast to the natural or supernatural, sublime. The devastating consequences of these destructive acts are intensified by the circumstance that their cause is usually trivial, insignificant, or simply unknown. Where natural disasters like earthquakes and hurricanes seem irrational because they defy reason and the principle of causality, human acts like murder seem irrational when they lack any plausible motive. The mind balks at such irrationality, maintaining that natural catastrophes must have causes, and murderers must have motives, although these often elude our comprehension.

It is a small but crucial step from the romantic assumption of writers like De Quincey and Schwob that apparently inexplicable murders are actually the result of secret, obscure combinations of circumstances that the human mind cannot fathom, to the modernist view of Gide, Camus, and others who present murder simply as an unmotivated act that is either gratuitous or absurd. The sublimity of acts like murder vanishes once we move from romanticism to relativism: an event is sublime when its cause is hidden; it is absurd when it has no cause at all. The prototype of the romantic criminal-hero was created when Milton, following exegetical tradition, gave the unidentified, motiveless serpent in the third chapter of Genesis the sublime identity of Satan, the fallen archangel who is driven to tempt Adam and Eve by motives of envy and revenge.

De Quincey, we know, was fascinated with the "involutes of human sensibility," as he called them, whereby unexpected or inexplicable actions are actually the result of complex combinations and endless causal chains of events. Throughout his autobiographical writings, he records his fascination with the phenomenon of movement across a vast distance or transmission through extended periods of time. He writes about Lord Rosse's new telescope that enables the eye to leap through space and "walk . . . into Orion" (8:23). He dwells at length on the acoustic marvel of the Whispering Gallery in Saint Paul's Cathedral which he had visited as a boy; he had been struck by the way the whisper of a friend, "after running along the walls of the gallery, reached me as a deafening menace in tempestuous uproars" (3:296). Already as a child he had been mystified by the story of Aladdin, and particularly by the African magician who could hear the boy's footsteps a continent away by putting his ear to the ground. Not only was the magician able to single out the sound of Aladdin's tread from the sound of all the footsteps on the earth, but he had "the power still more unsearchable, of reading in that hasty movement an alphabet of new and infinite symbols; for, in order that the sound of the child's feet should be significant and intelligible, that sound must open into a gamut of infinite compass . . . and thus the least things in the universe must be secret mirrors to the greatest" (2:156).

Senelick rightly remarks that the awareness expressed in this passage of the significance of the apparently insignificant has important implications for De Quincey's aesthetics of murder: "what could be more seemingly irrelevant than the *acte gratuit* implied by an unmotivated murder?"[50] Here again, what appears gratuitous and unmotivated turns out to have resulted from a secret combination of circumstances too complex even to be noticed, let alone explained. Only a magician could track down such elusive foot- or fingerprints. Similarly, in the view of his friend James Hogg, De Quincey's interest in the murderous Indian sect of the Thugs stemmed from the "far-reaching power of this mysterious brotherhood, the swiftness and certainty of its operations, the strange gradations of official rank, and the curious disguises adopted."[51] The fact that De Quincey was fascinated with the "far-reaching power" of this sect is noteworthy; as Senelick suggests, this phrase "recalls the African magician, ear to the ground, tracing footsteps thousands of miles away."[52] Like the "seeds . . . carried variously combined . . . into remote countries," the methods and motives behind the Thugs' assassinations were inscrutable because they involved so many intermediaries. In the case of such hierarchical, organized crime, the elaborate division of labor makes it impossible to trace a given killing to its source; the actual assassin is a hit-man who carries out the orders of an unknown party. Not only is the murderer's motive unknown in such institutionalized slayings, but his identity— or rather, the identity of the person who orders the execution— remains a mystery as well. In the case of a character like Balzac's Vautrin, the killer may take it upon himself to mastermind and execute untraceable crimes, acting on behalf of individuals he wishes to favor, and carrying out in secret their unspoken murderous impulses.[53]

As we approach the twentieth century, we find the artist-assassin not only acting without a motive, but sometimes even renouncing action itself. The modernist murderer is no longer interested in enacting another's lethal desire by ordering or executing a contract. Why kill on someone else's behalf, even in secret, when one can induce someone to commit murder for one's own aesthetic enjoyment? Such is the plan of the aristocratic des Esseintes in an episode from J.-K. Huysmans's 1884 novel *A Rebours*. Having once happened upon a wretched sixteen-year-old boy on the street, des Esseintes offered to treat him to an evening in an expensive brothel. While the boy enjoyed himself with a Jewish whore, des Esseintes explained his purpose to the incredulous madame: "The truth is that I'm simply trying to make a murderer of the boy" ("la verité c'est que je tâche simplement de préparer un assassin"). By exposing a virgin, who's "reached the age where the blood starts coming to a boil" ("l'âge où le sang bouillonne") to "luxury such as he's never known and will never forget, and by giving him the same treat every fortnight, I hope to get him into the habit of these pleasures which he can't afford." Leaving three-month's payment with the madame, des Esseintes looked forward to the day when the boy would turn first to robbery, and then to murder, in order to continue his debauches after the money ran out.

> Looking on the bright side of things, I hope that, one fine day, he'll kill the gentleman who turns up unexpectedly just as he's breaking open his desk. On that day my object will be achieved: I shall have contributed, to the best of my ability, to the making of a scoundrel, one enemy the more for the hideous society which is bleeding us white.

Ever since his payments for the boy's sentimental education have stopped, des Esseintes—more an aesthete than an artist—has scoured the Police Gazette for news of his protégé's involvement in some sensational slaying. When he's unable to find the boy's name in the papers, he suspects that he's been cheated. The drawback in engineering a murder at a distance, des Esseintes is forced to admit, is that he hasn't "been able to play a close game" ("il ne m'a pas été possible de jouer serré"). Too many "contingencies" ("aléas") were able to intervene to upset his plan: the madame could have pocketed the money for herself, one of the whores could have fallen for the boy and gratified his desires for free, or the boy could even have been scared off by the Jewess's "exotic vices" ("les vices faisandés de la belle Juive").[54] Murder by proxy turns out to be as physically impractical as it is aesthetically appealing. There's more certainty—although less art—in the act of killing someone outright (even when the deed is done on behalf of another, or when the deed is done without any motive at all) than in waiting for someone else to act out one's own fantasy and fulfill one's own desire.

In their respective treatments of the concept of murder committed at a distance, Balzac and Huysmans bridge the gap between the romantic insistence that action is motivated, no matter how obscure such motives may be, and the modernist idea of the *acte gratuit*. Whether human actions are necessarily motivated, or whether they may be motiveless, is crucial to a study of artistic representations of murder. No doubt, the issue has its roots in abstract scientific and philosophical thought. In physics, for example, the problems of impulse and impetus had been debated at length since the seventeenth century. Newton's formulation of his theory of gravitation had dramatically brought the problem into focus by compelling most natural philosophers to accept, on the basis of mathematical proof, the counterintuitive idea of a force operating through a vacuum across a distance. Such a phenomenon was supported both by theory and by scientific observation, but how could such a force be "real"? Unable to find a mechanical explanation for gravitational attraction, Newton and his followers simply deferred the problem. But for romantic writers and philosophers at the end of the eighteenth century who were preoccupied with the task of saving appearances in the face of the growing dominance of a mathematically abstract scientific discourse, such postponement of the problem was itself the problem. If gravity was a force, it must operate through a physical medium, and it must have a physical, or even a metaphysical, cause.

Several writers of the eighteenth and nineteenth centuries took issue with Newton's theory of gravitation on much the same grounds that they objected to the idea of murder as a gratuitous act: both entailed action over an extended distance through no perceptible medium. Like murder, gravitation was a convoluted phenomenon that appeared unmotivated because its causes were so complex. The agency as well as the sign of the Fall of Man itself, gravitation was associated by Laurence Sterne with digressive movement, deviation, and deceit;[55] like murder, its nature is to conceal the manner of its operation. By far the most vociferous opponent of Newton, however, was the visionary romantic poet William Blake, whose chief objection to gravitation was that it entailed the violent intervention of an external force on an inert object.[56] Such a physical force was analogous to murder insofar as it deprived a body of its own subjecthood, its own inner, spontaneous capacity to act. As the epigraph to this section indicates, Blake was unable to conceive of murder as De Quincey did in aesthetic terms: far from envisioning murder as a fine *art* that could be aesthetically appreciated, he could not even accept murder as a simple *act*. Murder was rather a "restraint on action"—a view that makes more sense when we recall that action, for Blake, was a necessarily positive phenomenon, a spontaneous impulse originating within the active body, in contrast to an external force violently imposed upon a passive object, as he believed to be the case in Newton's concept of gravitation. Blake's idea of action as a spontaneous outburst of energy, unmotivated and unmediated by any extrinsic factors, applied neither to gravitation nor to murder, which were better understood as what Deleuze, following Nietzsche, calls "reactive forces."[57] Such physical and human "mysteries" were not explicable as actions because they were matters of human artifice, of scientific or moral invention. What Tristram said of gravity was equally true of murder: its "very essence . . . was design, and consequently deceit" (*Tristram Shandy*, 1:12).

Since the phenomenon of gravity seemed to contradict both reason and nature, it was bound to strike its critics as being an artificial contrivance rather than a scientific truth or a natural "law." Similarly, as an "act" that was often in conflict with social norms of order and psychological theories of motivation, murder appeared to be more closely related to the irrationality and deviousness traditionally associated with the arts than to the rationality and virtue that was the supposed basis of human action. "Out-lawed" in real life as a moral transgression, murder could only be legitimated, and made socially acceptable, in art. Insofar as it defied reason itself, murder could only become minimally comprehensible *as* art.

Although it first seemed an outrageous joke, De Quincey's idea of murder as an art form has actually come to be accepted—if not acknowledged—as the only way to make common sense out of this social threat. As in the case of any mysterious "action at a distance" that eludes human understanding and control, it has been more expedient to pass murder off as aberrant fantasy or as deceptive artifice than to try to account for it logically. Murder has defied expla-

nation because to understand it would be to rationalize, and ultimately, to justify it. However inclined people are at first to scoff at the
idea of murder as an art form, they prove to be even more reluctant to
accept murder as a fact of life or as a characteristic of human nature.
As a result, the affinity between art and murder is far greater than all
but a few artists and killers have been willing to admit.

THREE

MURDER AS (CARNAL) KNOWLEDGE

> In that every action today leads to murder, direct or indirect, we can-
> not act until we know whether or why we have the right to kill.
> —Camus, *L'Homme révolté*

> To know and not to act is not yet to know.
> —Wang Yang-ming

From Aesthetics to Erotics: Bataille's Critique of Identity

In the writings of De Quincey and his successors, writes Dennis
Porter, the "shock of murder is no longer in the act" as in Sade and *his*
followers, "but in its aesthetic treatment."[1] It is the witness's role as
aesthetic spectator in the "Postscript" to the "Murder" essays that
turns what otherwise would have been the sensational description of
a grisly murder into a highly literary presentation of murder as art. In
his description of John Williams's slaughter of the Marr family, De
Quincey transferred the sense of trancelike "suspension" described in
the "Macbeth" essay ("Another world has stepped in; and the murderers are taken out of the region of human things, human purposes
and human desires") from the murderer to an innocent witness.
Standing inches away from the slayer of her employer's family, the
servant-girl Mary sustains what amounts to an aesthetic experience of
the supermundane sublime.

De Quincey's follower Marcel Schwob went a step further in his
story "The Veiled Man." The fact that the narrator-witness in Schwob's
story claims to have taken no action either to assist or to deter the
actual murderer (who, for all we know, may only be a figment of the

narrator's overworked imagination) emphasizes his attitude of extreme aesthetic disinterestedness, a form of paralysis that precludes
the possibility of action. So enthralled is the narrator during the
murder scene aboard the train that he suffers a seizure or suspension
of the will; consequently, he is unable to offer resistance, even when
the veiled traveler "incriminates" him by smearing him with the
victim's blood.

The obvious allusion in "The Veiled Man" is to the ineradicable
stain of blood/guilt in *Macbeth*. Beyond this allusion, however, is the
more significant affiliation with De Quincey's "Macbeth" essay. In the
paradoxical double role of passive-witness-accused-of-acting/active-
murderer-who-did-not-act, the narrator has experienced the same vertiginous, dreamlike sensation, the "deep syncope and suspension of
earthly passion," that befalls Macbeth in the brief interval between his
killing of Duncan and his hearing the knocking at his castle gate. A
mystical, if diabolical, trinity unites witness, murderer, and victim in
a fatal embrace. The ritualistic blood-daubing establishes an ineradicable double bond, on the one hand, of *brotherhood* between the narrator-
witness and the victim, and on the other hand, of duplicitous and
complicitous *otherhood* between the narrator-witness and the mysterious murderer—the double for whose crime the narrator will soon pay
with his life.[2] De Quincey, we recall, imagined the eerie possibility of
having to murder "a *doppel-ganger* who went about personating me,"
and then being hanged for the crime of "murdering a sham, that was
either nobody at all, or oneself repeated once too often" (11:460–61).
Schwob presents the terrifying possibility of a man finding himself
condemned to die not for murdering his double, but for a crime committed *by* his double. The hapless narrator bears witness to a murder
that he is powerless to prevent because the murderer is a simulacrum
of himself; the narrator tells his tale while waiting to be punished as
the murderer, even though his only role in the affair had apparently
been that of a passive witness.

Not content merely to follow De Quincey in presenting murder
from the perspective of the witness, Schwob suggests that the witness
himself may not be entirely innocent. By virtue of the fact that he sees
a crime without intervening, or without being able to intervene, he

becomes an accomplice in the crime, a *hypocrite lecteur.* The witness's voyeuristic fascination with the murderer and his victim implicates him in the murderer's guilt. Like the beholder of a painting or the reader of a literary work, the witness's eye is not innocent, but prejudiced—both by what it sees and by the way it sees. Such prejudices render any supposedly pure act of aesthetic "judgment" impossible. Schwob's tale raises the possibility that De Quincey was able to transfer the experience of sublimity from the point of view of the guilty murderer to that of the innocent witness because of a secret communality between the perpetrator and the beholder of a murder that suspends moral categories of innocence and guilt. "Guilty" murderer and "innocent" witness are united, not only by the aesthetic bond between artist and beholder, actor and voyeur, but by an epistemological bond of shared knowledge mediated through their secret relation to a dead body. The names of the principal figures in De Quincey's "Postscript" underscore the bond between victim and witness (Marr/Mary) and between victim and murderer (Williamson/Williams),[3] but the body of the victim engenders a yet more powerful bond between the killer and his beholder.

This intimacy between murderer and witness—the mutual experience of sublime suspension from worldly concerns that they share in the presence of the victim's corpse, their secret knowledge that they (and the reader) savor for a few interminable instants before the alarm is raised and the event is made public—has a distinctly erotic character. The commonplace reference to sexual climax as a *petite mort* takes on a deeper significance with respect to murder.

We have already encountered an explicit instance of homicidal erotics in De Quincey's "Postscript" when Williams's intention to kill the Williamsons' sleeping granddaughter was described as "a murder of pure *voluptuousness.*" It is doubtful, however, that such a murder can be considered either aesthetic or erotic. Although Williams was not motivated here, we are told, by a desire for revenge, personal gain, or by the need to protect himself ("no hostile witness was to be removed"), he was not "entirely disinterested" as the narrator claims—at least in a Kantian sense—because of the sensual gratification he expected to receive from such a "voluptuous" slaughter. Williams's supposedly gratuitous desire to kill the innocent Williamson girl actually passes beyond aesthetic experience (in which the beautiful or the sublime is beheld by a disinterested spectator), as well as beyond erotic enjoyment (in which the beautiful or the sublime is beheld by an interested voyeur/witness), into the domain of the pornographic (in which an engaged spectator/agent both beholds and participates in a primal scene of sexual violence and violation).

Where De Quincey's narrative borders on the pornographic in its almost Sadeian description of Williams's murderous intent against the Williamsons' granddaughter, it assumes a more erotic tinge in its account of the Marr slayings with its focus on the interplay between Williams and Mary. Here the scene is not described directly from the murderer's point of view as he bears down on his unconscious, prepubescent victim—who, besides being morally and sexually innocent, is ignorant of his crimes—but from the mediated vantage of a mature woman who is a potentially "hostile witness." Mary is by no means as completely innocent or helpless as the Williamson child in what promised to be "a murder of pure *voluptuousness*"; by virtue of her role as witness, Mary is implicated (however unwillingly) in the atrocities that nearly included her as a victim. An erotic bond of shared knowledge develops between Williams and Mary in their brief interval in the doorway that would be unthinkable between Williams and the Williamson girl.

A slight, but crucial, shift in perspective takes us from the sublimated eroticism of Mary's experience of murder as a horrified "innocent" bystander, to the unsublimated pornography that occurs when a violent spectacle elicits an immediate feeling of pleasure in an all too willing spectator. Susanne Kappeler cites the case of a white farmer in Namibia who invited friends to take pictures as he tortured a black farmhand to death. Even if one questions Kappeler's analogy between the situation of the black man who is forced to "pose" for the camera while being tortured/murdered and the situation of female models who are photographed in pornographic positions, her point cannot be denied that in the case of the black victim, "taking pictures was an integral part of the act of torture and an integral part of the enjoyment of the act of torture." The activity of taking pictures signals the presence of a third party besides the torturer and his victim who experiences enjoyment at the sight of this spectacle. "With an audience," writes Kappeler, "torture becomes an art, the torturer an author, the onlookers an audience of connoisseurs."[4] Insisting that what she calls the "spectator function . . . is crucial to the analysis of representation" (p. 31), Kappeler attributes "the voyeuristic titillation of the pornographic viewer" to "the notion of a third party looking on" (p. 29). The Namibian photographs indicate the presence of willing witnesses to the murder, which in turn suggests the staged, theatrical quality of the white men's torture of their victim and their gratuitous, sadistic enjoyment at the sight of the black man's agony. "Gratuitousness," observes Kappeler, "is the mark of the murderer's photography" (p. 10).

Reflecting on Sade's lascivious descriptions of pornographic cruelty, Georges Bataille has pondered the circumstances whereby the "sight or thought of murder can give rise to a desire for sexual enjoyment."[5] In contrast to sex performed for procreation, eroticism entails a death wish, the impulse toward the pure, unbroken continuity that lies beyond the discontinuity of selfhood. The impulse to close the gap, or to bridge the chasm, that separates individuals from each other as living beings is a supremely giddy experience:

> Mais je ne puis évoquer cet abîme qui nous sépare sans avoir aussitôt le sentiment d'un mensonge. Cet abîme est profond, je ne vois pas le moyen de le supprimer. Seulement nous pouvons en commun ressentir le vertige de cet abîme. Il peut nous fasciner. Cet abîme en un sens est la mort et la mort est vertigineuse, elle est fascinante.[6]

> But I cannot refer to this gulf which separates us without feeling that this is not the whole truth of the matter. It is a deep gulf, and I do not see how it can be done away with. Nonetheless, we can experience its dizziness together. It can hypnotise us. This gulf is death in one sense, and death is vertiginous, death is hypnotizing.

This phenomenon of "dissolution"—the submersion of separate subjectivity into unbroken continuity—is common both to erotic experience and to the experience of murder. The blurring of the separate identities of partners in the sexual "act" is essentially the same as—and, could conceivably lead to—the act of murder, in which, if no witness is present, the murderer simultaneously becomes both actor and witness to his deed. If there *is* a witness to the act of murder, actor and witness lose their respective identities and become, not each other or the same person, but *no-body*. The identification of murderer and witness through their mutual loss of identity may last only the briefest instant, but that instant will seem timeless. As De Quincey writes of the audience's and the murderer's shared experience in the "Macbeth" essay, "time must be annihilated" until, with the knocking at the gate and the resumption of mundane human affairs, "the pulses of life [begin] to beat again; and the reestablishment of the goings-on of the world in which we live first makes us profoundly sensible of the awful parenthesis that had suspended them."

Bataille's account of the connection between eroticism and murder offers a useful insight into the strange intimacy shared by killer and witness—an intimacy that is analogous to the relationship between exhibitionist and voyeur, artist and beholder. The act or sight of murder simultaneously terrifies and thrills the witness-beholder with an awareness of the close proximity of life to death, of the imminent prospect of his or her own dissolution as an integral but separate individual into seamless continuity with all existence. At the instant that he slays the King, Macbeth is rapturously freed from the demon of self-hood that has goaded him to commit murder; he is at one with his victim, and has thereby atoned for his deed, until his sense of self returns with the knocking at the gate. So profound is the servant Mary's sense of suspended selflessness when she returns from her errand that she is barely able to tear herself away from the door behind which the murderous stranger waits to add her to his victims. And now we know why the narrator in "The Veiled Man" was paralyzed in the murderer's presence, and why the murderer's face appeared to be invisible: at some level, the narrator was aware that the murderer he was watching was himself—or was no one. It comes as no surprise that the narrator has been (mis-)taken for the murderer, and that he awaits his execution even as he writes his incredible story. The reader suspects that at the instant of his death, the narrator/witness's disjointed identity will finally rejoin that of his murderous double.

Bataille's conception of murder as an erotic experience differs

netic presentation of murder in one crucial
cey focuses on the murderer's (in the case of
's (in the case of Mary) aesthetic experience of
nurder, Bataille zeroes in on the erotic event of
ted body overcomes its own limits in a burst of

Il y a u.. ible du mouvement qui nous anime: l'excès éclaire le sens du mouvement. Mais ce n'est pour nous qu'un signe affreux, sans cesse nous rappelant que la mort, *rupture* de cette discontinuité individuelle à laquelle l'angoisse nous rive, se propose à nous comme une vérité plus éminente que la vie. . . .

A la base de l'érotisme, nous avons l'expérience d'un éclatement, d'une violence au moment de l'explosion.

The stirrings within us have their own fearful excesses; the excesses show which way these stirrings would take us. They are simply a sign to remind us constantly that death, the rupture of the discontinuous individualities to which we cleave in terror, stands there before us more real than life itself. . . .

Underlying eroticism is the feeling of something bursting, of the violence accompanying an explosion.[7]

De Quincey's focus in the "Macbeth" essay is the knocking at the gate which interrupts the murderer's trance and which makes him and the spectator aware "that the transitory vision was dissolved"; Bataille is concerned with "dissolution" in precisely the opposite sense — in the erotic sense of dissolving and dispersing individual identity in the act(s) of sex and/or murder. Where De Quincey refers to the private, insulated world of the murderer during his trance, "cut off by an immeasurable gulf from the ordinary tide and succession of human affairs," Bataille uses the identical image of a gulf or abyss in the opposite sense: the phrase, "cet abîme qui nous sépare," refers to the chasm that separates us as living, discontinuous beings from each other in our everyday existence.

With respect to murder, the experience of sublimity can be handled in two opposed ways. De Quincey adopts an aesthetic perspective: the murderer Macbeth becomes conscious of his visionary experience only after it is over. The mundane act of the knocking on

the gate is a necessary precondition for Macbeth's (and our own) retrospective awareness of his ecstasy *as* ecstasy. Bataille, in contrast,
views the murderer's ecstatic condition prospectively: it is an ultimate
state or terminus to which our own inexpungeable erotic excesses
impel us. There is no need for a knocking at the gate to disrupt our
insular ecstasy and recall us back to ourselves; on the contrary, it is
our all-too-isolated condition as individuals that our erotic-criminal
excesses drive us to overcome. Both De Quincey and Bataille accept
the fundamental equation of God = Death;[8] however, where the artistic safeguards of interruption and digression enable De Quincey to
return (or retreat) from the abyss,[9] Bataille's excesses drive him further
and further to the edge.

The Tell-Tale Hand: Lacenaire and Gautier

An artist with a murderer's hands; that was the ticket, the hiero-
glyphic of the times.

—Malcolm Lowry, *Under the Volcano*

I respected the police. They can kill. Not at a distance and by proxy,
but with their hands.

—Jean Genet, *Journal du Voleur*

His hands were moving across my face almost like an artist on a
canvas.

—Marla Hanson, former model testifying about being
slashed with a razor blade in June 1986

The fashionably scandalous nineteenth-century idea of murder as
art generally referred to a way of perceiving or conceiving homicide in
a disinterested manner. As such, it was actually a way of domesticating
the most aberrant, sociopathic behavior—of converting a moral transgression into an amoral, aesthetic digression. Gide's aristocratic character Julius de Baraglioul can play with the idea of gratuitous murder in
his novel; Hitchcock's Rupert Cadell can banter philosophically with
his students about murder as an art form. Both characters, however,
are unable to accept these provocative notions in reality. Beyond the
limits of a novel's dust jacket or the housemaster's parlor, murder is in
excess: it is no longer art but act, and as such, it is intolerable.

As daring as the idea of an aesthetics of murder may have appeared in the writings of romantic artists and their followers, and however much this idea seemed to play with and to confuse the boundaries between criminality and art, it ultimately appears to have had the positive effect of reinforcing the fundamental distinction between the world of art and the world of action upon which the social order rests. Murder can be accepted as art when it is presented according to the institutionalized conventions of the art world—as a stable, interesting event to be regarded from different perspectives and debated from different points of view by critics and connoisseurs. Whenever murder erupts as an uncontrolled event, gratuitous or otherwise, in the unpredictable world of action, it eludes the strictly delimited realm of artistic objects. The *act* of murder remains a capital criminal offense.

Shortly after the appearance of De Quincey's essay "On Murder," Paris was buzzing with the news of Pierre-François Lacenaire, a man who had flagrantly violated the conventions determining murder as an art form. Lacenaire's trial and execution in 1836 would scarcely have attracted notice were it not for his pretensions as a poet. His verses consisted of a number of sentimental lyrics and political songs, which for the most part were unremarkable in their style and substance. Several of these poems accompanied Lacenaire's memoirs, which he composed in the Conciergerie while awaiting execution, and which appeared in a censored edition a half-year after his death. In the *Mémoires* Lacenaire describes his love of poetry, and claims that he was "born a poet" ("J'étais né poète enfin"), and that writing verse was for him a "natural gift" ("un véritable don de nature"). He modestly adds, however, that he "certainly [has] no special claim to being favored thus" ("je n'ai certes aucun mérite à en avoir été favorisé"), and that he is "certainly not the only [poet-murderer]" ("et qu'on ne soit pas étonné d'avoir pu trouver un poète assassin, je ne suis certes pas le seul").[10]

It is hardly for his poetry that Lacenaire was lionized in the nineteenth century or that he is remembered today. Rather, his fame stems from the fact that he was a poet *as well as* a murderer. Théophile Gautier judged him a "Vrai meurtrier et faux poëte": Lacenaire's artistic sensibility revealed itself, not in the sentiments expressed in his mediocre verse, but in the chillingly dispassionate attitude toward his crimes that he displayed during his trial and in his *Mémoires*. In contrast to the fictional characters of Julius de Baugloul and Rupert Cadell who entertained the idea of murder as a gratuitous act and as an art form but were unable to accept such ideas in actual life, Lacenaire compensated for his banality as a poet with his stylistic verve as an assassin.

Not that Lacenaire's murders were the sensational deeds that he made them appear. His principal victims were a con-artist and his aged mother. "What became important to Lacenaire's age," notes Senelick, "was not his crimes but his image."[11] Throughout his sensational trial and during the composition of his memoirs, he strove with scrupulous care to present himself in the role both of the Byronic hero and of the quintessential poet for whom murder was as much an art as his verse. He made no attempt to defend or to exonerate himself at his trial, but struck a pose as the meticulous craftsman who was fated to see his brilliant schemes of murderous revenge fall apart because of his reliance on faint-hearted philistines. As his final tour de force, Lacenaire turned his own trial into an instrument of revenge against his bungling accomplices whom he blamed for sabotaging his crimes. He took immense delight in implicating his cohorts, gladly volunteering information about them to the court, and demonstrating in his cross-examination of them how their lack of artistic finesse, their blunders and indiscretions, had led to his apprehension. The accomplices desperately sought to dissociate themselves from their accuser, but were no match for him. While they struggled to save their own skins, their former associate coolly disdained any kind of defense for himself. His withering criticism of their clumsiness and lack of professional skill was in keeping with his view that murder was as much an art as the verses that he desultorily penned, and with his conviction that murder ought to be defended and judged wholly on the basis of aesthetic, rather than legal or moral, criteria.

One unsympathetic reviewer welcomed the news announcing the forthcoming publication of the *Mémoires* by hailing its author as "the man who invented the metaphysics of murder" ("l'homme qui a inventé la métaphysique de l'assassinat").[12] More than a century later,

Lacenaire was celebrated as the dandified hero-villain in Marcel Carné's epic film *Les Enfants du paradis* (1945). So great was the cult surrounding Lacenaire that, after his execution, his hand was dismembered and embalmed, turning up finally as an eccentric conversation-piece in the salon of Maxime Du Camp. Here it caught the eye of Gautier, who made it the subject of his poem "Étude de mains" (1851). And so the hand that had so artfully dispatched human lives itself became a secular relic, an object of aesthetic veneration. The same hand that had once composed verses became, in its turn, the subject of a poem.

Gautier's "Étude de mains" belongs to a curious nineteenth-century literary subgenre in France devoted to body parts;[13] beyond this, it harks back to the occult tradition of the "main de gloire"—the severed hand of a hanged man used by thieves as a talisman to paralyze the inhabitants of the homes they trespass.[14] "Étude de mains" is actually a double-poem that combines a meditation on Lacenaire's embalmed hand with a reverie inspired by the sculpted hand of the Renaissance Italian courtesan Imperia. These anatomical parts—one dead flesh, the other stony marble—synecdochically represent a larger, elusive truth. Gautier invites the reader to glimpse this truth by making the connection between the hands of the courtesan and the assassin. What connection can there possibly be?

For one thing, both the courtesan and the killer are related through their violation of socially accepted norms and laws. (A decade after Gautier's poem, Dostoyevsky was to explore the spiritual dimension of the bond between the murderer and the harlot in *Crime and Punishment,* while Brecht would examine its socioeconomic aspect nearly a century later in *The Threepenny Opera.*) Bataille insists that eroticism and murder are inseparably related as transgressions: "What does physical eroticism signify if not a violation of the very being of its practitioners?—a violation bordering on death, bordering on murder?" For Bataille, the sexual act has a close connection with ritual sacrifice: "The lover strips the beloved of her identity no less than the blood-stained priest his human or animal victim."[15]

A more specific and pertinent sense in which the courtesan and the assassin complement each other in Gautier's poem has to do with the fact that both are artists whose respective crafts give them a double identity that makes them appear larger than life. Imperia is not only a courtesan but she is also a queen, and in a salacious fantasy Gautier wonders whether she holds

> Entre ses doigts si bien sculptés,
> Le sceptre de la souveraine
> Ou le sceptre des voluptés?[16]

> Between such beautifully sculpted fingers,
> The scepter of the empress
> Or the scepter of ecstasy?

Similarly, Lacenaire is the duplicitous "poëte assassin." In his hand he wields no "scepter" (sovereign or carnal), nor workman's tool ("la varlope ou le marteau"); the instrument of his art is the knife. (Some sixty years before Gautier's poem, Sade had drawn the connection between the penis-wielding prostitute and the knife-wielding murderer in his character Clairwil, the murderess in *Juliette* who masturbates with the penis of a young friar, which she has severed and embalmed.)

The hand of the artist-assassin does not create, but it destroys (or it creates *by* destroying). Lacenaire explains that he could not achieve a fulfilling union with the only woman he ever loved because "I feared lest my own hand destroy the idol I had made myself" (p. 118) ("je craignais de détruire de ma propre main l'idole que je m'étais créée" [p. 71]). He even regards the writing of the *Mémoires* as an act of self-unmaking:

> je me décide, moi, bien vivant, sain de corps et d'esprit, à faire de ma propre main mon autopsie et la dissection de mon cerveau. (p. 26)

> I have decided that I, while definitely in the land of the living, sound in mind and body, will perform my autopsy and dissect my brain with my own hands. (p. 56)

By setting down his memoirs, Lacenaire would beat the phrenologists at their game. That these "cranologues" (p. 25) should be called upon after his execution to give a scientific explanation of his character was, for him, an appalling prospect. He would show the world that the

secret of his character was not to be sought in the bumps on his head—
or even in the thought processes *inside* his head, which would be
explored by the phrenologists' successors, the psychoanalysts—but in
the murders committed by, and described in the memoirs written in,
his own *hand*. Lacenaire is at great pains in his *Mémoires* to decenter
the locus of his being from his head to his hand, the instrument of his
personal artistic signature. Those analysts who look for psychological
motives for his crimes essentially reduce Lacenaire to the "brains"
behind the murders—the "mastermind" who decided on the victim
and planned the attack but who left the actual killing to his hench-
men, François and Avril. Lacenaire is particularly anxious to correct
what he felt to be a mistaken and degrading view of himself as a
purely conceptual artist, a man of ideas, rather than a man of *praxis*,
a master of technique.

> J'ai donc dû être étonné lorsque j'ai appris qu'un de ces savants pro-
> fesseurs, qui ne procèdent en observations et en morale que par
> bosse et protubérances, avait dit de moi: *Le défaut de courage l'a porté
> à se contenter de diriger le meurtre et à le faire exécuter par un complice. On
> se rappelle cette phrase souvent répétée: Lacenaire était la tête, Avril était le
> bras.* Certes, c'est une bien ridicule prétention de ma part, de vouloir
> revendiquer une plus grande part de crime qu'on ne m'en accorde;
> mais, puisque je me présente pour être jugé, non plus par mon
> crâne, mais par mes sensations et qualités intellectuelles, il faut bien
> tout expliquer. Vous dites, vous phrénologues, qu'Avril était le bras.
> Était-il le bras à V . . . en Italie? était-il le bras dans la rue du
> Faubourg-Saint-Martin, n° 8, où j'ai lutté pendant un quart d'heure
> seul à seul avec ma victime qui n'a été sauvée que par une de ces cir-
> constances qui ne se rencontrent pas deux fois dans la vie? Vous dites
> que je me contentais de diriger le meurtre et de le faire exécuter par
> un complice! Oui, j'ai dirigé le meurtre de Chardon, mais qui l'a
> exécuté? qui l'a frappé le premier? qui a frappé seul la mère? Et dans
> la rue Montorgueil, qui a frappé encore Genevay? Est-ce ainsi que
> l'on se contente de diriger un meurtre? Parmi les penchants faibles ou
> nuls chez moi, vous placez la *combativité* ou *courage*. Voici ma
> réponse: Je me suis battu en duel huit fois dans ma vie et deux fois
> dans des combats à mort. Mes témoins existent probablement tous
> encore aujourd'hui. Qu'il y en ait donc un seul qui se lève et qui dise:
> J'ai vu trembler cet homme, je l'ai vu sortir de son sang-froid, autre-
> ment que pour entrer en fureur; j'ai surpris enfin chez lui un mouve-

ment de crainte. Non, il n'y en aura pas; non, personne au monde ne
le dira. Si au contraire j'ai une qualité absolue à l'abri de toute discussion, c'est le courage. Je n'ai jamais connu la peur de ma vie. Voilà ce
qui arrive, lorsque, dans une scène toute hypothétique, on cherche à
faire coïncider les raisonnements avec les faits, et que surtout on ne
se donne même pas la peine de les approfondir. Cherchez un autre
thème à exploiter pour me faire entrer dans vos rêveries phrénologi-
ques, messieurs, celui-ci ne vaut rien. (pp. 91–92)

I could not be other than astonished when one of those learned professors who make their observations and mental judgments only
from lumps and bumps said of me: "Lack of courage has always
inclined him to be content with directing the crime and having it carried out by an accomplice. The sentence so often repeated at the trial
comes to mind: *Lacenaire was the head; Avril was the arm.*" No doubt it
is very ridiculous of me to claim a greater part in crime than has been
allowed to me, but as I am putting myself forward for judgment on
my feelings and intellectual qualities and not on my skull, I must
explain everything. You phrenologists say Avril was the arm. Was he
the arm at V— — in Italy? Was he the arm at No. 8 in the Rue du Fau-
bourg Saint-Martin when I struggled alone for a quarter of an hour
with a victim who was saved by one of those things that only happen
once in a lifetime? You say I was content to direct the crime and have
an accomplice carry it out! Yes, I directed the murder of Chardon, but
who carried it out? Who alone struck the mother? And again in the
Rue Montorgueil, who alone struck Genevay? Is that how one is content to direct a crime? Among the feeble or nonexistent tendencies in
me you place "fighting-quality" or "courage." Here is my answer: I
have fought eight duels in my life, two of them to the death. Probably
all my witnesses are still alive. Let one single one of them rise and
say, "I saw him tremble; I saw him lose his composure — other than
to quicken to anger: I surprised him in a moment of fear." None of
them will do so; no one in the world will say it. On the contrary, if
I have one quality of which there can be no shadow of doubt, it is
courage. I have never known fear in my life. This is what happens
when, in a hypothetical case, people try to reconcile their reasoning
with fact and no one takes the trouble to go any deeper. You must
seek another theory to exploit, messieurs, if you want me to fit into
your phrenological fantasies; this one won't do. (pp. 148–49)

Lacenaire's self-portrait in the *Mémoires* is less defense than bravado,
and invites comparison with Vidocq's "exercise in self-aggrandize-

ment" in *his Mémoires* of the preceding decade. (In that work, it is the detective's—rather than the murderer's—boasts that "continually draw the reader's attention to his superhuman powers and achievements,"[17] without which the police would be altogether at a loss to solve most crimes.) By transposing the terms in the often-repeated remark *"Lacenaire était la tête, Avril était le bras,"* the poet-assassin identifies himself with the masculine arm (*"le* bras") rather than with the feminine head (*"la* tête"), with action rather than with thought, while at the same time exposing his accomplice Avril as weak and effeminate. Behind Lacenaire's boastful image of himself as a dauntless, cold-blooded killer is his determination to present himself as an artist—a man who works with his hands, a man who makes (and unmakes)—in contrast to the men of science—the men who (think they) know—who are his judges and critics, and whom he foresees fruitlessly racking *their* brains to come up with a theory about *his* brain.

The two figures yoked together by Gautier in his poem, the courtesan Imperia and the assassin Lacenaire, are both artists who have the power to make their lovers or unmake their victims with their hands. In contrast to tales in which the dismembered foot of an inaccessible woman is fetishized as an aesthetic object (Balzac's "Le Chef d'oeuvre inconnu") or a sexual object (Gautier's "Le Pied de momie"), Gautier's poem depicts hands that are in excess of the specular realms of aesthetics or erotics. Such hands are not static objects to be contemplated, but the sign—the instrument of signification and signature, as well as a signature in its own right—of artists who were above all else activists, skilled in their respective *hand*-icrafts. The hand of the courtesan-queen and the hand of the poet-assassin are treacherous, double-dealing signs, signs that don't represent but signs that act. These hands appear all the more manipulative in their immobile, dismembered condition as monumental relics or artifacts in which they are celebrated in Gautier's poem. Gautier's own artistic performance pales in the reflected glory of the erotic violence that it commemorates, much in the way that the novelistic art of Gide's fictional counterpart Julius de Baraglioul (and even of Gide himself) betrays, in the double sense of reveal and conceal, the irreducible act of Lafcadio's crime.

As agents of active artistic manipulation rather than as relics to be aesthetically (or voyeuristically) worshipped, the hands of Imperia and Lacenaire in Gautier's poem are instruments not only of making and unmaking, but of knowing and unknowing. In the act of "making" her lover, the courtesan "knows" him in the biblical sense of the word; similarly, the assassin acquires a certain privileged knowledge of his victim, as well as of himself, in the act of murder. Such knowledge is a secret, intimate insight that eludes all attempts at communication or comprehension, as the narrating murder-witness learns in Schwob's story "The Veiled Man." Underneath his portrait that served as the frontispiece for the original edition of the *Mémoires*, Lacenaire had theatrically penned the lines:

> Il est un secret qui me tue,
> Que je dérobe aux regards curieux,
> Vous ne voyez ici que la statue,
> L'âme se cache à tous les yeux.

> It is a secret that will kill me,
> That I conceal from inquisitive stares,
> Here you will see only the statue,
> The soul hides itself from all eyes.

The hands of the courtesan and the killer in Gautier's poem furnish the adroit means whereby an esoteric brand of practical knowledge—in contrast to speculative theory that is aesthetically or voyeuristically gathered through the *eye*—may be acquired through manipulation and violence, and through the violation of established moral values. This is the essence of the active art, the craft or *techne* of both Lacenaire and Imperia that affords them their duplicitous talent for assuming multiple, and seemingly conflicting, roles—assassin/poet and courtesan/queen.

In his *Confessions of an English Opium-Eater*, De Quincey had detected a far-fetched similarity between himself as a young impoverished philosopher and an equally impoverished prostitute named Ann based on their respective habits of walking the streets of London. "Being myself, at that time, of necessity, a peripatetic, or a walker of the streets, I naturally fell in, more frequently, with those female peripatetics, who are technically called street-walkers."[18] The activity of "street-walking" is useful in attaining intellectual as well as carnal knowledge. De Quincey's comparison between himself and Ann is based on the fact that they are both transgressors: the philosopher and prostitute are outcasts not because they both happen to be friendless and impoverished in London, but because they have violated epistemological and moral limits in their pursuit of forbidden knowledge. The young philosopher's speculative quest after intellectual knowledge is intimately related to the young prostitute's practice of carnal knowledge. Prostitute and philosopher are related by virtue of their feet, underscoring the connection between coitus and intellectual knowledge. In Gautier's poem, it is the prostitute and *murderer* who are related by virtue of their hands, thereby reinforcing the connection between coitus and *killing*. Knowing and killing are interrelated, interchangeable activities, mediated by their common reference to sexuality. De Quincey's pairing of prostitution and philosophy lends support to the view that knowledge is the hidden key to "Étude de mains." Reciprocally, Gautier's pairing of prostitution and murder leads us to suspect that behind De Quincey's confession of himself and Ann as the peripatetic pair of philosopher-prostitute lurks the more demonic, hand-related pairing of the *murderer*-prostitute that we might expect De Quincey to have revealed, had he actually written his projected *Confessions of a Murderer*.

Historically, we are at the point of transition from the romantic recognition of knowing-as-action (illustrated by Faust's rendering in Goethe's drama of the opening sentence of the Gospel of Saint John— "Im Anfang war das Wort!"—as "Im Anfang war die Tat!" [I, 1237]) to the modern formulation of action-as-knowing. Consider the statement by the terrorist Chen in André Malraux's novel *La Condition humaine:* "A man who has never killed is a virgin." Jan Kott has called this "one of the most terrifying sentences written in the mid-twentieth century," and he has offered the following gloss: "This sentence means that killing is cognition, just as, according to the Old Testament, the sexual act is cognition."[19] What sets killing and coitus apart from conventional cognitive activities is precisely the fact that they are not mere activities, but modes of action. They are not mere exercises in ratiocination, but forms of manipulation. They refer not to thoughts, feelings, fantasies, wishes, or motives conceived by the mind, but—as in Gautier's poem—to deeds done by the hand. As Sting croons in the tune "Murder by Numbers," "If you can find that your *hands* are still willing, then you can turn a murder into art." And when murder, like prostitution, ceases to be a cool-headed, resolute "hand-job" and becomes instead an irresolute, labyrinthine "mind game," then we have the post-homicidal dementia of Lady Macbeth, hopelessly trying to wash the hallucinated bloodstains from her hands.

But Kott extends his analysis of Malraux's sentence even further: "it also means that the experience of killing cannot be communicated, just as the experience of the sexual act cannot be conveyed." Killing and coitus are pre-eminently *private* acts, intensely intimate personal experiences that are completely sealed off from intersubjective discourse because they impart a wordless kind of knowledge mediated by the body. The carnal knowledge shared by lovers, or by the murderer and his victim or witness, does not involve the communication of discursive meaning between two discrete individuals, but rather a communion at the instant of death between bodies that are no longer distinct from each other. As Bataille wrote in his essay on Nietzsche, "'communication' cannot take place from one full and intact being to another: it requires beings who have put the being within themselves *at stake*, have placed it at the limit of death, of nothingness."[20]

This is why sex and murder are ultimately inaccessible to psychoanalytic inquiry and judicial decision. As the purest kinds of intersubjective action, killing and coitus are the two experiences that cannot be psychologically explained, but that at most can only be phenomenologically, tactfully, described. Factors such as motivation, intention, consciousness, sanity, and guilt—terms that are indispensable to the "tact-less" scientific discourse of jurisprudence and psychoanalysis— are suspended or "bracketed" in such "pure" descriptions. Hence Lacenaire's relatively taciturn account of his own crimes in his otherwise boastful *Mémoires*. Even De Quincey, despite his claim that human action is always motivated, and despite his appreciation of Shakespeare's psychological treatment of murder in *Macbeth*, scrupulously avoids psychologism and refrains from assigning any definite motive to the Williams slayings. Williams's experience as a murderer is simply too intense, his motives too profound, his knowledge too personal to be communicated or vulgarized. Like the narrator in Schwob's "The Veiled Man," De Quincey's narrator is aghast, paralyzed, and utterly incapable of accounting for a murder of such exquisite, erotic "voluptuousness." Rather than adopt the psychological, motivational discourse of murder that informs the great oeuvre of Shakespeare, Dostoyevsky, and (to some extent) Gide, De Quincey develops an alternative, more "tactful," aesthetic description of murder that is closer to the writing of actual killers like Lacenaire and his contemporary Pierre Rivière, as well as to the later productions of literary stylists like Schwob and Robbe-Grillet, and directors like De Palma and Polanski.

Creative Murder: Abbott, Genet, Rezzori, Girard

> Il n'éxiste que trois êtres respectables:
> Le prêtre, le guerrier, le poète.
> Savoir, tuer, et créer
> —Charles Baudelaire, *Mon coeur mis à nu*

> There will be time, there will be time
> To prepare a face to meet the faces that you meet;
> There will be time to murder and create . . .
> —T. S. Eliot, "The Love Song of J. Alfred Prufrock"

> Nowadays you have to be a scientist if you want to be a killer.
> —Humbert Humbert, Nabokov's *Lolita*

In Nietzsche's synthesis of literature and philosophy, we have not only to do with the ultimate subversion of ethics by aesthetics, but we also find the modern displacement of traditional epistemology by hermeneutics to be already under way. Knowledge of the truth is revealed to be (merely) interpretation; philosophy is exposed as (and by) rhetoric. It would appear that both the great projects of Kant's first and second critiques—the transcendental philosophy of the conditions of knowledge in the *Critique of Pure Reason,* as well as the transcendental philosophy of the basis of moral action in the *Critique of Practical Reason*—are undermined by the very philosophy of aesthetics which

Kant had himself introduced in the *Critique of Judgment* and which, ironically, had been intended to bridge the gulf between the separate philosophical domains treated by the two earlier critiques. By considering murder as an art form rather than as a moral transgression (if only for the purpose of pointing up the shortcomings of Kant's moral philosophy), De Quincey unwittingly prefigured Nietzsche's radical subversion of Kant's—and everyone else's—ethical system by aesthetics. It remained for later writers like Dostoyevsky and Gide to show that murder may not only be a moral transgression or an artistic performance, but can be considered a cognitive, and even a creative, act as well. Modernist writers who recognized this possibility in effect performed the post-Nietzschean feat of upsetting Kant's philosophy of art by a literature—or even, as in the case of Lacenaire, a life—of action.

Writing to Norman Mailer in 1983, the writer Jack Abbott—presently serving a prison sentence for manslaughter—has commented on Kott's insight about killing as cognition, and offered a compelling critique of Kant's conception of knowledge. Cognition is limited because it is a theoretical, speculative activity; its objects are restricted to the realm of sensible phenomena. Like De Quincey whom he claims never to have read, Abbott suggests that there is a kind of knowledge that has direct access to the supersensible realm of the noumena, the things-in-themselves. In episodes of human conflict, the noumenal essences that normally elude the understanding can become the objects of an intensely personal knowledge. This kind of action that appropriates the knowledge and the suffering of the other is guided neither by reason nor by morality, but consists of sheer terror.[21]

In a section on prison violence in his book *In the Belly of the Beast*, Abbott presents bullfighting as "a surrogate gladiator conflict" in which "the matador is in a sense fighting another man to the death." The matador is compared to "an ingenious maestro who can bring out excellence in the most inexperienced of musicians by sheer dint of the talent he sees in them." The spectators at a bullfight are not so much watching a sport as they are witnessing an artistic performance that "brings into play esthetic, sublime qualities which move men to contemplate *moral* elements of the spectacle, the way drama does in theatre."[22] The spectators, in other words, are not merely entertained by the violence they witness, but like the audience at a Greek tragedy, they gain access through it to a kind of moral wisdom. Abbott has since developed this idea, writing in a Nietzschean vein of the origin of tragedy in "the *appropriation of suffering* by those who wanted to acquire the experience of others." Far from feeling pity for the characters in tragedy, the Greeks envied and admired these figures. "This envy, this *desire* for the terrible (and the terrible wisdom it would impart), was perhaps the leading motive in appropriating it." Abbott speculates that "*watching* the suffering of others from outside" provides an explanation of how cruelty came into being.[23] Cruelty is rooted in a desire for an intimate knowledge of human suffering that goes beyond mere cognition and is "not intellectual" (p. 135).

An example of such knowing appears in a controversial passage from *In the Belly of the Beast* in which the murder of one prison inmate by another is described. As in the bullfight, so in prison violence, the weapon of choice is the knife: "A knife is an intimate weapon. Very personal. It unsettles the mind because you are not killing in physical self-defense. You're killing someone in order to live respectably in prison. Moral self-defense." The intimacy between the killer and his victim has a distinctly erotic character:

> You can feel his life trembling through the knife in your hand. It almost overcomes you, the gentleness of the feeling at the center of a coarse act of murder. You've pumped the knife in several times without even being aware of it. You go to the floor with him to finish him. It is like cutting hot butter, no resistance at all. They always whisper one thing at the end: "Please." You get the odd impression he is not imploring you not to harm him, but to do it right.[24]

Although this passage—which is part of what Abbott has since called "The Killer Vignette"—was read as evidence against him at his trial for the stabbing death of Richard Adan in 1981, and although Norman Mailer himself seems at first to have assumed that the passage was a firsthand account of a fatal assault in 1965 in which Abbott was involved, Abbott has insisted that the passage was written from "the point of view of an observer" (p. 61), and "was a synthesis—a universal emblem of prison murder" (p. 129). There is no reason to doubt

Abbott's claim that his "description was *designed* to charge the emotions of the reader" (p. 103), in which case he was unwittingly following De Quincey's technique of presenting murder in all its terrifying sublimity to an awestruck beholder. But it is easy to see how this scene of suffering could have been read (and condemned) as a killer's account of his own cold-blooded deed: "*watching* the suffering" of his victim "from outside," and acquiring a "terrible wisdom" in the act of appropriating that suffering.

Gide had already explored the philosophical ambiguities of murder in *Les Caves du Vatican*. Gratuitous murder was ultimately incomprehensible and scandalous to the novelist Julius, while Lafcadio regarded it coolly as an authentic, creative action. "One imagines *what would happen if*," muses Lafcadio only minutes before he throws his brother-in-law out of the moving train, "but there's always a little hiatus through which the unexpected creeps in. . . . That's what makes me want to act. . . . One does so little! . . . 'Let all that can be, be!' That's my explanation of the Creation. . . . In love with what might be. If I were the Government I should lock myself up" (p. 179; "On imagine *ce qui arriverait si*, mais il reste toujours un petit laps par où l'imprévu se fait jour. Rien ne se passe jamais tout à fait comme on aurait cru. . . . C'est là ce qui me porte à agir. . . . On fait si peu! . . . 'Que tout ce qui peut être soit!' c'est comme ça que je m'explique la Création. . . . Amoureux de ce qui pourrait être. . . . Si j'étais l'État, je me ferais enfermer" [7:328]). By carrying out his transgressive impulse of hurling his fellow-traveler out of the speeding train, Lafcadio, like Macbeth, hopes to bridge the gulf "between the imagination and the deed" (p. 186; "entre l'imagination et le fait" [7:337]) once and for all. Insofar as murder is spontaneous and gratuitous—insofar as it "kills time" by annulling the gap between thought and action—it can be said to be genuinely "creative." It is not a matter here of transforming murder into a creative act by presenting or beholding it aesthetically. Rather, murder is *already creative as an act*—on the level of immediate, pre-aesthetic action. Murder *is* the act of creation itself, not despite its destructive violence, but because of it.

This is what Nietzsche seemed to say when he urged his readers to undertake "*the creation of our own new tables of what is good*" and to "stop brooding about the 'moral values of our actions.'" Nietzsche was prompted to call for the re-creation of morality by his realization that the causes, the essence, and the meaning of human action are fundamentally unknowable, and that action therefore eludes both moral and aesthetic judgment: "as one contemplates or looks back upon *any* action at all, it is and remains impenetrable"[25] ("*jede* Handlung, beim Hinblick oder Rückblick auf sie, eine undurchdringliche Sache ist und bleibt" [12:246]). Especially impenetrable are violent acts whose gratuitous destructiveness strikes terror into everyone who witnesses or hears of them—everyone except the terrorist himself who claims to have acquired an intensely personal kind of knowledge through his violence. As Gautier implies in his poem about Lacenaire's hand, the assassin gains a secret knowledge in the act of murder that—like carnal knowledge, and unlike conventional types of cognitive or even "literary" knowledge—is noncommunicable: Lacenaire is a "vrai meurtrier et faux poëte."

The claim that murder and coitus are private, noncommunicable forms of knowledge can never be philosophically justified, however—at least in any discursive sense. What guarantee does the assassin or the lover have that he has been initiated into *gnosis?* What proof can he offer that his act of violence or love has ushered him into a type of secret knowledge—of his victim or partner or of himself? What certainties can there be in the face of the flagrant contradiction that Abbott discerns in American society whereby the "*same* act"—namely, sexual penetration—is seen "as a consecration and expression of love" when performed on a woman, and as "a *desecration* and expression of the deepest contempt" when performed on a man?[26] If Nietzsche wrote that "*every* action is unknowable," and "*any* action . . . is and remains impenetrable," Abbott shows that the most impenetrable act of all is the act of penetration itself. Yet does this mean that action is fated to contradict and undermine itself since one can never really "know" what one is doing, or, as Abbott seems to say elsewhere in his writings, that the intrinsic unknowability of action enables it to arrive at wisdom that surpasses human understanding? Far from solving the Kantian problem of knowledge, the supposition that creative or destructive actions can provide access to higher reaches of wisdom only leads back to Kant's epistemologically bound system. Nietzsche's principle about the fundamental unknowability of human action would pre-empt any attempt to make action the basis of knowledge.

An alternative to the secret wisdom supposedly obtained by the murderer is the insight into the mystery of human existence acquired by his witness, or better still, his confessor. In the *Journal du Voleur* (1949), Jean Genet writes of his envy of police inspectors like his friend Bernardini in Marseilles who is able to "draw to himself the most unexpected, the most unhappy situations, to take upon himself the most humiliating confessions, which are the richest." "It is not the more dazzling crimes [contained in the police files] that I would like to know about," Genet admits, "but rather the more dismal, those which are called sordid and whose heroes are gloomy. As a result of the emotional shufflings they cause, crimes bring about enchanting situations." He proceeds to enumerate such aesthetic murders: "those twins, one of whom was a murderer, the other dying when his brother was beheaded; the babies choked by hot bread; a wonderful device in a macabre setting to delay the discovery of a murder; the stupor of the criminal who gets lost, turns about, goes back, and is caught in the neighborhood of the crime," etc. Genet savors the interplay of chance and fate entailed in crime and detection, "the grandiose chance discoveries which culminate in the beheading of a man." He treasures the confessions of these criminals that afford a singularly intimate knowledge of human nature, and he attributes the "vastest intelligence . . . to the lucid and sympathetic witness of so many wretched confessions"—namely, the police inspector ("Au témoin lucide et sympathique de tant d'aveux misérables, l'intelligence la plus vaste semblait permise"). Ultimately, he speculates that this voyeuristic curiosity is at the root of his own insatiable homoerotic and criminal impulses: "Perhaps it was also the quest of this intelligence that led me to those incredible adventures of the heart" ("C'est peut-être sa recherche aussi qui me conduit vers ces incroyables aventures du coeur"). Genet's thievery was not merely a means for him to obtain "earthly profit" ("profit terrestre"); "what I have sought most of all," he wrote, "has been to be the consciousness of the theft whose poem I am writing" ("ce que j'ai recherché surtout c'est d'être la conscience du vol dont j'écris le poème"). And again, "poetry lies in [the thief's] full awareness of being a thief" ("La poésie consiste dans sa plus grande conscience de sa qualité de voleur").[27] Genet aspires to become a witness in both a criminal and a sacred sense—indeed, for him the two are one and the same. Both murder as well as lesser crimes reveal the poetic/erotic mystery of existence to which Genet bears witness as a poet-saint. This poetic realm that becomes accessible through sovereign acts of transgression is to be distinguished from merely prosaic, discursive celebrations of murder like that of the prose-writer Julius in Gide's *Les Caves du Vatican*.

Where Julius is only capable of sanctioning murder in the literary context of his novel, the unnamed novelist-narrator of Gregor von Rezzori's *The Death of My Brother Abel* (1976) affirms that "a murder, no matter how vile its motive, no matter how despicably committed, no matter with how much literary hedonism it may be grasped, goes beyond the private and the literary sphere." In Rezzori's late-modernist work, a writer again attempts to produce a novel in which he meditates on murder as a creative act, but as he is also the narrator of the metanarrative in which the fragments of his novel-in-progress are embedded, he displays a good deal more awareness than Gide's novelist. Rezzori's novelist-narrator shares Kott's insight into Malraux's work, recognizing that murder entails a higher-order of communication, an intimate, nonverbal knowledge which the killer shares with his victim: "A murder (and presumably only a murder), despite all modern-day problems of interpersonal communication, establishes a relationship with the other—and indeed one that instantly becomes transcendental." This insight is continued in the narrator's novel-in-progress:

> —for everyone carries the murderer inside himself and is simulta-
> neously a murderer's victim. And thus the terror aroused by a
> murder is a primal terror, the immediate realization of the Evil that
> dwells in us—more thorough, more intrinsic, more involuntary than
> all drives (and, incidentally, contained in all drives). And such a con-
> frontation with this terrible thing in us, bloodily witnessed by a mar-
> tyred victim, who is I, and a murderer who is I, instantly raises the
> question of the why and the wherefore and, thus, of the how of crea-

tion. Why is man born with this terrible thing in him? Who created
him in this way and for what purpose?

The illusion of individual identity dissolves in the erotic experience of
murder, and the intimate communion between slayer and slain. All
differences collapse in the kiss of Judas that makes him one with
Jesus, that Christian re-enactment of Cain's murder of Abel whereby
the sinner is indistinguishable from the savior, and the evil brother
identical with the good. Such "murder mysteries" constitute the mystery of creation: "every street ballad about murder is actually primal
history, and even the most inane whodunit (beyond the silly hunt for
the murderer, who could be anyone, and not just for the sake of suspense) is a circuitous search for God."[28]

Because of its mystery, and what Nietzsche called its unknowability, human action is potentially both transgressive and creative: transgressive because it violates existing epistemological categories and
ethical values, and creative because it requires "the creation of our own
new tables of what is good" and, presumably, of what is "true." The implications of the originating power of the act of murder have been most
fully elaborated in René Girard's observations about the mimetic
nature of violence—namely, that all human institutions have their origin in a conflict between rivals who are actually doubles. (Genet
expresses much the same insight, we have seen, with respect to the
relation between criminal and cop;[29] Rezzori, in the relation between
the murderer and his victim.) This conflict is resolved in murder, and
subsequently either ritualized as sacrifice—that religious "subter-
fuge," as Bataille calls it, whereby "the sacrificer identifies with the
animal struck by death," and thus "dies while watching himself
die"[30]—or secularized as Abbott's bullfight in which "the matador and
the bull become *equal*" in the "moment of truth" when "the matador
pierces its heart."[31] Girard ponders the cultural significance of such
sacrificial legends as Romulus's slaying of his brother Remus (the act
that made possible the founding of Rome), and Jacob's covering of his
body with the skins of slaughtered goats (the ruse that enabled him to
pre-empt his elder brother Esau's blessing and birthright from their
father Isaac).[32] (We shall see that Abraham Lincoln may also be consid-

ered a sacrificial victim of the rivalry between a pair of actor-brothers, the Booths.)

Not surprisingly, Girard accords the biblical story of Cain's primal murder of *his* brother a special importance. He regards it as an indication of God's judgment in favor of cults that practice animal sacrifice in contrast to supposedly nonviolent cults that do not—and that ultimately have recourse to murderous violence against fellow humans instead. The first-born human is the first murderer who also happens to be the brother who tills the soil, and "who does not have the violence-outlet of animal sacrifice at his disposal. . . . To say that God accedes to Abel's sacrificial offerings but rejects the offerings of Cain is simply another way of saying—from the viewpoint of divinity—that Cain is a murderer, whereas his brother is not" (p. 4). By drawing a crucial anthropological distinction between animal and human sacrifice, the story of Cain and Abel signals a divine prohibition against the latter, a taboo against murder upon which any social order must be based. "The murder of Abel in Genesis has an exceptional value," Girard writes in a later study. "It owes this value to the fact that it is the first foundational murder [*meurtre fondateur*], and the first biblical story to raise a corner of the veil that has always been thrown on the crucial role of homicide in the founding of human societies."[33]

Girard further suggests that in those primitive acts of collective murder which ultimately give rise to sacrificial practices, we find the origin not only of all cultural laws and institutions, but of human thought itself. The sacrificial act organizes and neutralizes the violent forces of disorder in primitive societies, thereby laying the foundation for a new, more "advanced" social order, but it also serves a fundamentally cognitive, heuristic purpose. "Sacrifice is an instrument for exploring the world," Girard writes. "There is something in [sacrifice] that is akin to scientific research in the modern world."[34] Humbert Humbert's paradox that "nowadays you have to be a scientist if you want to be a killer" finds its inverse formulation in the ritualized violence of primitive societies: In *those* days man had to be a killer if he was ever going to become a scientist, a thinker, a rational being.

In this sense of sacrifice as primitive science, murder is revealed to be both an act of knowing and an act of creating because it is a fundamental, originating act. But its originating potential is inseparable from its violent, destructive, excessive character which goes beyond both Kant's moral universe and De Quincey's aesthetic-visionary perspective. The great problem confronting the post-romantic epoch, and addressed by such cultural theorists as Freud, Bataille, and Girard, is how to deal with this smouldering discontent, this erupting excess, this sudden violence. In the absence of a rational enlightenment ethics that could outlaw, condemn, and at least contain their natural excesses—indeed, the excesses of reason have proven to be even more vicious than man's instinctual proclivities—and in the absence of a romantic aesthetics that could serve as the secure playground upon which their murderous impulses would be sublimated and sublimed, men and women of the twentieth century have found themselves confronting the open space of irrational, pre-aesthetic action in which humanity's Dionysian lunges at and plunges into—self-knowledge are repeatedly performed.

ILLUSTRATIONS

Caspar Walter Rauh, *Haus des Mörders*. Pen and ink drawing from *Niemands-land* (Munich: Verlag Kurt Desch, 1947). The drawing is accompanied by Rauh's text: "Temples are built to honor successful murderers. They stand in a bog of blood and tears."

Félicien Rops, *Le Bonheur dans le crime* (1879). Collection Carlo de Poortere, Courtrai, Belgium. This illustration is from a series accompanying Barbey d'Aurevilly's short stories, *Les Diaboliques*. J.-K. Huysmans has offered this description: "On a socle, topped by the pale visage of Medusa in its mane of serpents, the murderous couple embraces, while death, disinterred in her shroud and dragging herself on her knees, howls curses and implores vengeance from the Gorgon who smiles with her impassive lips and her blank eyes."

Théodore Géricault, *Portrait of a Kleptomaniac* (ca. 1822). Oil on canvas, 61.2 × 50.2.
Museum of Fine Arts, Ghent. This portrait is from a series of studies of mental
patients painted by the artist in the last years of his life. Each portrait depicts a
different "monomania," Esquirol's term for a delusion that appears logical in
itself but is based on a distorted view of reality. Although the subject of this particular portrait is usually identified as a kleptomaniac, the painting is frequently
called *The Mad Assassin*. Thus, the painting illustrates the curious connection
between theft and murder that is a recurrent theme in Genet's writing.

Paul Cézanne, *The Murder* (ca. 1870). Walker Art Gallery, Liverpool. Where Géricault's portraits of lunatics gave them a normal, almost dignified appearance, this early work by Cézanne belongs to a period when the artist, in John Rewald's words, "wished to externalize the agitations of his inner life" by turning to "violent and erotic subjects." As one critic described Cézanne's aggressive technique, he painted "not only with a knife but with a pistol." The impact of the painting—which Robert Simon suggests is indebted to the *canards*, the sensational "journalism of blood and lies"—results from the viewer's assumption of the role of a stunned passerby, a paralyzed witness to a brutal slaying he is powerless to stop.

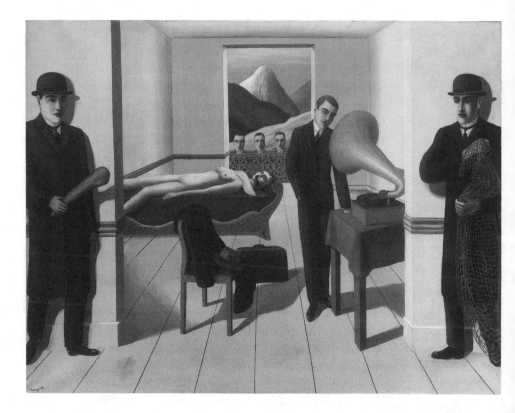

René Magritte, *The Menaced Assassin* (1926). Oil on canvas, 59¼″ × 7′4⅞″. Collection, the Museum of Modern Art, New York. Kay Sage Tanguy Fund.

In this sequence from De Palma's
Dressed to Kill, Kate (Angie Dickinson)
is assaulted inside a closed elevator by
a transvestite slasher. When the elevator door opens, Liz (Nancy Allen) is
horrified to find Kate sprawled on the
floor, her arm extended in a plea for
help. (*Continued on next page*)

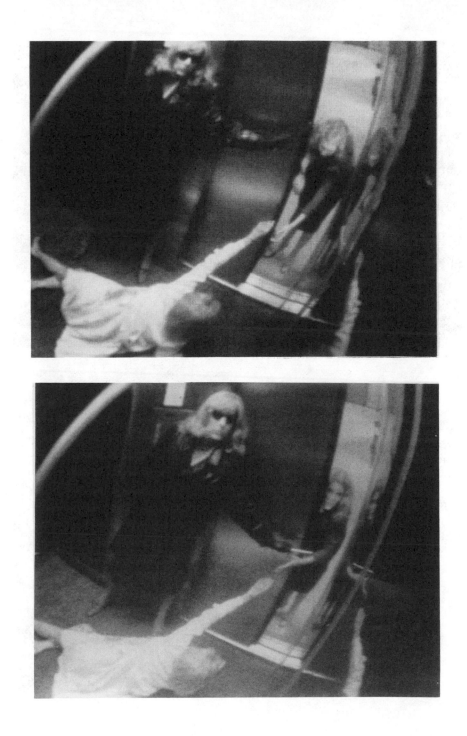

Liz cannot see the killer who is standing just inside the half-open door, but his reflection is visible to the viewer in the elevator mirror. In a brief close-up of the mirror, the viewer assumes the gaze of the killer, who watches Liz's reflection as she reaches her hand toward Kate. The killer then begins to extend *his* hand (in which he holds the darkened razor) along the door's interior. Just as the razor is poised above Liz's wrist, and the hands of bystander and victim are about to meet, light glints off the blade and alerts Liz. She raises her eyes to the mirror, and in a second close-up of the same shot, the viewer's gaze becomes identical with that of the witness and the killer. This suspended instant ends abruptly when the distracted killer drops the razor which Liz retrieves as the door closes. She thus avoids becoming a second victim. (Still of Allen courtesy of the Museum of Modern Art/Film Stills Archive; other stills courtesy of Orion Pictures Corporation.)

In the climactic scene from Alfred Hitchcock's *Rope*, the publisher Rupert Cadell (James Stewart) is determined to find out if his former prep-school students Phillip (Farley Granger, left) and Brandon (John Dall, right) have actually killed their classmate who has mysteriously disappeared. Brandon vaguely tries to dissuade Cadell from opening the chest in which he has concealed the body, but his behavior earlier in the evening and his remarks about murder have aroused Cadell's suspicions. As Phillip has come to realize, his accomplice really wants his one-time housemaster to behold his "masterpiece." "Alright! Go ahead and look," Brandon finally tells Cadell. "I hope you like what you see."

Far from appreciating the young men's deed, Cadell is stunned by the sight of the corpse. Brandon brazenly defends himself, explaining that he and Phillip have only followed Cadell's idea that "moral concepts of good and evil, and right and wrong, don't hold for the intellectually superior. . . . That's all Phillip and I have done. He and I have lived what you and I have talked." Cadell rather lamely insists that Brandon has perverted his idea. "You've thrown my own words right back in my face . . . You've given my words a meaning that I never dreamed of, and you've tried to twist them into a cold, logical excuse for your ugly murder!" (Museum of Modern Art/Film Stills Archive; © Universal/MCA Inc.)

John Ford's western *The Searchers* presents the five-year search of Ethan Edwards (John Wayne) for his niece Debbie who was kidnapped by Comanches during a raid on his brother's home. The trail leads Ethan and Debbie's half-brother Martin to the tepee of Chief Scar where they discover that the kidnapped girl has grown up to become her captor's squaw (Natalie Wood). In this recognition scene, Debbie fails to acknowledge her would-be liberators. Instead she dutifully displays Scar's lance from which hang his victims' scalps, including those of her own family. Since Debbie has accepted her Indian identity and refuses to be "rescued," Ethan not only disowns his niece, but resolves to take her life. (Museum of Modern Art/Film Stills Archive. Copyright © 1956. Warner Bros. Inc.)

Another girl who refuses to be rescued is the 14-year-old prostitute Iris played by Jodie Foster in Martin Scorsese's and Paul Schrader's *Taxi Driver*. When the quixotic cab driver Travis Bickle (Robert De Niro) fails to persuade her to leave her pimp, he arms himself, acquires a mohawk haircut, and wages a one-man war against the mobsters who are exploiting her. In John Hinckley's adaptation of this film to his life—or of his life to the film—in 1981, the actress Foster was cast in the role of a prisoner at Yale University (where she was in fact a freshman), while the former actor and newly elected President Ronald Reagan was assigned the part of the assassination victim. On the day of his assault, Hinckley wrote to Foster, "I'm asking you to please look into your heart, and at least give me the chance, with this historical deed, to gain your respect and love." (Museum of Modern Art/Film Stills Archive. Copyright © 1976. Columbia Pictures Industries, Inc.)

Guido Reni, *St. Sebastian* (c. 1611). Capitoline Museum, Rome (Alinari/Art Re-
source, New York, N.Y.). Mishima writes that it was his discovery of this painting in one of his father's art books that occasioned his first ejaculation. In his
biography of Mishima, John Nathan calls this figure "the central image in
Mishima's sadomasochistic eroticism," and notes the young Japanese writer's
particular regard for Wilde's poem "The Grave of Keats":

> Taken from life when life and love were new
> The youngest of the martyrs here is lain,
> Fair as Sebastian, and as early slain.

Shortly before his death in 1970, Mishima conceived the idea for a series of
photographs by Kishin Shinoyama to be called "Death of a Man." He posed in
various death scenes including this one in which he recreated the Reni St.
Sebastian. (Photo courtesy of Kishin Shinoyama.)

P   A   R   T

FOUR

MIMESIS AND MURDER

On est soi de nature, on est un autre d'imitation.
—Diderot, *Paradoxe sur le comédien*

Media-Mediated Murder

Where the phenomenon of pure murder, of homicide committed without any motive or idea of self-interest on the part of the assailant, was a recurrent feature in nineteenth- and early twentieth-century fiction, it has now become the all too familiar subject of news headlines. The dramatic rise in the number of sensational, senseless killings—of assassinations and multiple murders—since the 1960s has been well documented.[1] Inevitably, this escalation of violent crime has been attributed to the cultural impact of television.[2]

It took some time, however, for the mass media's effect on patterns of murder to become evident. The sensational homicides of the 1960s and 1970s continued for the most part to fall into one of two categories.[3] On the one hand, they were politically motivated to some degree (either acts initiated and executed by private citizens as in the deaths of the Kennedys, Malcolm X, and Martin Luther King, Jr., or state-sponsored assassinations as in the slayings of Patrice Lumumba of the Congo, the Diem brothers in South Vietnam, President Salvador Allende of Chile, and Egypt's President Anwar Sadat).[4] On the other hand, they were evident psycho- or sociopathic acts as in the Manson cult slayings, the Moors murders of 1965 (in which Myra Hindley and Ian Brady recorded the deaths of their child victims "as an art statement"), or the serial killings by Richard Speck, David Berkowitz, Ted Bundy, and Albert DeSalvo. But by the late 1970s several note-worthy assassination-episodes occurred that could not be written off either as being politically motivated or as resulting from a condition of madness or social malaise. The "Kool-Aid" suicides in Jonestown, Guyana, that took place immediately after the slaying of an investigat-ing U.S. Congressman, and the "Twinkie defense" invoked on behalf of the disgruntled civil servant who killed San Francisco Mayor Mos-cone and Supervisor Harvey Milk presaged the bizarre, quasi-political, media-mediated violence of the 1980s. This violence needs to be understood in the historically unprecedented context of a hyperaes-theticized mass-culture.

Our survey of literary fictions of the past two centuries has demon-strated that murders not committed on the basis of political, or even personal, motives needn't be written off as psychopathic acts. Never-theless, the judicial system and the medical establishment have been reluctant to admit the possibility of motiveless murders committed by disinterested, sane assailants. (In this respect, the institutions of law and medicine share the view of the novelist Julius de Baraglioul in Gide's *Les Caves du Vatican* who refused to accept the possibility of a disinterested murderer in real life, although he had himself created just such a character in his own fiction.) Traditionally, the legal and medical discourses have sought to rationalize violent crimes in the form of a confession elicited from the perpetrator. The police interro-gation, the courtroom cross-examination, and the psychoanalytic ses-sion are modern institutionalized modes of the much older religious confession of the Catholic church or the literary, autobiographical con-fessions of writers like Augustine, Rousseau, and De Quincey. Often working in partnership, criminal and psychoanalytic confessions cus-tomarily try to determine not only *that* a suspect has committed a par-ticular act, but also the reasons *why* he did it. This is especially true in criminal cases in which the defendant is known to have committed a crime, and in which it is his sanity that is in question. In such cases, the defendant is likely to be judged insane not so much on *legal* grounds—his being judged to have been at the time of his crime alter-natively incapable of distinguishing right from wrong (the M'Naghten rule), lacking the capacity to appreciate the wrongfulness of his action (the Brawner rule), or lacking the specific intent to commit a criminal act (the *mens rea* test)—but on the *logical* grounds that no plausible motive for his deed can be found.

The medical and the legal professions understandably have trouble accepting the possibility of pure, motiveless murder because they tend to view individuals as autonomous willing agents who act in their own self-interest. Such a view has proven to be hopelessly inadequate in the case of Mark David Chapman's 1980 killing of John Lennon and John W. Hinckley, Jr.'s 1981 assassination attempt against a newly elected President Reagan. In both cases, the medical-legal professionals failed to extract a plausible confession from the defendants explaining why they did what they did. This failure in turn stems from a general inability to recognize, first, that the assaults by Chapman and Hinckley are related, and second, that they belong to a different category of assassinations from that of political and psychopathic murders. "Traditional" assassinations belonged to an Age of Meaning, or Age of Transgression, where party politics and ideologies were worth fighting for, and occasionally, killing for. The assassin's mental condition was readily intelligible so long as insanity was regarded simply as the Other of intelligibility, the absence of meaning. Hinckley's assassination attempt and his 1982 trial abruptly brought home the problematic nature of clinical diagnoses and legal judgments of insanity,[5] particularly at a time when the categories of meaning and madness were increasingly being determined by the media, if they hadn't been outmoded altogether. We don't hesitate to call Hitler mad, but what do we say of a parodic tyrant like Idi Amin?

Our post-transgressive age marks the fulfillment of McLuhan's dictum about the medium becoming the message, the final phase of what Christopher Lasch calls the transformation of "horrible events into images."[6] "Meaning" at this juncture repeatedly reveals itself to be merely a function or fictional "special effect" of the mass media. It is no accident that the decade of the presidency of former movie actor and television host Ronald Reagan coincided with a hyperreal phase of mass culture when the media (literature, film, TV, and all the other arts) came to mediate as never before the general public's sense of "reality." This is no longer simply a case of life imitating art but, as Jean Baudrillard has insisted, of life being indistinguishable from, or unimaginable without, art—art being understood not merely in the restricted sense of the "fine" arts, but, as the Pop artists of the 1960s had demonstrated, in the far broader sense of advertising and the commercial arts. In the new media-mediated "reality" thoroughly awash in art-as-advertising and advertising-as-art, acts of violence like those of Chapman and Hinckley need to be studied as media-simulations, as quintessentially mimetic acts.

Thomas De Quincey's insight into the aesthetics of murder, and beyond this, into the violence inherent in aesthetic experience itself, will have to be substantially revised if it is to be applicable to our own cultural situation. For one thing, the relation of the ethical and aesthetic domains to one another has been inverted in the twentieth century, especially in its later phase. The social norm in postindustrial society and in postmodern culture is no longer the ethical world of the real, but the aesthetic realm of the hyperreal. The romantic artist-assassin has become the postmodern performance artist. Both resort to violence, but while the violence of the former enables the murderer to achieve an aesthetic suspension from the ethical norm, as in Macbeth's trance upon killing King Duncan, the latter's violence attempts to shatter the ubiquitous aestheticized image-world so that the all-but-forgotten ethical world may be revealed, or if necessary, created. Instead of vaulting in the manner of Hedda Gabler from hum-drum, middle-class ethical reality to aristocratic-aesthetic hyperreality, the contemporary performance artist often employs bold, aggressive means to penetrate the surrounding world of hyperreality in order to reveal the "real." "Art or the world of appearances becomes ethics or the world of action through crime"[7]—this formulation has increasingly become the norm in the twentieth century, an epoch that "has been taken up," in Greil Marcus's words, "with the attempt to prove that the beautiful, the poetic, and the call to murder are all of a piece."[8]

Neither Mark David Chapman nor John Hinckley, Jr., committed their attacks under the influence of drugs—the romantics' view of the murderer's psychology. Rather, Chapman and Hinckley were operating under the influence of the mass media. A popular novel and a pop-

ular film were sufficiently powerful stimulants to trigger a total collapse of these media-junkies' already tenuous sense of the distinction
between ethics and aesthetics, reality and fiction. The assaults against
media-heroes John Lennon and Ronald Reagan were a response to
this collapse, a desperate attempt to restore the ethical/aesthetic and
reality/fiction distinctions. For Chapman and Hinckley, the media
functioned much in the manner of the Indian hemp that the original
assassins, the Moslem *hashshashin*, consumed in preparation for their
deadly deeds. Indeed, Chapman's and Hinckley's apparently random
acts of violence exemplify the global situation of American society
itself in the late twentieth century. For the United States' role in world
affairs has become precisely that of De Quincey's artist-assassin, of
the religious fanatic feeding on hashish in order to psych himself up
for undercover murder. It is no coincidence that as the world's leading
importer of illegal drugs, America—the *soma* culture prophesied by
Aldous Huxley—also happens to be the world's leading exporter of
arms and media entertainment.[9]

Turning from the beginning to the end of the 1980s, we find a curious twist of the Hinckley scenario. Instead of an artist manqué acting
under the influence of the media and attacking a head of state, a head
of state called for the assassination of an artist. If we judge Hinckley
and Chapman to be insane because they were unable to distinguish
between fiction and reality, what are we to say of the Ayatollah Khomeini and his followers who refused to buy the Western notion that
artistic fiction has a different order of validity than historical reality, but
who take literature and its artistic devices of parody and satire in absolute seriousness? Khomeini's death sentence against Salman Rushdie
for having written a novel that was considered blasphemous against
the Islamic faith was hardly without precedent, but was in keeping
with the longstanding tradition of the *hashshashin*, the fanatic followers
of an Islamic religious leader known as the Old Man of the Mountains
who sent them out on secret murderous missions during the time of
the Crusades. Chapman and Hinckley's acts of violence were not all
that different from the deeds of the *hashshashin*; instead of acting
under the influence of drugs, however, they acted under the influence
of the mass media, the Huxleyan *soma* of our brave new world.

Celebrity Assassins

The assassin Czolgosz made President McKinley a hero by assassinating him. The United States of America made Czolgosz a hero by the same process.

—Shaw, *Man and Superman*

Because it has become a commonplace to observe that American culture celebrates violence, many U.S. citizens have accepted the stereotype and become inured to this condition. Americans must turn to outsiders, like the Canadian anthropologist Elliott Leyton, to remind them of what is only too obvious: that "no single quality of American culture is so distinctive as its continued assertion of the nobility and beauty of violence—a notion and a mythology propagated with excitement and craft in all popular cultural forms, including films, television, and print" (p. 287).

The United States is only the most glaring example of a global phenomenon found in all industrialized nations where the celebration of violence through the media is not limited to literary and electronic technology. Leyton gives the example of the multiple murderer Peter Kurten, who ravaged Germany during the 1920s. After his capture, the

> authorities rooted through his past and discovered that as a youth he had spent much time in the Chamber of Horrors, a waxwork exhibition in Kölnerstrasse. A childhood friend recalled that he always gravitated toward the wax figures of murderers. Kurten once said to him, "I am going to be somebody famous like those men one of these days." (p. 282)

If murderers were celebrated early in the century by wax effigies made in their image, and if such icons could inspire a troubled boy to become famous by embarking on a career of violent murder, one can imagine what the social impact would be of the celebration of violence by the advanced media technologies of television and film. As Leo Braudy remarks in his cultural history of fame,

> Whatever political or social or psychological factors influence the desire to be famous, they are enhanced by and feed upon the available means of reproducing the image. In the past that medium was usually literature, theater, or public monuments. With the Renais-

sance came painting and engraved portraits, and the modern age has added photography, radio, movies, and television. As each new medium of fame appears, the human image it conveys is intensified and the number of individuals celebrated expands.[10]

Every communications medium is a "medium of fame" that acquires its cultural prestige by appealing to people's "desire to be famous." Killers like Peter Kurten discover their heroes in the media; they learn about their "chosen precursor through some medium of communication."[11]

But some killers find not only their precursors in the media, but also their victims. The would-be murderer can gratify his "desire to be famous" in two ways: either by emulating a murderer celebrated by the media, or by choosing a victim from among the pantheon of media celebrities. In either case, the media's role is decisive—a fact that has become most evident in recent years in the case of those sensational instances of homicide where the murderer first takes his cue for violence from the media, and then exploits the media's constitutive role in society in such a way as to become a celebrity in his own right.

The first option available to the individual who wishes to become famous through murder is to emulate a celebrated killer, an assassin or a multiple murderer. Of multiple murderers there are two kinds— those who commit a sensational series of killings over a period of time, and those who slaughter a number of innocent victims in a single, deadly massacre. In the latter case, the mass murderer[12] kills his victims during a violent rampage that often culminates in his own death, either by suicide or in a police raid, thereby ending his spectacular career as a killer as soon as it begins. He is unlikely to give much thought to his reputation, but tends to act out of a personal quest for retribution and perhaps martyrdom. The serial murderer, in contrast, is often motivated by a quest for identity and celebrity. "How many times do I have to kill before I get a name in the paper or some national attention?" wrote the "Wichita murderer" to the police in 1976.[13] The serial killer need not perish in the course of his crimes, but may even go on after his capture to promote his renown. Typically, he is tracked down and arrested after his reputation has already been established during his reign of terror; then his prestige is further enhanced by a sensational trial, followed by his incarceration. This in turn can lead to the publication of an account of his deeds, or even of his prison memoirs, which may be followed by the release of television, movie, and video docudramas. As Leyton summarizes, multiple murderers who "no longer wish to live . . . will stage a mass killing whose climax is their execution; but should they wish to live, and to achieve notoriety—even celebrity—they will prepare their careers in serial murder" (p. 28). (The mass murderer who elects to sacrifice himself in a blaze of violence is an example of a cathartic rather than a mimetic phenomenon, and will be discussed in the following chapter.)

Once the life of the serial murderer becomes a matter of public record and he is dubbed a newsworthy subject by the mass media, the consequences are unpredictable. In 1986 the TV-film *Deliberate Stranger* was aired about the deceptively genial serial coed-killer Ted Bundy. (It is believed that John Hinckley saw this film at St. Elizabeth's Hospital, prompting him to try to correspond with Bundy.)[14] The film was rerun two years later in July 1988. Six months afterwards, after more than a decade on death row and several stays of execution, Bundy abruptly went to the electric chair in January 1989 to the cheers of an enthusiastic crowd waiting outside the prison. In this instance, the attention given by the media to a convicted serial murderer may have worked against him, and may even have been exploited by others as a way of calling attention to themselves.[15] But if actor Mark Harmon's televised re-enactment of Bundy's crimes inflamed public feeling against the justice system for stalling his execution, the media's coverage of the event and of the anti-Bundy vigil created a backlash of sympathy for the executed convict. The media may present the multiple murderer as an object of either public outrage or public pity. The TV docudrama may turn its viewers into a lynch mob, while cooler journalistic commentary in the aftermath of the execution is likely to bestow a certain immortality on the convict as a kind of religious martyr or sacrificial scapegoat. We have seen such literary celebrations of historical serial murderers as De Quincey's account of John Williams and Marcel Schwob's rendition of Burke and Hare. And we are familiar with the legends that the popular press has created in the case of Jack the Ripper, and more recently, the Boston Strangler and the Son of Sam.

Who is to say what may be the ultimate fate of Ted Bundy?

Just how unpredictable the multiple killer's celebration/condemnation by the media can be is illustrated by the case of Jeffrey MacDonald, the physician convicted in 1979 for the murder nine years earlier of his pregnant wife and two children in Fort Bragg, North Carolina. MacDonald invited author Joe McGinniss to attend his trial and to write a book about his case as a means of subsidizing his legal expenses; after his conviction, MacDonald hoped the book would reveal his innocence. At the trial, however, McGinniss became convinced of MacDonald's guilt, and presented him in his 1983 book *Fatal Vision* as a cold-blooded killer. The following year, MacDonald filed suit against McGinniss for misrepresenting him and for having betrayed his trust. Although the trial ended in a hung jury, all but one of the jurors sided with the convicted murderer MacDonald against the journalist McGinniss. Janet Malcolm focused her articles about the MacDonald-McGinniss affair in *The New Yorker* on the enigma that a journalist and literary author managed to appear more guilty in the public eye than a mass murderer.[16] Malcolm portrayed McGinniss as an opportunist who sought to promote his journalistic reputation at the expense of his notorious subject. The journalist-artist appeared as a monster who was guilty of an act of "character assassination" that turned him into a kind of murderer himself. But perhaps it would be more accurate to say that the artist's monstrosity in this case consisted in the fact that he was *not* an honest-to-goodness murderer, but only an impostor. The artist was more guilty than the murderer because he had parasitically fed off of the latter's tragic, quasi-sacred vocation. As Genet declared, "The utilization of crime by an artist is impious. Someone risks his life, his glory, only to be used as ornament for a dilettante."[17]

Besides achieving renown by becoming a *celebrated* killer who takes the lives of a succession of innocent, anonymous victims, the homicidal individual in search of fame has the more direct option of becoming a *celebrity* killer. Like the multiple murderer who, Leyton argues, is likely to be found "among the ambitious who failed—or who believed they would fail—and who seek another form of success in the universal celebrity and attention they will receive through their extravagant homicides" (pp. 297–98), the celebrity assassin is often, as in the case of Chapman and Hinckley, a frustrated middle-class youth engaged in a desperate quest for social identity and recognition. But in contrast to the multiple murderer, his victim is a single individual, a media-hero whom the assailant looks upon as a kind of model or double.

The celebrity assassin's extreme identification with his model should not be simply explained away as a psychotic aberration. The recent vogue of celebrity assassination attempts[18] is undoubtedly related to the unprecedented role played by the media in contemporary society as a mimetic mechanism. In the world of the hyperreal, identity is contingent upon image, and individuals exist insofar as they are able to identify themselves with an image generated by the mass media. The individual who lacks a sense of identity may seize upon the image of a public figure that can serve him as a model. Such behavior is quite innocuous when the celebrity-model is already dead, as in the increasing number of Elvis-impersonators who have appeared since the "King"'s death. The problem arises when an anonymous individual tries to appropriate the image of a living celebrity as his own. The progress from celebrity qua model to celebrity qua double culminates in the celebrity qua victim. This is to be expected in an age of mass-(re)production when uniqueness seems impossible to achieve: the anonymous individual tries to appropriate the celebrity's unique aura for himself. It takes a violent act of self-creation to transform the anonymous individual from a Nobody to a Somebody.

Although the victim of a celebrity assassination must of necessity be a Somebody, he might just as well be an Anybody, because the assailant has no compelling reason for singling out his particular celebrity-victim from a pool of Hollywood or Washington media-heroes. The innocent victim in the case of celebrity assassinations is selected as arbitrarily, it turns out, as the innocent victims of multiple murders (both serial killings and mass murders), or for that matter, as the innocent victims killed or maimed in a terrorist bombing or the innocent hostages taken in a hijacking or kidnapping. In the case of most multiple murders and terrorist acts, the victims are unknown to the killer, in contrast to the victims of conventional single murders whom the killer usually knows personally.[19] In this respect, celebrity assassinations constitute a special, paradoxical case that lies midway between single and multiple murder. In one sense, the celebrity assassin, like the assailant in cases of single murder, certainly "knows" his victim; however, his knowledge of the victim is not based on immediate, personal experience, but only on the victim's public persona as transmitted by the media. So the celebrity assassin really doesn't know his victim at all, or knows him only through his media-mediated image. As in the case of multiple murder and terrorist violence, the celebrity-killer's victim is actually a stranger to him; if the celebrity were not a stranger, it is doubtful the assailant could kill him in cold blood.

The assailant's apparent disregard of his victim's identity distinguishes multiple murders and celebrity assassinations as "aesthetic" murders from political assassinations, crimes of passion, and personal vendettas where the killer has a decided interest in his victim's identity, or in his victim's nationality or religion in the case of terrorist violence. It is precisely the assailant's arbitrary selection of the victim that makes the "aesthetic" violence in such cases all the more chilling.[20] But the most troubling aspect of celebrity murders in the age of mass media—slayings where the murderer identifies with a victim who is so familiar and yet at the same time a total stranger—is that the victim is perceived as a false double who must be destroyed. In this respect, celebrity assassinations are a contemporary manifestation in our hyperaestheticized culture of the romantic phenomenon of the murder of one's double explored by Hoffmann, De Quincey, and Poe.

Double Fantasy: Mark David Chapman and John Hinckley, Jr.

Most of us are diers. We don't have the disposition, the rage or whatever it takes to be a killer. We let death happen. We lie down and die. But think what it's like to be a killer. Think how exciting it is, in theory, to kill a person in direct confrontation. If he dies, you cannot.
—Don DeLillo, *White Noise*

An idolater is also a murderer.
—Tertullian, *De Idololatria*

Although the assassination of former Beatles leader and pop superstar John Lennon on December 8, 1980, received enormous publicity, the event was soon overshadowed by the shooting less than four months later of President Reagan. The accelerating pace of these events—the attack against Reagan was itself succeeded two months later by the shooting of Pope John Paul II—resulted in the suppression, rather than the revelation, of the striking similarities between Mark David Chapman's and John W. Hinckley, Jr.'s respective acts of violence. Both acts were committed by troubled young men of the same age against public figures whom they had no reason to dislike, and whom they in fact admired. It wasn't that the parallels between these assassination episodes escaped everyone's notice; on the contrary, the media may have wanted to cover up these similarities in order to avoid triggering a rash of copycat celebrity killings, thereby putting the lives of their own progeny of media-heroes at risk.

The close relation between the two events ought to have become especially evident during Hinckley's trial in the spring of 1982. Psychiatric testimony documented Hinckley's reaction to Lennon's murder—his ensuing depression, and his suicidal and homicidal fantasies—in the nearly four-month period leading up to his own attempt on Reagan's life. The expert testimony focused public attention on the issues of Hinckley's mental and emotional condition at the time of his assault, and particularly on the problem of the legal definition of insanity that ultimately led Hinckley's jurors to find him not guilty. Yet apart from the psychiatric and legal questions associated with the case which received such widespread attention, there remains the issue, virtually neglected by the media, of their own role concerning Hinckley's psychological condition during the weeks that preceded his assassination attempt. Hinckley's response to pop culture, his cultural conditioning by the mass media (which he himself criticized as being "out of control"),[21] bears an unmistakable resemblance to Chapman's case. Both youths were overexposed—as to some degree we all are—to the media images of cult-heroes and superstars who provided them with fantasy role-models. Both were victims of their own emulation and simulation of Lennon, the pop-star who was transformed by obsessive media coverage into an exemplary cult-figure, a secular idol.

So powerful were the identification fantasies of Chapman and Hinck-ley that it is not surprising that these secular idolaters should in turn become—as Tertullian wrote nearly two millennia ago in an explicitly religious context—murderers. Why this should be needs to be explored in some detail.

The youth of each succeeding generation identifies itself with—and is in turn identified by—its idols. As Sinatra and Elvis had been the pop heroes of American adolescents during the 1940s and 1950s, John Lennon was a cult figure for the generation growing up in the 1960s. His leadership of the most successful band in modern music history assured his popularity even after the group's breakup in 1970, when his outrageous antics, such as the "peace-ins" in bed with Yoko Ono, were diligently reported. Then Lennon abruptly dropped out of sight.

Earlier statements and lyrics hint at his quasi-religious notion of withdrawal from public life—his controversial quip that the Beatles had become more popular than Christ, and the prophetic refrain to the ballad he recorded with Ono: "The way things are going, they're going to crucify me." Lennon was hypersensitive to his status as an idol/martyr. After Elvis Presley's untimely drug-related death in 1977, he became obsessed with the idea that martyrdom was the fate of secular as well as religious idols. Embarking on a new family life, Lennon tried to "divest his divinity" before it killed him as, he suspected, it had killed Presley. For a time, it seemed he had actually succeeded in ceasing to be an idol. Then in 1980 he emerged from the quiet life of house-husbandry and fatherhood with the release of the album *Double Fantasy.* This joint collaboration with his wife celebrated the domestic bliss of de-idolization even as it confirmed his status as a pop idol. With hindsight, it seems less ironic than inevitable that Lennon's comeback after nearly half a decade of self-imposed exile from public life should prove to be the occasion of his death.

For no one had Lennon been more of an idol than for his assassin, Mark David Chapman. His idolatry had gone to extraordinary lengths, verging on total identification with his hero. He had been a devoted fan ever since his father bought him the Beatles' first album when

Chapman was nine years old. He had learned to play the guitar so he could perform the Beatles' tunes. Two months before shooting Lennon he used the ex-Beatle's name when quitting his job as a security guard at a Honolulu condominium; his ambition was to imitate Lennon's relationship with Yoko Ono, becoming a house-husband to the Japanese woman whom he met in Hawaii in 1978, and whom he married the following year.[22] The shock felt by Lennon's mourners at his death would have been even more numbing had they realized that the slaying was the result—and perhaps even the confirming proof—of a fan's extreme idolatry. (The word "fan," after all, is short for "fanatic," which itself is derived from *fanum*, the Latin word for temple, the place where the god inspires madness.) The critical difference between Lennon's legions of admirers and Chapman was the latter's acute feeling that he lacked an identity. Without a sense of who he was, he could not subordinate "himself" to his idol in the manner of other idolaters; he required Lennon's image to fabricate an identity for himself.

Idolatry cannot remain a reverential state of submission when one's own identity is at stake. The behavior leading up to the assault—Chapman's sustained imitation and "stalking" of his victim—suggests that Lennon had become not just an idol for him (someone to be worshipped or desired), but a model (someone to be imitated). It was as if Chapman had tried to invest in himself the divinity of his model, John Lennon, with the same care that Lennon had sought to divest himself of his precursor Elvis's aura. Chapman's meticulous imitation and appropriation of Lennon's life, carried out to the most minute detail, turned him into Lennon's "double." Perhaps this might have been a workable arrangement so long as Lennon remained in relative isolation—so long as he remained invisible and determined to renounce his divinity. But when Lennon again appeared in the role of idol with the release of the *Double Fantasy* album, Chapman was moved to take action against the model who had become an obstacle to his desire to be Somebody. Rather abruptly, Lennon appeared to Chapman as a "bastard," a "phony," who preached peace and love but courted wealth and fame. And so, posing as an autograph hound at the entrance to the Dakota apartment building where Lennon lived—and even getting him to sign a copy of *Double Fantasy* as he rushed off to a recording session—Chapman waited patiently for him to return. It was then that the would-be double fired his fatal shots.

The double fantasy, however, was only just beginning.

Born the same year as Chapman, 1955, John Hinckley also suffered from an acute lack of self-image and desperately sought a media-hero upon whom to fashion an identity. His enthusiasm for the Beatles prompted him, like Chapman, to learn to play the guitar in junior high school, and "from about the age of eight" he wanted "to be a Beatle or a dictator."[23] Professing his admiration for Reagan after his crime, Hinckley added that "the only person I ever idolized throughout my life was John Lennon, and look what happened to him."[24] During Hinckley's trial, his lawyers produced a paper written after Lennon's death titled "I read the news today, oh no," after a line from a Beatles song. In this paper Hinckley recorded his own response to the death of his idol, observing that Lennon's loss overshadowed the death of Elvis. "The dream is over," Hinckley lamented. "In America, heroes are meant to be killed. Idols are meant to be shot in the back." For Hinckley, not only had the dream died, but "I died. You died. Everyone died. America died. The world died. The universe died"— along with, presumably, God Himself.[25]

Lennon's murder in December 1980 had a profound impact on Hinckley's already depressed and obsessed imagination. The most immediate result was that Hinckley's plans to stalk the newly elected President were momentarily interrupted. According to William Carpenter, the leading psychiatric expert for the defense at Hinckley's trial, "the stalking of President Reagan . . . suddenly became no longer important, and what was important was the loss of his idol in the world. He immediately identified in that process with both Chapman and Lennon."[26] Even the scene of Lennon's murder provided Hinckley with an incentive and a model for his own violent apotheosis. He joined the mourners at Lennon's funeral in New York City. Two months later, on Valentine's Day, he returned to the Dakota and stood at the very spot where Chapman had opened fire. This time, however, he had not come to New York to offer his respects. In his pocket was a .38 caliber Charter Arms handgun that he had purchased the previous month, the same type of gun that Chapman had used to shoot down Lennon. Hinckley had returned to the murder scene with the specific intention of taking his own life at the exact location where Lennon had been shot. He did not go through with his plan, however. Instead, a little more than a month later, he ambushed President Reagan as he was leaving a reception at the Washington Hilton Hotel, wounding not only the President, but Press Secretary James Brady, a Secret Serviceman, and a police officer as well.

At Hinckley's trial, the prosecution sought to repudiate the grounds for an insanity defense. It repeatedly emphasized Hinckley's inability to turn his gun against himself, while he *had* succeeded in firing at the President. In their cross-examination of Dr. Carpenter, the prosecuting attorneys attempted to characterize Hinckley's failed suicide attempt—and, by implication, his actual assassination attempt—as a conscious, controlled decision:

> Q. Whatever you say, he was able to control his behavior and not kill himself on Valentine's Day.
> A. I say he was unable to get his behavior to culminate in his death at that time.
> Q. He couldn't psych himself up, right?
> A. He could not take that act.
> Q. He couldn't psych himself up, right?[27]

The difference between "taking the act" and "psyching oneself up to take the act," between suicide or homicide as a blind act and as the outcome of an intent to commit the physical act of suicide or homicide *(mens rea)*—this was the delicate balance on which the verdict concerning Hinckley's innocence or guilt, his insanity or sanity, ultimately hung.

In 1977, Chapman had come even closer than Hinckley to taking his own life. He failed when a hole burned through a vacuum hose he had rigged to his car's exhaust pipe in Hawaii. With a failed suicide attempt behind him, Chapman's thoughts turned to murder. His behavior in the days before he shot Lennon in December 1980 repeated his activities before his suicide attempt three and a half years before—first checking into an expensive hotel to live it up one last time before the big event, eventually moving into a seedy YMCA to conserve funds, then flying home to his girlfriend in Georgia (1977) or wife in Hawaii (1980) where he pledged to renounce his violent plan, and finally shuttling back to Hawaii/New York to carry out his suicide attempt/actual murder.[28]

The different verdicts in the trials of Chapman and Hinckley—the former eventually withdrew his insanity defense and pleaded guilty to Lennon's murder,[29] while the latter was found not guilty by reason of insanity in the sensational verdict of 1982—obscure the significant parallels between the two cases. Like Chapman, Hinckley failed to commit ignominious suicide, and instead returned to his earlier fantasies of notorious homicide. "Guns are neat little things, aren't they?" he had written in his "I read the news today" essay about Lennon's murder. "They can kill extraordinary people with very little effort." As soon as Hinckley and Chapman ceased to be a menace to themselves, they became a threat to others. And not a threat to anyone in particular: who their victim was did not really matter as long as he was "extraordinary," in Hinckley's words. Hinckley may have "identified," as Dr. Carpenter suggested, "with both Chapman and Lennon," assassin and victim. But since there was no assassin to make him a celebrated martyr like Lennon, the only alternative was to assume the assassin's role himself. Because Hinckley could not be Lennon, he must be Chapman; because he could not be Reagan, he must be Reagan's assailant; because he could not be Christ, he must be Judas.

In the pocket of the coat worn the day he fired at the President was a button of John Lennon, the idol who had unsuccessfully tried to divest himself of divinity. Lennon's death—and more particularly, Lennon's status as an idol—was a largely overlooked but crucial factor in the events leading up to Hinckley's act of pulling the trigger of the gun aimed at the President.

The Arbitrary Victim

The murderer is the last man who still seeks human contact; the remaining members of the species merely continue to ride past each other on escalators. In such a world, murder and conflict govern humanity.

—Heiner Müller

We have to become murderers in order to experience ourselves as real . . . isn't that horrible?
—Gregor von Rezzori, *The Death of My Brother Abel*

In both Chapman's murder of Lennon and Hinckley's attempted assassination of President Reagan a few months later, an individual with virtually no self-image contemplated suicide, and then abruptly sought to kill a public figure whom he admired and emulated. In the self-less loner's desperate quest for identity, any esteem he may have for his idol is beside the point. Since he feels he has no identity of his own, it is of no consequence that his idol is a personal role model, an object of private veneration. All that matters is that his idol/model be the celebrated object of *public* interest, of *others'* attention.

Having stalked President Carter during his re-election campaign, Hinckley was in Washington, D.C., in March 1981, en route to New Haven where he planned to take either his own life or that of actress Jodie Foster. In a copy of the *Washington Star*, he happened to notice President Reagan's schedule, and decided on the spur of the moment to shoot him instead. (Other options he had contemplated included assassinating Senator Edward Kennedy or storming a session of the U.S. Senate.)[30] His victim's identity did not really matter as long as he or she, like Lennon, was "extraordinary."

Similarly, when asked by his attorney and psychiatrist when the idea of murder had occurred to him, Chapman answered that he first thought of killing George Ariyoshi, the governor of Hawaii where Chapman had taken up residence after leaving Georgia. When asked why, Chapman replied, "I don't know. I guess because he was the governor. He was popular." Asked who else he had thought of killing, Chapman named Johnny Carson. Again, the only explanation he could offer was Carson's popularity. "Actually, I kind of like Johnny," he admitted. Among Chapman's other possible targets were Jackie Onassis, Paul McCartney, Elizabeth Taylor, George C. Scott, and Ronald Reagan. He harbored no ill will toward any of these celebrities, and could give no reason for wanting to harm them. In the case of Scott — "I like him. He's great" — he even seemed surprised himself.[31]

Hinckley, too, revered his victim Reagan, calling him "the greatest president of the century." When asked after the assassination attempt which political leaders he most admired, he responded that there was no one, "except perhaps, Mr. Reagan."[32] Hinckley's emulation of Reagan, while not as constant or as monomaniacal as Chapman's emulation of Lennon, underscores the strikingly similar nature of the two cases: both were instances of idolatry in which the idol suddenly became the victim of an act of violence. As idol and as victim, however, the celebrity in question was selected arbitrarily—less for who he was, what he had achieved, and what he represented than for the fact that he was popular and widely recognized by virtue of his media exposure. As a sure-fire method of achieving instant celebrity, nothing beats taking a celebrity's life.

Can aspirations to stardom really explain Chapman's and Hinckley's murderous acts? This was indeed the prosecution's argument in both trials. Park Dietz, the government's leading psychiatric expert in its case against Hinckley, maintained that the defendant was obsessed with fame: "He displayed a considerable concern with the media . . . [a]nd he indicated his interest in assassination through . . . comparisons he made between himself and other assassins."[33] As an explanation for this interest, Dietz noted that Hinckley "hadn't been occupationally successful. That is why he had to turn to high-publicity crime." Dietz called attention to Hinckley's concern the night of the shooting about whether the Academy Awards would be televised as scheduled, or pre-empted by his deed.[34]

It is misleading, however, to suggest that Hinckley and Chapman had the specific intention of becoming celebrities through murder. It was not primarily celebrity but identity that they were after. (Among Chapman's cherished possessions was a photograph showing Judy Garland as Dorothy in *The Wizard of Oz* consoling the lion in search of courage; did Chapman see himself similarly embarked on an identity quest?) Hinckley and Chapman reached adulthood at a time when identity, and indeed reality itself, had become in large part a fabrication of the mass media. To be somebody is to be Somebody—to be a media-personality, to have one's personality mediated by the media. As Chapman described a childhood fantasy to defense psychological expert Milton Kline, "I used to fantasize that I was a king and I had all these little people around me and that they lived in the walls. . . .

And that I was their hero and was in the paper every day and I was on TV, their TV, and that I was important. . . . They all kinda worshipped me, you know."[35] Chapman was the man who would be king in a hyperreal world where media coverage defines and confers existence—existence, however, which is no longer anything more substantial than image.

Because of their celebrity status, Lennon and Reagan were arbitrary victims for Chapman and Hinckley. These would-be assassins sought to acquire identities by taking the lives of public figures, thereby assuming their aura of uniqueness and, in the process, becoming celebrities in their own right. At the same time, the available evidence suggests that Chapman and Hinckley did not perceive their victims as real people at all, but as "bit players,"[36] mere media-images or *Wizard of Oz* fantasies whose insubstantiality they may have felt a need to expose. If Lennon and Reagan were either divine idols or mere images, there could be no harm in shooting (at) them; alternatively, if they were real flesh-and-blood people then they were not worthy of people's worship, and ought to be exposed for the false gods they were. Instead of dismissing Chapman and Hinckley as criminal lunatics, or diagnosing them as sociopaths in search of fame and stardom, we need to consider them in the context of a hyperaestheticized culture where they appear in an altogether different light: as disenchanted secular idolaters, self-proclaimed iconoclasts in a media-saturated world. We may even begin to see them as belonging to the same tradition we read of in the apocryphal story of the youthful Abraham who smashed the idols in his father's workshop to reveal them for what they were, as well as for what they were not.

Scripts for Assassins

Many Ugandans believe that [Presidents Idi] Amin and [Milton] Obote and that bunch learned their methods of murder from the movies.
   —Jackson Nduwala, director of the Ugandan Theater Groups Association

The goddam movies. They can ruin you.
   —Holden Caulfield, in *The Catcher in the Rye*

Lennon's and Reagan's status as media-heroes exposed them to the violence of self-less assailants who were motivated to perform sensational iconoclastic acts, and in the process, to create an identity for themselves. But what was it that specifically motivated these iconoclastic killers? It is doubtful that as individuals with a severely damaged sense of their own identity who were as likely to commit suicide as homicide, Chapman and Hinckley would have been able to take the initiative of carrying out their assaults without some form of mediation, some intervening script that could spur and guide their actions. Chapman and Hinckley were compelled to enact fictions provided by literature and film, without which they would have been incapable of acting out their plans, and possibly even of conceiving them in the first place.[37]

In Chapman's case, the fiction that obsessed him to the point that he began acting out his own interpretation was itself a respected work of literature—J. D. Salinger's 1951 novel, *The Catcher in the Rye*. Chapman first read the book when he was sixteen, the same age as the novel's protagonist Holden Caulfield, with whom he closely identified. Shortly before he shot Lennon (whose own name he already had occasion to adopt), Chapman wrote to the state attorney general's office in Hawaii about changing his name to Caulfield.[38] Lacking an identity of his own, Chapman assumed the names of both a real celebrity and a fictional character. Lennon's murder was, in part, a way of playing both identities off each other, and perhaps of testing which was more real—the media-star Lennon or the literary anti-hero Caulfield.

In a letter written to *The New York Times* after Lennon's death, Chapman maintained that his motive for the killing was contained in *The Catcher in the Rye*. A Bible that Chapman conspicuously left in his New York hotel room before going off to shoot Lennon was inscribed "Holden Caulfield." (In the same Bible, he had added Lennon's name to the Gospel according to John.)[39] For his fatal meeting with Lennon, he had outfitted himself in a black fur Russian hat with earflaps in imitation of the red hunting hat worn by Caulfield in the novel, and called by him "a people shooting hat."[40] Chapman picked up a copy of the novel on his way to the Dakota and wrote in the title page: "To

Holden Caulfield, From Holden Caulfield," followed by the words, "*This* is my statement." In his prison interviews with James R. Gaines, Chapman reported a fantasy that he expected to take place after the shooting: when the police came to arrest him, he would shout to them, "I am Holden Caulfield, the catcher in the rye of the present generation";[41] then he would actually turn into Salinger's fictional character.[42]

While awaiting trial, Chapman came to believe that although he had not yet become Holden Caulfield by killing Lennon, he *had* become "the catcher in the rye of the present generation"—a kind of martyr-savior who had murdered Lennon for the express purpose of promoting Salinger's novel and the messianic message it contained. He continued to hint that the key to his shooting of Lennon was to be found in the novel, along with an explanation of his own role as a messianic prophet, although he was either unwilling or unable to express these dark mysteries himself. "*Everybody's* going to be reading this book," he told his defense psychiatrist before his trial, "—with the help of the God-almighty media. And I'm going to use it like it's never been used before."[43] If prior to his crime Chapman had been the autograph hound who solicited Lennon's and other celebrities' signatures, after the crime he himself became the celebrated autographer of Salinger's novel, dozens of copies of which were brought to him to sign.

Chapman's crime had indeed turned him into a celebrity, a fact his prosecutors intended to use against him by arguing that his promotion of Salinger's book after his arrest was simply another way of promoting himself. While his own attorneys were busy preparing his insanity defense, Chapman continued to hype himself as the catcher in the rye of the present generation. Two weeks before he came to trial, however, he decided against his attorneys' advice to withdraw his insanity defense and to plead guilty to murder. As he was about to be sentenced, he read aloud in court this passage from *The Catcher in the Rye:*

> Anyway, I keep picturing all these little kids playing some game in this big field of rye and all. Thousands of little kids, and nobody's around—nobody big, I mean—except me. And I'm standing on the edge of some crazy cliff. What I have to do, I have to catch everybody

if they start to go over the cliff—I mean if they're running and they don't look where they're going I have to come out from somewhere and *catch* them. That's all I'd do all day. I'd just be the catcher in the rye.[44]

Based on his interviews with Chapman, Gaines concluded that the decision to forswear the insanity defense was a way of exorcising his Holden Caulfield identity, much as his murder of Lennon had effectively negated his identification with the former Beatle. "Just as his fantasy of becoming Holden Caulfield was dispelled only after the murder of John Lennon," Gaines writes, "he would not cease to believe in himself as the catcher in the rye of the present generation until he had decided to plead guilty."[45] This observation supports the view that Chapman had assumed two conflicting identities based alternately on pop and literary culture—the Lennon identity as the media-star, and the Caulfield identity as the alienated savior. When Lennon came out of semiretirement in 1980, Chapman rejected the Lennon pop-star identity as being inauthentic—or in his "own" (or rather Caulfield's) words, a "phony." His wife recalled that several months before his crime, he had been enraged by a book he had read about Lennon, and had called the singer a "bastard": "he was angry that Lennon would preach love and peace but yet have millions."[46] By killing Lennon, Chapman may have hoped to expunge this fake identity so that he could give himself over completely to the more-real-than-life Caulfield persona; hence his fantasy of becoming Salinger's anti-hero immediately after the shooting.

In his subsequent interviews with teams of lawyers and psychiatrists, Chapman was particularly sensitive about being regarded as a fraud himself. "Do you think I am a phony?" he asked one psychiatrist for the prosecution.[47] And to a psychiatric expert for the defense he maintained that every generation needs a catcher in the rye—someone like himself "who speaks out against phoniness and corruption."[48] By the time of his trial, Chapman had directed his crusade against his own lawyers, and even against his own obsession with Holden Caulfield. Six months after the Lennon murder, he phoned his attorney to tell him, "You're all fakes, you're all a bunch of phonies." Gaines reports that he then "tore up his copy of *The Catcher in the Rye,* explaining that his fascination with it had been 'a delusion. . . . The book to me now represents an illness, a sickness.'"[49] More than two years later, he continued in this self-critical vein, telling Gaines that "it's the greatest cop-out in life to allow yourself to become insane."[50]

In Chapman's case, this iconoclastic impulse to strip away all media- or literature-mediated personas as inauthentic masks, regardless of their supposed intrinsic value, comes as a (perhaps inevitable) response to his original idolatrous impulse to acquire an identity by emulating media-stars and literary figures. The progression goes from identification with a celebrity figure who symbolizes iconoclasm and the rejection of false values, to rejection of this role model as a false idol himself, to a rejection of all idols and all fictions as deceptive. In the process, the individual creates an "authentic" identity for himself—not the false identity of his idol, but the true identity of the destroyer of idols.

In the hyperreality of the 1980s, such practices of appropriating, simulating, exchanging, and denying media images and narrative fictions became an indispensable means of fashioning a social identity. In a narcissistic culture awash in inauthenticity, murder seemed to offer a desperate means of clarifying the real. As Chapman confided, "We create our own definitions, we fill our own dictionaries with our own words, and until they are utterly proved false because of facing reality, they just grow stronger."[51]

John Hinckley was in the crowd gathered to welcome President Reagan when he arrived at the Washington Hilton on March 30, 1981, but only shot the President as he left the hotel less than half an hour later. The prosecution used this fact as evidence that Hinckley was not desperate but cool-headed at the time of the shooting, waiting for the best opportunity to fire his gun.[52] But this "waiting period" is significant for other reasons. Mark David Chapman loitered in the vicinity of the entrance to the Dakota for most of the day before he killed Lennon. He could have shot the celebrity as he left for a recording session in the mid-afternoon. Instead he asked for an autograph, and then waited another six hours for Lennon to return before he attacked.

This might be regarded as one more, perhaps trivial similarity between Hinckley's and Chapman's assaults on celebrities. Hinckley's suicide attempt at the site of Lennon's murder and his subsequent attempt to assassinate President Reagan suggest that he could have been following a script that had been unwittingly prepared by Chapman. Gaines has called Hinckley's attempt on Reagan's life "a grim coda to the Lennon celebricide,"[53] and one of the books found in Hinckley's Washington, D.C., hotel room after his assassination attempt was a copy of The Catcher in the Rye. However, the principal script that Hinckley followed has an altogether different source that dates almost five years before the Reagan shooting: Martin Scorsese's 1976 film Taxi Driver.

In this film's climactic scene, Travis Bickle (played by Robert De Niro) shoots a pimp at point-blank range at the entrance of a New York apartment building. Then, instead of storming the building, Bickle walks down the street, sits down in a neighboring entrance-way, and waits. Finally he gets up, walks back to the scene of the shooting, enters the building, and engages in a bloody shoot-out with the wounded pimp and his underworld cohorts. This brief scene was overlooked in all the close analyses of Taxi Driver in the aftermath of Hinckley's assassination attempt. Yet the scene is relevant not only to Hinckley's but to Chapman's crimes: it portrays a killer pausing before committing an act that is as much a suicidal as a homicidal act of violence. The reason that the killer waits is not (as Hinckley's prosecutors argued) so that he can have the best shot at his victim(s), but so that he can compose himself in a dramatic scenario that he has himself composed.

Despite the great differences between the film and the novel, Taxi Driver and its lead character Travis Bickle played a strikingly similar role in Hinckley's shooting of Reagan as The Catcher in the Rye and its protagonist Holden Caulfield played in Chapman's murder of John Lennon. Hinckley believed the film had been addressed specifically to himself, much as Chapman had been convinced that he was the intended reader and appointed interpreter of Salinger's novel. We should remember that the lead characters of both the film and the novel are anti-heroes—down-and-out drop-outs who are sick of society's filth (*Taxi Driver*) and phoniness (*The Catcher in the Rye*), and who are eventually moved to take some action against what they perceive to be the cause of all these social ills. It is not surprising that such narratives should appeal to disaffected youths like Chapman and Hinckley. Their extreme identification with Caulfield and Bickle is only too comprehensible given their own fragile sense of identity. Lennon's murder and *The Catcher in the Rye* were only secondary "scripts" for Hinckley, which he adapted to his primary script of *Taxi Driver*—the principal model that he followed as he tried to collect his thoughts and plan his actions in the months, weeks, and days leading up to his shooting of the President.

Like Chapman, Hinckley became caught up in an ongoing interplay between art and real life whereby literary and cinematic fictions repeatedly mediated actual events, and vice versa.[54] Hinckley was partly aware of this interplay, or at least he became aware of it when both the prosecution and the defense made it a crucial issue in their respective arguments. In its case against him, the government reported Hinckley's own explanation for his "insane state of mind": "the adverse influences upon him of various works of art and literature." The government's team of psychiatrists interpreted this to mean "the failure of his identification with literary characters to produce personal satisfaction"—an explanation the team placed last in its list of "the most salient [themes] in the development of Mr. Hinckley's behavior eventuating in the shootings of March 30, 1981."[55] The government's report on Hinckley's sanity endorsed Dietz's argument that Hinckley's interest in "art and literature" was nothing more than a sign of his obsession with fame and of his desire to become a media star.

Notwithstanding the prosecution's skepticism regarding Hinckley's remark about "the adverse influences . . . of various works of art and literature," there is much to be said about this statement. In Los Angeles, where he had moved in 1976, Hinckley allegedly saw *Taxi Driver* fifteen times after its release that year. The original object of his interest in the film appears to have been the character Betsy, a sophisticated woman played by Cybill Shepherd, who works for a presidential candidate. Bickle idealizes the campaign worker (who in turn idealizes the candidate) and tries to strike up a relationship with her that soon fails, although he writes his parents that he is continuing to see her. After seeing the film, Hinckley fabricated an imaginary girl friend named Lynne Collins whom he mentioned in letters to his parents, and who was modeled on Betsy in *Taxi Driver*. Hinckley invented Lynne, it seems, for the purpose of keeping up an appearance of normalcy with his parents so that they would continue to support him in his creative endeavors as a songwriter. Defense psychiatrist David Bear testified that Hinckley had told him that "the idea of making up a girlfriend, . . . exaggerating how good the relationship was going, was directly from Travis Bickle. He was a washout with the girls and yet would write home, 'I am doing well with Betsy. Things are just fine.'"[56] After his arrest, Hinckley was accused by the prosecution of feigning madness; before his attack on the President, however, his chief concern had been to feign normalcy.

Soon Lynne became a means for Hinckley to disguise his developing obsession with the actress Jodie Foster, who plays the part in the film of Iris, a fourteen-year-old prostitute. De Niro's character Bickle first meets Iris when she tries to get into his cab, but is prevented from doing so by her pimp. After his abortive relationship with Betsy, Bickle seeks Iris out and unsuccessfully tries to persuade her to give up her work as a hooker. His alienation soon drives him to plot the assassination of the presidential candidate for whom Betsy works. (From Bickle's perspective, the professional relationship between the candidate and Betsy is yet another exploitative pimp/prostitute arrangement.) Once again Bickle's plans are thwarted, and in a feverish frenzy he returns to Iris—staging a raid on her tenement, slaughtering the pimps and pushers who have exploited her, and finally turning his gun against himself only to find he is out of bullets. When the police arrive, they find Bickle covered with blood, holding his hand up to his head as if it were a gun—a suicidal pose imitated by both Hinckley and Chapman.[57] In a highly unlikely ending, Bickle recovers from his wounds and emerges as a hero.

Before Lennon's death, Hinckley had already made several half-hearted attempts to contact Jodie Foster who, he learned in the May 1980 issue of *People* magazine, had entered Yale as a freshman. On Valentine's Day of 1981, the day he tried to take his own life at the entrance of the Dakota, Hinckley wrote a poem to Foster called "A Reluctant Swan Song." In this poem he explained that his death would not be in vain because he was killing himself for her. A few days later, Hinckley was fantasizing about a skyjacking venture in which he and Jodie would replace the Reagans in the White House. On the day of the attempted assassination, Hinckley wrote a note to Foster that he left in his hotel room in which he characterized his crime as a sacrificial act and as proof of his love for her: "By sacrificing my freedom and possibly my life, I hope to change your mind about me. This letter is being written only an hour before I leave for the Hilton Hotel. Jodie, I'm asking you to please look into your heart and at least give me the chance, with this historical deed, to gain your respect and love."[58] And in a thank you note he added, "Jodie, after tonight, John Lennon and I will have a lot in common. It's all for you."[59] An hour before he left to shoot the President, Hinckley saw himself more as a murder victim (John Lennon) or as a suicide than as an assassin. He seems to have imagined his destiny at that critical instant to have been more that of a martyr than of a celebrity. Where Chapman fantasized about becoming Holden Caulfield by killing Lennon, Hinckley (according to Dr. Carpenter) expected to die while shooting the President, and through his death "to accomplish his ideal union with Jodie Foster."[60]

Hinckley's desperate attempts to work Foster into his life led him to make a recording of his rendition of a song written by Lennon to Yoko Ono in which he substituted Jodie's name for Yoko's. The recording was played at the trial:

> In the middle of the night,
> In the middle of the night I call your name.
> Oh, Jodie,
> Oh, Jodie,
> My love will turn you on.[61]

Chapman had also tried to appropriate Lennon's songs and life as his own, but in the end turned to Salinger's novel as his primary model. (Nearly nine years later, Chapman and Hinckley would be imitated in this respect by Robert Bardo in his slaying of starlet Rebecca Shaeffer; Bardo had included Lennon lyrics in fan letters which he sent his victim before the shooting, and a copy of *The Catcher in the Rye* was found in his possession after his arrest.) Like Chapman, Hinckley found Lennon's lyrics to be of only limited use in constructing an identity for himself, and he eventually adopted Scorsese's film as his principal script.

Where the prosecution tried to portray Hinckley as a man driven to "art and literature" because of an obsession with fame, lawyers for the defense focused more pointedly on the defendant's obsessive imitation and enactment of scenes in the film. Relying on the testimony of specialists like Dr. Bear that Hinckley "felt like he was acting out a movie script,"[62] Hinckley's attorneys portrayed the defendant's experience of the film as a program that he meticulously followed. In its rejection of the defense's argument that Hinckley was compulsively acting out a script, the prosecution hinted that the defense psychiatrists had deliberately or inadvertently coached the defendant to make his mental condition appear to be worse than it was. However, even if it was true, as Dietz charged, that the defense had adopted the "legal strategy" of making Hinckley appear to have followed the script of *Taxi Driver*,[63] this would have only shown that since his arrest Hinckley had been following *another* script—a version of events provided by his attorneys. But the evidence was overwhelming that *Taxi Driver* was indeed Hinckley's script of choice. As one defense lawyer maintained, "Travis Bickle became a standard and a model and a hero for John Hinckley . . . to the extent that his conduct and his actions and his thoughts and his lifestyle imitated and copied and followed Travis Bickle."[64] As evidence of Hinckley's imitation of Bickle, such details were cited as his keeping a diary, his compulsive pill-popping, and his purchases of clothing (an Army jacket, flannel shirt, boots) and weapons (three handguns and two rifles) used by Bickle in the film. Hinckley even took to drinking peach brandy, Bickle's favorite drink. In Dr. Carpenter's words, "Mr. Hinckley was, in a literal way, identifying with the character in this movie."[65]

True to his faithful imitation of Travis Bickle, Hinckley began stalking President Carter during his campaign appearances in Dayton and

Nashville in the fall of 1980. His pistols and ammunition were confiscated in Nashville when he tried to board a plane to New York, where
John Anderson was campaigning. He then "went back to Dallas to
replenish [his] arsenal," as Dr. Carpenter put it;[66] and by the time of
Lennon's murder in December, he was back in New York stalking
President-elect Reagan. Hinckley was, according to Carpenter, "bor-
rowing an identification, taking an identification, taking on content,
. . . taking on almost a script that doesn't exist in reality, but is made
to develop a life of its own and existence within his own mind."[67] The
culmination of Hinckley's identification with Travis Bickle was his
assault on President Reagan. As Dr. Bear summarized the message
that Hinckley had derived from *Taxi Driver*, "Violence, horrible as it is,
was rewarded."[68]

Taxi Driver was only one of the scripts that Hinckley followed in the
events leading up to his assassination attempt. He had also read the
book that had inspired Paul Schrader to write the screenplay for the
film—*An Assassin's Diary*, by Arthur Bremer, the man who wounded
George Wallace in 1972. James W. Clarke has suggested that the real individual Bremer rather than the fictional character Bickle was Hinckley's
principal role model; since the diary established a direct link between
Bremer and Hinckley, it exerted a more powerful effect on the latter
than the indirect intermediary provided by *Taxi Driver*.[69] My own sense
of the matter, which I develop in a different context at the conclusion of
this study, is that fiction often has a more powerful effect on impressionable imaginations than factual reporting. Precisely because of fiction's
mediated, intermediate status, it can engage the reader-viewer's imagination in ways that unmediated, immediate "reality" cannot. Although
Hinckley was exposed to both Bremer's nonfictional diary and the
fictional film based on that diary, *Taxi Driver* unquestionably affected
Hinckley more strongly than *An Assassin's Diary* or any other work.
Clarke himself makes the telling point that although Bremer confided
that he had turned to New York prostitutes after being rejected by his
lover, he "didn't meet an Iris" among them[70]—the crucial character in
Taxi Driver who became Hinckley's obsession.

Besides *Taxi Driver*, *The Catcher in the Rye*, and *An Assassin's Diary*, several other books furnished Hinckley with models that he set out to enact. Among the literature found in his hotel room after his assassination attempt was *Romeo and Juliet*—the paradigm of star-crossed lovers and of double suicide—and a book called *The Fan*, by Bob Randall, which describes a man who falls in love with a movie star whom he believes has the power to save his life. He writes fan letters to her and when he receives no response, he murders her, her secretary, and himself. Hinckley's skyjacking fantasy originated in David G. Hubbard's *The Skyjacker*, and in a book based on a true story called *The Fox is Crazy Too*, by Eliot Asinof. In this book, a troubled character skyjacks a plane to New York where he demands that a sum of money and certain people be brought to him. At his trial he feigns mental illness as a way of covering up his actual insanity in order to escape the consequences of his crimes. Hinckley actually copied a skyjacking note from this book in the winter of 1981, which he planned to use in his own skyjacking attempt. The note, found by police in a Band-Aid box in Hinckley's Washington, D.C., hotel room, read: "This plane has been hijacked! I have a bomb with me. Plus flammable liquid and a knife. A companion is also on the plane with a firearm. Act naturally and lead the way to the cabin. Stay calm!"[71] Hinckley intended to demand that Reagan resign as president, and that he himself occupy the White House with Jodie Foster.[72] He even went so far as to imitate the skyjacker in *The Fox* by purchasing shoestring (to tie up his victims), an electric switch (to fool people that he had a bomb), lighters (to give the impression he would burn the plane up), and a toy gun.[73]

Referring in his testimony to these and several other books that served as models for Hinckley's fantasies, Dr. Bear speculated that, "The real question is—I am still wondering—was there anything he read that did not go into his mind? Everything I could find, every story of a sick, bizarre character somehow entered into this man's mind."[74] How could Hinckley have been sane and planned to kill President Reagan, Bear queried, when he was responding to books and films as scripts that were sending certain signals specifically to him? In Bear's view, such behavior could hardly be called rational—a view the jury ultimately agreed with.

Hostages and Defectors

I still think about Jodie all the time. That's all I think about really.
That, and John Lennon's death. They were sorta binded together.

—tape of John Hinckley's 1981 New Year's monologue

I say this a lot, and I probably shouldn't: the difference between rape
and seduction is salesmanship.

—Bill Carpenter, mayor of Independence, Missouri (July 1990)

Certainly the most sensational revelation to come to light during
Hinckley's trial was his obsession with the actress Jodie Foster. All the
psychiatric testimony and media coverage devoted to this obsession
succeeded in doing little more, however, than to present it as a bizarre
aberration of Hinckley's depressed psyche. Yet why this overwhelming interest in a young actress and her role in a film, an interest that
induced him to attempt to take the life of the President of the United
States? To say he got the idea of assassinating a political figure from
Taxi Driver, or from any of the literary thrillers he consumed, does not
explain his particular obsession with Foster. Why did he shift his interest from the more sophisticated character, Betsy, to the twelve-year-old
prostitute, Iris? We overlook a very important cultural phenomenon if
we simply explain away Hinckley's obsession as evidence of his psychological derangement. There are compelling reasons having to do
with the media-mediated nature of contemporary experience, and
with the American psyche as a whole, that explain why Hinckley's—
as well as Chapman's—delusions took the specific form they did.

Shortly before they carried out their respective acts of violence,
Chapman and Hinckley both sought the company of young prostitutes, less to assuage their sexual desire than to enact their literary
and cinematic scripts. In one scene of *The Catcher in the Rye,* the narrator Holden Caulfield arranges for a prostitute named Sunny to be sent
to his New York hotel room, but when she arrives he only wants to
talk to her. On December 7, 1980, the day before he shot Lennon,
Chapman called a massage parlor to request that a prostitute be sent
to his hotel room at the Sheraton Centre in Manhattan. He recalls the
conversation he had with the massage parlor personnel: "I said, man,
I've got to have a woman up here, you know. I'm getting horny, like

Holden Caulfield." Instead of having intercourse with the prostitute, or even letting her massage him, Chapman claims that *he* massaged *her*: "My thing with prostitutes was, I'd say, 'This is your rest period,' you know? I did everything for them—rub their back, I'd do everything for them. . . . That's what a real man does, you see, a real man gives to a woman."[75]

Chapman was not the only celebrity assassin to traffic with prostitutes in anticipation of his crime. Five days after Chapman shot Lennon, Hinckley followed his own script—*Taxi Driver*—by picking up a teenage prostitute in New York City.[76] Exactly two months later, on February 13, 1981, he tried to find this same prostitute—a day before his attempted Valentine's Day suicide at the Dakota.[77] "For the first time," writes Lincoln Caplan, "rather than thinking of them as untouchable idols, he found himself interested in sex with women."[78] It is misleading, however, to say that Hinckley suddenly felt a spontaneous desire for sex. His "desire" did not originate immediately within him, but, as with all his fantasies, was an imitation of someone else's desire;[79] it was a desire mediated by the mass media. Hinckley was on the prowl for a certain kind of woman: barely pubescent prostitutes like Iris in *Taxi Driver*. With such girl-women he could enact his fantasy, based on Bickle's role in the film, of being a self-styled savior of the exploited and corrupted underclass.

Chapman and Hinckley were inversions of Jack the Ripper: instead of killing prostitutes, they professed a solicitous regard for them—and turned to killing celebrities instead. Both men modeled their behavior on artistic fictions that betokened a grandiose messianic fantasy. Where Chapman imagined himself to be a savior of children, "the catcher in the rye of the present generation" as he repeatedly proclaimed, Hinckley thought of himself as the savior of underage prostitutes, and fantasized about saving one in the manner of Bickle's "rescue" of Iris in *Taxi Driver*. In Hinckley's quixotic fantasy, the redemption of the world was to begin with the rescue of an innocent maiden who was being held hostage as a whore, but who in her innocence somehow managed to remain a virgin. He addressed a picture postcard of the President and Mrs. Reagan to Foster; the card read, "Dear Jodie, Don't they make a darling couple. Nancy is downright sexy. One day you and I will occupy the White House and the peasants will drool with envy. Until then please do your best to remain a virgin. You are a virgin, aren't you? Love, John."[80] After discovering that Foster was a freshman at Yale, Hinckley wrote a poem called "Liberation" in which he imagined her as a prisoner in the university who, like her alter-ego Iris in the New York brothel, was in need of rescue. "No force beneath the Milky Way," he wrote, "can prevent me from carrying out my goal of being the first saint to win the academy award for bravery while attempting to rescue an actress . . . As I liberate that young lady from the concentration camp."[81] And in another poem called "Prince Valium," Hinckley fantasized about rescuing Jodie from the rabble so that she could assume her appointed destiny as his princess: "I'm here to protect your honor, but do not be afraid of my method. It is the only way I know how to make things real."[82]

The idea of abduction as a means of seduction most likely came to Hinckley from another literary source: a novel by Nathaniel Benchley called *Welcome to Xanadu*. In this work, a patient named Leonard Hatch escapes from a mental institution and decides to kidnap an innocent, pure-hearted woman whom he loves. He brings the terrified woman to an isolated cabin where he finally succeeds in arousing her affection for him by showing her his poems. The idyll ends when the couple are tracked down by the police, and Leonard kills himself rather than lose the woman he adores. Hinckley's interest in this book—he praised it in a book report he wrote for a sociology class at Texas Tech University in 1975—centered on the idea of a romantic kidnapping. He envisioned such an act not as a crime, but as a heroic rescue mission. That interpretation seemed to him to be borne out by the situation in *Taxi Driver*: despite Iris's unwillingness to be "rescued" from her pimp, Bickle's violent raid on her tenement was justified by the fact that Iris was too confused to understand, and therefore to resist, her abject condition. Iris's exploitation by the mob prevented her from giving up prostitution and provoked Bickle to carry out his raid; in the all too likely event that Foster/Iris should prove unwilling to be liberated from Yale, Hinckley would similarly be compelled to take drastic action—either abduction or assassination, or some combination of the two.

Bickle's raid on Iris's apartment building in *Taxi Driver*, and his shootout with her pimp and his confederates, is a chilling but plausible action.[83] But, as Dr. Bear conjectured at Hinckley's trial,

> if John got the idea there and then, he took that idea and transferred it to Jodie Foster and said, "Jodie at Yale University, she is the prisoner the same way Iris is in the slums of New York," that is a bizarre thought. . . .
> Jodie was at Yale University of her free accord. She freely chose to go to Yale University. John thought she was a prisoner, thought she was trapped.[84]

It was Hinckley's idea that Foster was a prisoner at Yale that was bizarre, not his sense that she was unwilling to be "rescued," which, after all, was precisely Iris's attitude in *Taxi Driver*. (The reluctance of actual inmates to be released from prison is not as farfetched an idea as it may seem.)[85] Because Foster was unwilling to be released, Hinckley made up his mind to abduct her. He acquired a set of handcuffs that were confiscated by the police along with his guns at the Nashville airport in October 1980. He sent an anonymous note the following month to the FBI in which he described a plot to abduct Foster from her Yale dorm. In the note he explained that there would be no ransom, and that Foster was "being taken for romantic reasons."[86] And on March 6, 1981, he conveyed the following rescue letter to Foster: "Jodie Foster, love, just wait. I will rescue you very soon. Please cooperate. J. W. H."[87]

Hinckley's "method" of liberation, then, was to be abduction. This was a desperate, but necessary, measure in the case of an unaware or unwilling victim like Foster, and it had been suggested to him by his cinematic and literary models. According to Dr. Bear, the "idea that Jodie was a prisoner at Yale . . . may have started from *Taxi Driver*. . . . But the idea that he could get her to fall in love, I think that came from *Welcome to Xanadu*."[88] And in his sketch of the plot of *Taxi Driver*, Dr. Carpenter explained that when Bickle "failed to establish a love relationship with the woman [he] wanted [i.e., Betsy/Cybill Shepherd], and when he failed in the attempt to assassinate a presidential candidate, [he] turned to the saving of the young prostitute [i.e., Iris/Jodie Foster]."[89] Viewed in this way, *Taxi Driver* presents the scenario of a failed seduction that gives way to an abduction, which the protagonist is able to rationalize as a romantic rescue mission.

A curious paradox is involved in the propositioning of prostitutes: since their services can only be purchased, they cannot be seduced. The supposed non-seduceability of prostitutes has long appealed to the male imagination. The patriarchal fantasy that lies behind a pulp thriller like *Welcome to Xanadu* is essentially the same as that behind the classic erotic tale *Behind the Green Door:* namely, that for all its coercive crudity, abduction is sometimes a necessary prerequisite for seduction. This male fantasy is even present in the more cultured fictions of literate society, where the seduction qua abduction of an underprivileged girl is routinely sublimated as education or salvation. Millions have been charmed by the *Pygmalion/My Fair Lady* story in which a cultivated gentleman undertakes to reform, if not an actual whore (as *is* the case in the popular 1990 film *Pretty Woman*), then a woman from the lower classes. This classic narcissistic fable always has the same ending: not only does the male demigod fall in love with his female creation, but he gets her to fall in love with him too.

The story of the rehabilitated whore belongs to a long and distinguished literary tradition that goes back at least to the tale of Mary Magdalen in the Gospels. The principal literary source of this theme as it appears in *Taxi Driver* and in *The Catcher in the Rye* is the narrator's treatment of the prostitute Liza in Dostoyevsky's *Notes from Underground.* The Underground Man succeeds in getting Liza to give up her degrading work and to become half-enamored of him. Then, in an abrupt inversion of the "Pygmalion" story, the Underground Man balks at his role of lover/savior. Unable to reciprocate Liza's love, he humiliates her out of spite. The Underground Man's inadequacy and his inability to engage in a fulfilling relationship with another person stem from his lack of any social identity; he can't even identify himself by name. The only action he is capable of taking is to enact the Russian romantic fictions that he habitually devours. In these respects, the Underground Man is the prototype for Caulfield and Bickle, as well as for all the other alienated, media-consuming, urban antiheroes in modern literature who pattern their social identity on the heroic or romantic fictions they have encountered.

Hinckley's case is of interest because it literalizes the traditional literary theme of the reformed prostitute. His method of reform was to
stage a heroic *rescue* of a "prostitute" from what he believed to be her
exploited circumstances. What would appear to the rest of the world,
as well as to the victim herself, as the forcible abduction of a freshman
actress at Yale, was from Hinckley's perspective a glorious act of liberation. In this respect, Hinckley exemplifies the "love for a harlot" syndrome analyzed by Freud in his 1910 paper on "A Special Type of
Object Choice Made by Men":

> The trait in this type of lover that is most astonishing to the observer
> is the desire they [sic] express to "rescue" the beloved. The man is
> convinced that the loved woman has need of him, that without him
> she would lose all hold on respectability and rapidly sink to a deplor-
> able level. He saves her from this fate, therefore, by not letting her
> go.[90]

We needn't assent to Freud's explanation of what he calls this "rescue
phantasy"—the son's complete identification with the father as part of
"the wish to be the *father of himself*"[91]—in order to see the relevance of
the "love for a harlot" syndrome to Hinckley's case. What is most striking in this instance is that Hinckley's need for a prostitute—or rather
his need to rescue a prostitute—was based on a film, and his obsessive
quest for a *particular* prostitute was determined by the part played by
a real-life actress *in* that film.

This point is missed in James W. Clarke's psycho-social analysis,
which maintains that "while Hinckley was attracted to the character
Jodie Foster played in the film, Iris, he did not fall in love with Iris.
There was never any confusion between the character and the actress;
it was always the real Jodie Foster he pursued, not the fictitious Iris."[92]
Once we appreciate the extent to which Hinckley was following a
script, we see that matters are just the reverse: he was less interested
in Foster herself than in her character, her role. Hinckley's obsession
with Foster resulted from the arbitrary circumstance that she happened to be the actress selected to play the part of Iris in the film. Had
another actress been selected for the part, one suspects that Hinckley
would have developed a similar obsession with *her*.[93] Clarke's judgment that "John Hinckley never lost his ability to distinguish between

the real world and characters he saw portrayed on the screen"[94] under-
estimates the media's power not only to represent reality, but to determine it, and in the case of an artistic work like *Taxi Driver*, to re-
capitulate mythic narratives and cultural fictions with compelling
force. It oversimplifies matters to say that when Hinckley "wanted to
see Jodie Foster, he went to New Haven; when he wanted sex with a
teenage prostitute like Iris, he went to New York";[95] the "real" Jodie
Foster sought by Hinckley in New Haven was more of a media-fantasy
in his mind than the "fictional" Iris whom he presumably bedded in
New York.

Hinckley's alleged ability to distinguish fantasy from reality isn't
really the issue. What is significant about his fantasy life is the way it
combines the traditional, "high," literary theme of the reformed prostitute and the "low," literal, mass-mediated scenario of the attempted
rescue and liberation of a terrorized captive who, for whatever reason,
is unwilling to be set free. In recent years, this curious scenario has
been a recurrent feature in "art and literature," to use Hinckley's
phrase. A quick look at several examples reveals that for all its strange-
ness, his fantasy recapitulates a specifically American myth.

The story of the female captive who refuses to respond to the val-
iant and persistent efforts of her would-be liberators has very ancient
analogues. In Western culture, it goes back at least as far as the Homeric tale of the Trojan War, which the Greeks fought in order to
recover the "abducted" but fickle queen Helen. The Old Testament
story of Joseph is an early variation involving a male captive: instead
of being rescued, he is sold into slavery by his brothers; rather than
bringing him back to Palestine, the Hebrews emigrate to Egypt where
he becomes the means of *their* salvation. The key literary example of
the romantic era occurs at the end of the first part of Goethe's *Faust*
when the protagonist enlists Mephistopheles' help to rescue his
beloved Gretchen from prison. Resolved to meet her fate and to accept
heavenly judgment, Gretchen renounces Faust's offer of escape. By
refusing to let Faust "save" her, Gretchen ensures her everlasting spiritual salvation.

In modern literary examples, the theme of the prisoner who
refuses to be rescued has received a darker, more ambiguous treat-

ment. If the captive in such works is unwilling to return to her native turf, this is because she may not be a captive at all. Rather, the "captive" plays an active part in her own "capture," and thus is actually a defector from his or her own homeland. This theme of the captive-turned-defector figures prominently in the short fiction of British writer Angela Carter. Her story "Our Lady of the Massacre" (1979) is narrated by a seventeenth-century English peasant girl who is orphaned and brought up by a Catholic woman. After her benefactor's death, she is driven to prostitution until she is arrested and brought to the American colonies as a slave. She eventually escapes and joins a tribe of Indians, where she discovers a sense of kinship and community that she has never known among the civilized white man. She is adopted by an Indian woman, and marries a brave by whom she gives birth to a son. But after her husband and the rest of the tribe are massacred by English soldiers, she is told by her captors to "thank God" that she has "been rescued from the savage," and that she should "beg the Lord's forgiveness for straying from His ways."[96] The English maintain that the narrator is a bonded servant-girl who had been carried off by the Indians; "if they choose to think I was forced into captivity," says the narrator, "then they have my leave to do so, if it makes them happy, as long as they leave me be" (p. 55).

The defector theme appears in an even starker form in Carter's story "Peter and the Wolf" (1982), in which an infant girl is carried off and reared by wolves that have devoured her parents. Some years later, the wolf-child is discovered and tracked down by her remaining relatives who capture her and bring her home. She refuses to be reclaimed, however, and her incessant howling summons the wolf pack to descend on the cabin where she is trapped and to take her away with them. As the English orphan girl in "Our Lady of the Massacre" was more at home with "savage" Indians than with "civilized" colonial settlers, the wolf-child in "Peter and the Wolf" is more at home with a pack of wild beasts than with her own human relatives who only make her feel a trapped animal.

It is in the American cinema, however, that the scenario of the hostage-turned-defector has been most evident. Besides its presence in *Taxi Driver*, in which the Vietnam vet Bickle must liberate Iris by force when she proves unwilling to leave her captors, the renegade hostage theme informs two major films of the late 1970s that deal with the Vietnam War. In Michael Cimino's *The Deer Hunter* (1978), a veteran soldier (again played by Robert De Niro) returns to Asia to try to bring back his shell-shocked buddy who continues to haunt the Saigon bars where he makes a precarious living out of playing Russian roulette in a compulsive re-enactment of a torture-ritual to which he and his would-be rescuer were subjected during their imprisonment by the Viet Cong. And in Francis Ford Coppola's *Apocalypse Now* (1979), an Army captain undertakes a perilous mission to reclaim a maverick U.S. military commander who has gone native and organized his own private army of guerrillas in Cambodia. We can trace the renegade hostage theme in these early post-Vietnam era films back to John Frankenheimer's cold-war era film, *The Manchurian Candidate* (1961). In this psychological thriller, Lawrence Harvey plays Raymond Shaw, an American POW in Korea who is welcomed home a hero at the end of the war. Unbeknownst to everyone, including himself, the Russians have brainwashed Shaw to carry out acts of sabotage in the United States. Shaw's former army buddy (played by Frank Sinatra) discovers the ploy and tries to de-program him before he can carry out a political assassination.

The film credited as being the classic example of the theme of the captive who refuses to return home is John Ford's classic 1956 western *The Searchers*. John Wayne plays an ex-Confederate soldier named Ethan Edwards on an obsessive quest to recapture his niece Debbie (played by a young Natalie Wood) who has been abducted by a tribe of Commanches during a bloody raid on Ethan's brother's Texas ranch. (Note how Carter in "Our Lady of the Massacre" ironizes the plot of *The Searchers*[97] by showing that what seems to be abduction is really a matter of defection: although the female protagonist in the story is said by her colonial captors to have been carried off by Indians, she actually joined them of her own free will.) After a grueling five-year search, Ethan finally locates Debbie, only to learn that she has become a squaw of Chief Scar, the leader of the tribe that massacred her family. After this discovery, and Debbie's avowal that she has become an Indian and will never return to white man's ways, Ethan is

determined to wreak his vengeance upon her as well as on her captors. "Living with a buck" is reason enough for Ethan to resolve to kill
his niece whom he considers to be permanently tainted. The same
"better dead than red" logic holds for Indians in Civil War America
that will hold for Communists in cold-war America.[98]

Film critic Stuart Byron has dubbed *The Searchers* a "cult movie of
the New Hollywood," finding traces of its theme of thwarted rescue
and injured honor in *Taxi Driver, Apocalypse Now, The Deer Hunter,* and
other post-Vietnam films of the 1970s. Byron reports that Paul Schrader
and Martin Scorsese, *Taxi Driver*'s writer and director, admitted to seeing *The Searchers* at least once a year, and Schrader has acknowledged
that "Scorsese and I agree that *The Searchers* is the best American film,
a fact that must have influenced *Taxi Driver*."[99] Since Hinckley's assassination attempt against President Reagan and his fantasy about
abducting/liberating Jodie Foster were modeled on the film *Taxi Driver,*
they can ultimately be traced back to John Ford's *The Searchers,* which
is the cinematic source of *Taxi Driver* and which was released exactly
two decades before Schrader and Scorsese's film — ironically at a time
when Ronald Reagan was still making movies, before his near-fatal
career change from acting to politics. (Reagan's final film, *The Killers,*
was released in 1964.)

As a key example of the hostage-turned-defector theme in the
American cinema, *Taxi Driver* became Hinckley's principal script for
his abduction/assassination attempt. A year after Hinckley's attack on
Reagan, Scorsese released *The King of Comedy,* a parodic revision of the
hostage-turned-defector theme. In this film, the aspiring comedian
Rupert Pupkin (yet again played by De Niro) is frustrated in his effort
to gain the recognition of TV talk-show host Jerry Langford (played by
comedian Jerry Lewis). He arranges to abduct Langford, and threatens to kill him unless he is allowed to perform live on Langford's
show. The plan succeeds, and Pupkin emerges as a celebrity — the king
of comedy — after serving an obligatory two-year jail sentence. The
film's message could not be clearer: the most direct route to stardom
in the Age of Showbiz is the same route that *Taxi Driver* showed was
the way to achieve heroism in a violent society — namely, crime. Ordinarily the means whereby the masses are manipulated, the mass

media may themselves be manipulated by an individual who is willing to resort to crime as a way of becoming a celebrity and turning his private fantasy into a public reality.

The relationship between Scorsese and Hinckley indicates the degree to which artists and criminals may inspire each other. (Scorsese makes a cameo appearance as a psychopathic killer in *Taxi Driver* and as an artist in *The King of Comedy;* in the former film he is a jealous lover bent on murderous revenge, while in the latter he has a bit part as a television director.) In *Taxi Driver,* Scorsese unwittingly provided Hinckley with the would-be liberator fantasy that he set out to enact in his attempt to abduct Foster and assassinate Reagan. In *The King of Comedy,* Scorsese responded to Hinckley's abduction fantasy by turning the hostage theme on its head. De Niro no longer plays Bickle, the violent liberator, but Pupkin, the genial kidnapper; his "hostage" Langford is by no means averse to being freed, and in fact arranges his own escape. In marked contrast to Travis Bickle, Rupert Pupkin is no longer the quixotic hero aiding a damsel in distress, but—and here we see the resemblance to Chapman—an inveterate autograph hound and self-promoting entertainer who turns against his own role model in order to establish himself as a media-celebrity.

In the aftermath of Hinckley's rampage, Scorsese exposed the hostage-turned-defector theme that he had taken over from *The Searchers* in *Taxi Driver* as just another romantic fiction. Despite their differences, however, *Taxi Driver* and *The King of Comedy* share a crucial insight. In a world of mass-media-mediated fictions, the individual in search of an identity is free to choose whatever script he wishes to enact: Travis Bickle enacts the script of quixotic liberator, Rupert Pupkin assumes the role of king of comedy. (Pupkin actually prepares and memorizes his *own* script, the stand-up routine he performs on Langford's show.) Both Bickle's and Pupkin's roles are, of course, pure fictions: Bickle is less a liberator than a terrorist, while Pupkin is less a king than a pretender or a usurper. After all, comedians have traditionally occupied the role of jesters and fools whose social function was to entertain a melancholic king. For the jester to become a king himself implies that the comedian is, at the very least, an impostor, if not a full-fledged regicide. (One thinks of Mosca's deception of his master in Ben Jonson's comedy *Volpone.*) In both cases, the fictions enacted by these characters lead directly to violence when they encounter a "reality" composed of competing fictions.

Historically, the post-Vietnam War period furnishes the most notable instances of the hostage-turned-defector scenario, not just in high art and popular culture, but in key news events of the 1970s. Vietnam became a symbol in the American consciousness of a hostage nation, a land that the United States had tried unsuccessfully to save from Communist occupation partly as a result of that nation's unwillingness to be liberated. America's foreign policy and even its domestic unrest in the aftermath of Vietnam repeated this scenario. The energy crisis of the mid-1970s made Americans feel that they were hostages of the mid-Eastern oil-producing nations. That feeling became especially vivid after Jimmy Carter's unsuccessful attempt to rescue the fifty-two Americans who were actually held hostage (albeit against their will) in Iran—an event that brought the decade, and Carter's presidency, to an ignominious end. "In 1979," as Leon Wieseltier has written of that low point in national morale, "it was established that the United States could be held hostage to hostages." Even the commercial cinema reflected this feeling of impotence. "By 1980," writes Carol J. Clover in her study of the slasher film, "the male rescuer is either dismissably marginal or dispensed with altogether; not a few films have him rush to the rescue only to be hacked to bits, leaving the Final Girl to save herself after all."[100]

The most glaring example of the abduction-turned-defection scenario in the news events of the 1970s—of the failure of patriarchal melodrama at "the moment that the Final Girl becomes her own savior"[101]— was Patty Hearst's 1974 "abduction" by the Symbionese Liberation (sic) Army and her subsequent "induction" into that underground terrorist group. (Small wonder, then, that Paul Schrader should have taken the heiress's abduction, seduction, and re-assimilation as the subject for his 1988 film *Patty Hearst*,[102] or that Brian De Palma should have made the kidnapping of a Vietnamese girl by a U.S. army platoon the focus of his 1989 Vietnam film, *Casualties of War.*) It is against the background of these events of the 1970s that Hinckley's 1981 assassination attempt against President Reagan should be seen, and that we may appreciate Jodie Foster's all-too-comprehensible reluctance to be "liberated," like the reluctance of her cinematic counterpart Iris, through the agency of a go-for-broke world-reformer.

The Assassination Scene

> Politics . . . is like a pistol shot in the middle of a concert.
> —Stendhal

Although Hinckley's attempt to assassinate the President of the United States may clinically and legally be judged insane, it should be recognized that this "insanity" assumed a specific, culturally conditioned form, determined in large part by a whole range of media fictions and mythic scenarios which, in the absence of any socially recognized identity of his own, he made it his business to enact.

Taxi Driver's critics and Hinckley's analysts overlooked a crucial point when they failed to recognize that the gestures of attempted assassination and liberation performed by Travis Bickle and Hinckley— as well as by Lennon's murderer Mark David Chapman—are characteristically *quixotic* acts. They hark back to Cervantes's tale about the Spanish gentleman who goes mad from reading too many chivalric romances, and who fancies himself a knight-errant as a result. Imitating the adventures he has read about, Don Quixote sets out on a series of misguided missions to reform a society that has no will to be reformed, and to do honor to his idealized lady, Dulcinea del Toboso, who has no desire to be so honored. Like Don Quixote's eminent fictional successors Flaubert's Emma Bovary and Dostoyevsky's Underground Man—both great dreamers and consumers of romantic novels in their own right—Hinckley and Chapman were imitators of literary models. As real-life human beings, however, they could only enact the scenarios provided by their principal media-scripts either by turning themselves into their fictional models (Chapman's expectation of being transformed into Holden Caulfield), or by appropriating the script for themselves (Hinckley's fantasy about "rescuing" Foster in imitation of Bickle's liberation of Iris).

"The line dividing Life and Art can be invisible," Hinckley observed as he awaited his trial. "After seeing enough hypnotizing movies and reading enough magical books, a fantasy life develops, which can either be harmless or quite dangerous."[103] This allusion to Plato's metaphor of the line separating the authentic realm of ideal forms from the shadowy realm of perceptible phenomena is used by Hinckley—as always, with a view to his own defense—to invoke the Greek philosopher's warning about the threat posed by poets to the security and well-being of the state. (Hinckley characterized himself as a "psychopathic poet" to the doctors who examined him after his arrest.) But it is Hinckley's actions more than his words that bear out Plato's mimetic view of the relation between art and life, and of the violence inherent in such mimesis. For the medium of film is "mimetic" in a way that narrative, or any written or spoken text *as text* is not. Film belongs to the dramatic arts, in which actors and actresses perform before spectators by impersonating—by miming or mimicking—characters other than themselves. Textual narrative, on the contrary, is not an impersonated performance; it is a representation or recitation of events by a voice that may be present or absent, embodied or disembodied. Don Quixote repeatedly praises the mimetic or dramatic arts for being indistinguishable from the reality they represent;[104] Plato and his followers were suspicious of these arts precisely because they blurred the fundamental distinction between fiction and reality, thereby giving rise more readily than the nonmimetic or narrative arts to violent disorder and confusion.

This is what seems to have happened during Hinckley's repeated viewings of the film *Taxi Driver.* By merging the fictional role of the prostitute Iris with the real-life actress Jodie Foster, Hinckley could imagine Foster, on the one hand, as an exploited girl in need of rescue, and, on the other hand, as the chaste, idealized object of his desire. The fact that Hinckley's script was presented to him in the form of a film rather than a written text assisted him in making these transformations from art to life, from fiction to reality. A medium consisting of images of real actors who impersonate fictional characters may seduce the viewer into denying the actor's inherent double-identity, into forgetting the actor's role, and into seizing on the shred of reality of the actor himself who can be made to play whatever part the viewer assigns him in his own life-fiction.

Paul Schrader, *Taxi Driver*'s writer, has distinguished what he calls "productive" fantasies from "modelmania" fantasies that alienate the subject from his feelings.[105] In Hinckley's case, both his actions and his desire were modeled on a fictional film portraying a quixotic fantasy. Appropriating the starlet in *Taxi Driver* as his own Dulcinea, he contrived his personal quixotic quest—first, the rescue of Foster from her imprisonment/enchantment at Yale University, and second, his seduction of Foster through a heroic action. In order to accomplish "this historical deed, to gain your respect and love" (as he described it in his final note to Foster), he settled on the idea of enlisting the services of an ex-actor, Ronald Reagan. In the realm of the hyperreal, the actor who can become president should be able to play any part—even the part of the evil enchanter whose death by the knight Hinckley would be a love-token for his lady. The shots fired at Reagan would somehow release Foster from the prison of her Ivy League brothel, and awaken this sleeping beauty from the enchantment that prevented her from recognizing Hinckley as her heroic lover. Failing to do that, the shots fired at Reagan would at least awaken the assailant from *his* quixotic fantasy, much as Julien Sorel's gunshots at Madame de Rênal in Stendhal's *Le Rouge et le Noir* brought him back to a sense of his self, or as Macduff's knocking at the gate (in De Quincey's analysis) jarred Macbeth out of his trance.

From an aesthetic perspective, Hinckley appears to be the scourge of the hyperreal, that dizzying, "through the looking-glass" condition coinciding with the Reagan presidency in which nothing was quite what it seemed (spy swaps that weren't spy swaps, summit meetings that weren't summit meetings, arms deals that weren't arms deals, etc.). A man without an identity of his own, Hinckley was himself an actor whose profession was the impersonation of others. He alone knew the secret about the President who was not really a president. It was up to him to expose the emperor's new clothes for the tissue of lies they were. In the final analysis, the violence of Hinckley's assassination attempt has less to do with his imitation of the violence in the film *Taxi Driver* than it has to do with the violence of imitation itself. The act of shooting Reagan was an act of mimetic violence: an actor shooting another actor, a con-artist shooting his double.

The attack against a president who was a former actor reverses the circumstances of the classic American assassination: Abraham Lincoln's murder by John Wilkes Booth 116 years earlier. In that theatrical slaying, it was the assassin Booth, rather than the victim Lincoln, who was an actor by profession. One of Booth's greatest roles was the murderer Macbeth, the object of De Quincey's fascination. And as Ken Burns has suggested in his 1990 documentary about the Civil War, Booth's 1864 performance in *Julius Caesar* may be seen as a rehearsal of his assassination of Lincoln.[106]

Acting had been a family tradition among the Booths: John's father, Junius Brutus Booth, was a successful tragedian in England before coming to the United States, and John's oldest brother, Edwin Thomas Booth, was in his time the most renowned Shakespearean actor on the American stage. John's reception as an actor was a good deal warmer in the South than in the North, where his brother Edwin reigned supreme, and it was widely believed that "one of the chief reasons for [John's] attachment to the cause of the South was a jealousy of his brother Edwin, who was a good Union man and who cast the first and only vote of his life for Mr. Lincoln."[107] The mimetic violence that René Girard finds lurking in sibling rivalry and in theatrical representation was probably more of a motivating factor than politics in Booth's assassination of Lincoln.[108]

"Raised in the cultured, if eccentric, environment of a theatrical aristocracy," writes James W. Clarke of Booth in his study *American Assassins*, "the transition to the stage was swift, smooth, and highly successful."[109] All the more reason to wonder, as Clarke does, why the successful actor should open fire at Lincoln during a theatrical performance: "Why did Booth choose a public theater for the act?" (p. 35). Clarke's answer that Booth settled on Ford's Theater for purely practical reasons—"As a famous actor, he had unlimited access to Ford's"—is no doubt convincing,[110] but intellectually unsatisfying. We begin to suspect a connection between acting and assassination that goes beyond merely practical considerations. In light of the mimetic nature of Chapman's and Hinckley's celebricides, we might amend Clarke's statement—"Probably no group of political actors is more poorly understood than American assassins" (p. 4)—to read, "Probably no aspect of assassination is more poorly understood than the relation it bears to acting." The theatricality of assassination calls out for investigation.

De Quincey's essay on *Macbeth* is concerned precisely with the theatrical representation of murder. Besides investigating the effect of a dramatized assassination on the fictional killer and his audience, De Quincey characterized the actual murderer John Williams as a celebrated actor in his own right: "At length, in 1812, Mr. Williams made his *début* on the stage of Ratcliffe Highway, and executed those unparalleled murders which have procured for him such a brilliant and undying reputation." The conceit of the murderer-as-actor (a version of the romantic motif of the criminal-as-artist) is inverted in Antonin Artaud's formulation in his essay "The Theater and the Plague" of the actor as a more authentic kind of murderer (an instance of the modernist notion of the artist-as-criminal). In the frenzy of his role-playing, the actor achieves a sustained suspension from the contradictions of Western views of art and reality, good and evil, that exceeds in purity the emotional release felt by actual murderers at the moment of their deed.

> Once launched upon the fury of his task, an actor requires infinitely more power to keep from committing a crime than a murderer needs courage to complete his act, and it is here, in its very gratuitousness, that the action and effect of a feeling in the theater appears infinitely more valid than that of a feeling fulfilled in life.
> Compared with the murderer's fury which exhausts itself, that of the tragic actor remains enclosed within a perfect circle. The murderer's fury has accomplished an act, discharges itself, and loses contact with the force that inspired it but can no longer sustain it. That of the actor has taken a form that negates itself to just the degree it frees itself and dissolves into universality.[111]

Far from providing a means of transcending the murderous contradictions of civilization, however, theater has conventionally functioned in Western societies as a homeopathic, cathartic form of emotional release, a site of controlled chaos and ritualized violence carefully regulated within the strict boundaries of the stage. The double-fantasies of mistaken identity so popular inside the theater are intolerable outside of it, in everyday "reality," where such confusion is bound to result in violence.

This is what is so scandalous about those assassinations that take place in a theatrical location such as a ballroom (Malcolm X), a motorcade (John Kennedy), or a political speech (Robert Kennedy), if not at a theater itself, as in the slayings of Lincoln and John Dillinger. (One should also mention the example of Stanford White, the architect who was shot dead in 1906 on the opening night of a musical revue in the roof garden of the old Madison Square Garden, a building that White had himself designed.)[112] Instead of defusing or sublimating violence as Aristotle's dramatic theory proposes, the theater periodically validates Plato's fear of mimesis by becoming a stage for spectacular killings that transform the immediate audience, as well as the general public, into shocked witnesses of a celebrity's death.

Jorge Luis Borges's tale "Theme of the Traitor and the Hero" reveals a conspiratorial metaphysics behind such killings. An Irishman named Ryan undertakes to write the biography of his great-grandfather, the revolutionary hero Fergus Kilpatrick, who was shot "on the 6th of August, 1824, in a theater box with funereal curtains prefiguring Lincoln's."[113] In the course of investigating the unsolved mystery of the murder, Ryan discovers that certain details bear a striking resemblance to scenes in Shakespeare's tragedies *Julius Caesar* and *Macbeth*. (Remember that these were the plays in which Booth achieved renown.) Ryan learns that one of Kilpatrick's co-conspirators named James Nolan had previously translated some of Shakespeare's works into Gaelic. Putting the pieces of the puzzle together, Ryan (in the manner of Hamlet) uncovers the secret of his great-grandfather's death: Kilpatrick had been a party to his own murder after the supposed "hero" had been unmasked by Nolan as a traitor. Rather than execute Kilpatrick for his betrayal, Nolan proposed—with Kilpatrick's consent—"that the condemned man die at the hands of an unknown assassin in deliberately dramatic circumstances which would remain engraved in the imagination of the people and would hasten the revolt" (p. 74). Pressed for time, Nolan patterned the historical "tragedy" of Kilpatrick's assassination on literature; "he had to plagiarize another dramatist, the English enemy William Shakespeare. He repeated scenes from *Macbeth*, from *Julius Caesar*" (p. 75). A theater was the logical location for Kilpatrick's murder because this supposedly chance event was actually a staged dramatic performance. "Kilpatrick was killed in a theater, but the entire city was a theater as well, and the actors were legion, and the drama crowned by his death extended over many days and many nights" (p. 74).

If theaters lend themselves to assassination, and if assassinations seek out theatrical situations, this is because theater is the mimetic art form par excellence that undoes the differences upon which ethical behavior and social reality is founded. Theater creates a condition of aesthetic suspension in which the impossible suddenly becomes "real" because the "real" is reduced to make-believe.

President John F. Kennedy was not shot in a theater, but his alleged assassin, Lee Harvey Oswald, was apprehended in a Dallas movie house. In *Libra* (1988), Don DeLillo's fictionalized account of a CIA conspiracy behind the assassination, Oswald's arrest takes place in the nick of time, before a co-conspirator seated behind him in the darkened theater can shoot him in the head to prevent him from betraying his accomplices. After the arrest, mob members pressure Dallas nightclub-owner Jack Ruby to shoot Oswald in the downtown police station, an execution staged in full view of everyone with a television set.

DeLillo's novel not only incorporates the Lincoln-Dillinger motif of assassination in the theater, but it dramatizes Oswald's susceptibility to the media. In a scene that takes place a few days before he shoots Kennedy, Oswald watches a TV double-feature with his wife Marina. The first film is the 1954 movie *Suddenly* in which Frank Sinatra plays a deranged presidential assassin. Oswald's reaction—"They were running a message through the night into his skin"[114]—is similar to Hinckley's belief that a series of Jodie Foster films that happened to air on TV over a short period of time had some personal reference to himself.[115] Unlike Hinckley, however, DeLillo's Oswald remains fully aware of the difference between fiction and reality; thus he can predict the fate of Sinatra's character in the film. "Lee knew he would fail. It was, in the end, a movie. They had to fix it so he failed and died."[116] (Oswald actually saw this film shortly before carrying out his assassination of Kennedy; when Sinatra discovered this several years later, he ordered United Artists to withdraw *Suddenly* and *The Manchurian*

Candidate, in which he also starred, "ostensibly to prevent other warped minds from being so inspired.")[117] DeLillo then depicts Oswald's reaction to the second film, *We Were Strangers* (1949), in which John Garfield plays an American revolutionary in Cuba during the 1930s who plots the assassination of the dictator and the explosion of his cabinet. Again, Oswald's reaction anticipates/reflects Hinckley's. "Lee felt he was in the middle of his own movie. They were running this thing just for him."[118]

Is there some secret connection between murder and acting, between assassination and theater? Does the assassin, or even his victim, actually *stage* the moment of death, as Burns, Borges, and DeLillo suggest in entirely separate contexts? As acts of violence that were mediated by some fictional script or text, Chapman's murder of Lennon and Hinckley's shooting of Reagan lend credence to this possibility. One must stress, however, that these events of the 1980s were not simply instances in which violent works of fiction were imitated in real life with violent results. Chapman's and Hinckley's murderous deeds were a postmodern phenomenon that occurred at a time when the distinction between the real and the imaginary had all but dissolved. Borges's line that "Kilpatrick was killed in a theater, but the entire city was a theater as well," suggests the hyperreal condition of contemporary America in Baudrillard's view (the entire country as Disneyland), or, for that matter, of Rome under the rule of Caligula and Nero for whom, as Leo Braudy notes, "all that was left of the position of emperor was its theater."[119] Braudy composed his history of fame during the Reagan presidency, a time when his remarks about Rome under the mad emperors were particularly pertinent.

> The power of the performer is essentially a power over minds and feelings (especially his own) within the compass of the performing situation. But when the entirety of a reign or an administration is a performance, the spectators may lose the ability to disentangle what is real from what is not.[120]

Describing Hinckley's assassination attempt as an assault carried out against a former movie actor in order to prove his love for a rising young actress, Braudy suggestively interprets Hinckley's act as a sign

of his disillusionment with "stars" who give up their roles as perform-
ers to become "real people": Hinckley was "willing to sacrifice Reagan, the actor turned politician, to his love for Jodie Foster, the actress
who has preserved her relation to fame untarnished and even enhanced."[121] As different as Reagan and Lennon may have been, both
were retired media-stars who drew assassins' fire at the very moment
that they made a comeback. "Real people" can become "stars," and
"stars" may even be permitted to go into retirement as "real people";
but by stepping back and forth between the private and public
domains, the actor calls attention to the artifice—or in Chapman/
Caulfield's terms, the "phoniness"—of his role-playing, and suggests
that his "real" identity is itself just a pretense. This unsettled relation
between reality and fantasy is what provokes the postmodern
assassin's violence. If you're a celebrity, it's alright to step out of the
limelight, but very dangerous to step back in again.

Actually, the problem in the media-saturated 1980s was not so
much the public's loss of a sense of the distinction between the imaginary and the real as the trivialization of this distinction to the point
of irrelevancy. The man in a late-'80s television commercial announces, "I'm not really a doctor, but I play one on TV"; in spite of
this disclaimer he goes on to recommend a pain reliever. This is not
deceptive advertising; who could be deceived? The commercial openly
acknowledges the difference between a real doctor and a pretend doctor, but proceeds as if the difference doesn't matter. During the same
period, "Joe Isuzu" made grossly exaggerated claims about the Japanese vehicle he represented. Again, no viewer believed him—the on-
screen caption even said, "He's lying"—but this hardly deterred consumers from buying an Isuzu. The selling ploy in the era of the actor-
president Reagan ("I'm not really a president, but I play one on TV")
was for the advertiser to acknowledge to his cynical audience all the
lies, the deception, and the hype that characterized his discourse. By
doing this, he showed that at least he was on the up and up, and that
he respected the intelligence of his audience, which presumably knew
the difference between reality and appearance and would have no
trouble telling them apart. In fact, such winking acknowledgment of
the distinction between the real and the fake, between ethics and aes-

thetics, freed advertisers, campaign managers, and even news agencies from having to take these distinctions seriously. The trivialization of difference intensified a hyperreal condition conducive to sudden, apparently gratuitous outbursts of violence.

In the world of Show Business, where nearly everything is appearance, we should expect a proliferation of simulacra. And so, when NBC decided in 1985 to make a movie about John Lennon and Yoko Ono for television, it happened to settle after an exhaustive search on an unknown British actor named Mark Lindsay, only to learn two weeks before production that Lindsay's real name was Mark Chapman. Even though, as NBC acknowledged, this was "purely a coincidence"—Lindsay adopted his stage name in 1979, before Lennon's murder, when he applied for a British Equity card and discovered that another member of the union was named Mark Chapman—network executives felt "it is in the best interest of this project that another actor be cast as John Lennon."[122] Evidently, NBC was sufficiently wary of such coincidences that it was willing to scramble to find a replacement for Lindsay at the last minute rather than risk the consequences of spinning yet another double fantasy.

FIVE

CATHARSIS AND MURDER

Murders are exciting and lift people into a heart-beating awe as religion is supposed to do, after seeing one in the street young couples will go back to bed and make love, people will cross themselves and thank God for the gift of their stuporous lives, old folks will talk to each other over cups of hot water with lemon because murders are enlivened sermons to be analyzed and considered and relished, they speak to the timid of the dangers of rebellion, murders are perceived as momentary descents of God and so provide joy and hope and righteous satisfaction to parishioners, who will talk about them for years afterward to anyone who will listen.

— E. L. Doctorow, *Billy Bathgate*

Aesthetic Violence: Mass Murder, Gang Warfare, and Staged Suicide

Mark David Chapman's celebricide of John Lennon and John Hinckley, Jr.'s attempted assassination of President Reagan were neither politically motivated acts of terror nor psychologically motivated acts of passion. They were aesthetic acts, mediated by literary fictions and films, that then became media events in their own right. The media provided the assailant not only with a victim but also with a role to play (that of savior or iconoclast), and in Hinckley's case, even with a script to follow. Once the deed was done, the media offered the assailant a means of publicizing his act, and even of creating his own audience — in short, of becoming an overnight sensation.

What of those spectacular killings that are not overtly imitative acts mediated by the artistic text or image, yet that aspire through their controlled or explosive passion to a kind of artistic sublimity? What of those murderers and suicide victims, in real life or in fiction, who shun mediation and the media (Hedda Gabler, after all, was afraid more than anything of the publicity of scandal), but who seek an unmediated, immediate experience of release, fulfillment, or transcendence in their deeds? For such killers the prospect of renown holds no attraction. Living off a sensational crime is irrelevant for the rebel and the fanatic who don't expect to live beyond their violent apotheosis. This sort of violence is less a matter of mimesis, or the imitation of an action, than of catharsis, or a spontaneous action in its own right, a sudden discharge of pent-up passions. Where does the passionate killer, who follows no script and who is oblivious to any audience, fit into an aesthetics of murder?

Most murders involve some kind of cathartic mechanism. Elliott Leyton notes that as "crimes against the *person*," offenses like "rape, assault, or even homicide . . . tend to be little more than a demonstration of individual power and a cathartic release of rage."[1] And Jack Katz detects a recurring emotional pattern in what he calls "righteous slaughter," where the assailant's experience of abject humiliation suddenly flares up as rage:

> For the impassioned killer, the challenge is to escape a situation that has come to seem otherwise inexorably humiliating. Unable to sense how he or she can move with self-respect from the current situation, now, to any mundane-time relationship that might be reengaged, then, the would-be killer leaps at the possibility of embodying, through the practice of "righteous" slaughter, some eternal, universal form of the Good.[2]

This "leap" occurs when the downward emotional sensation of the humiliated (debased, degraded) individual reaches a lower limit, and reverses itself as rage which "proceeds in an upward direction." "It may start in the pit of the stomach and soon threaten to burst out of your head. 'Don't blow your top' and 'hold your lid on,' we counsel the angry" (Katz, p. 27).

Having acknowledged the cathartic character of most acts of murder, Katz and Leyton make some significant qualifications. Katz takes issue with commentators who

> place the passion in homicidal and assaultive events before and as the immediately determining cause of the attack—often with metaphors suggesting catharsis or an image of the mind as a munitions

dump. Thus, they describe the attackers as finally feeling that they cannot take any more pressure and "exploding" into violence, as "giving vent" to their disturbance through attacking, and as "exhausting" or "expending" their passion through violence. (p. 39)

Katz objects to Truman Capote's description in his 1965 nonfiction novel *In Cold Blood* of Perry Smith's assault on the Clutter family as a "mind explosion." "The immediately antecedent experience was anything but emotional." Perry and his accomplice "drove four hundred miles across Kansas in one day to arrive at the scene" (p. 277). Katz argues that it is misleading to regard most homicides as cathartic emotional outbursts since "close accounts reveal a frequent pattern in which an assailant moves into an attack and then rage builds" (p. 39). This pattern of behavior challenges the customary notions of "crimes of passion" and murders committed in "blind rage"; in many of these cases, the would-be assailant deliberately puts himself in a situation where a cathartic outburst of violent rage culminating in a "righteous slaughter" is virtually inevitable.

Similarly, when Leyton observes that murders "tend to be little more than a demonstration of individual power and a cathartic release of rage," he is referring to conventional homicides involving a single victim. In cases of multiple murder, which are the subject of his study, the killer "transcend[s] mere catharsis and temporary gratification." Multiple murderers are typically social rebels who have undertaken "a kind of sustained sub-political campaign," a "protest . . . not on behalf of others, only themselves." Their crimes are not simply demonstrations of individual power, but a way of making "a demonstration to the authorities" (in the words of the serial killer Edmund Kemper) through a radical inversion of social values (p. 261). Multiple murders entail a complex sociopolitical set of attitudes that, Leyton claims, are altogether different from the relatively simple cathartic release of emotions that characterizes most single murders.

There are, however, two kinds of multiple murders—serial killings and mass murder. Where the serial killer, like the celebricide, is intent on making a name for himself, of acquiring an identity through his deeds, the mass murderer is fully prepared to sacrifice himself in his rampage, and is thus engaged in a cathartic enterprise. In his description of one such killer—Mark Essex, a young black Navy veteran who went on a racial shooting spree in New Orleans in 1975—Leyton observes that his "final hours were theatrical," and that "his goal had been merely to release his own personal anger, to stage his private rebellion" (pp. 220–21). Such cathartic killing is designed to culminate in the killer's own violent annihilation under police fire, and so can be considered as a type of suicide. ("I will fight to gain my manhood or die trying," Essex wrote in his last letter to his mother; as Leyton concludes, "He was suicidal in the sense that he was willing to sacrifice himself for the cause" [pp. 214, 218].) The fact that the mass murderer often regards himself as a sacrificial victim or martyr underscores the cathartic nature of his last stand.

Actually, Leyton and Katz both prefer the term *transcendence* to *catharsis* with respect to the specific types of murder that are the subject of their investigations. Leyton claims that the killer of multiple victims "transcend[s] mere catharsis." And despite Katz's objections to writers who make irresponsible use of the cathartic model of murder, he finds the term "transcendence" useful as a description of many killers' experience. Especially in the case of gang violence, the paramount impulse of urban youths is to "transcend" their abased situation and conventional notions of morality and material success. When black teen-agers speak of "getting over," "getting across," "making it," or "stepping fast," this language is less expressive of "aspirations for material status," in Katz's view, than "it captures the objective of transcendence." The "deviance" of social misfits is not limited to the means they use to achieve the conventional aim of material prosperity advertised on television and by the commercial media. Rather, the aims themselves "are specifically unconventional: to go beyond the established moral definitions of the situation as it visibly obtains here and now." For ghetto youths, the aim is typically not to achieve the establishment's signs of material success, but "to be a star—something literally, distinctively transcendent" (p. 315).

The aesthetic or theatrical violence of cathartic or transcendent killings has institutional parallels in very different cultures, from the mass murderer's last stand, to the mayhem of American street-gangs, to the ritual suicides of the warrior class in Japan. For all their cultural diversity, these violent forms of death are similar in that they are characterized by a certain artistry on the part of the murderer or suicide. What Leyton says of the mass murderer Mark Essex can be said of the fictional character Hedda Gabler and of the writer-suicide Yukio Mishima: they "stage" their own violent ends in such a way that their deaths assume an artistic form and become an artistic gesture.

Purgation and Purification

The concept of catharsis as the discharge of such pent-up passions as rage, aggression, and revenge is pertinent to the psychology of homicide, and especially to cases of mass murder. This is far from the sense, however, in which Aristotle used the term in his famous definition of tragedy. Most commentators agree that catharsis in the *Poetics* does not describe the psychological experience of the tragic character (who was often a murderer and always a victim), but rather the aesthetic experience of the spectator. (De Quincey conflates the two perspectives, as we have seen, in his "Macbeth" essay.) It is generally accepted that in his definition, Aristotle drew on the medical significance of the word *katharsis* which, according to D. W. Lucas, had to do with "the removal or evacuation of morbid substances from the human system." Catharsis is employed in the *Poetics* "in a sense partly religious, partly medical, for the psycho-therapeutic treatment of emotional disorders by ritual and music."[3] This sort of homeopathic process is what Aristotle seems to have had in mind when he described the purpose of tragedy as the catharsis of the spectator's emotions of pity and fear. In tragedies like Aeschylus' *Oresteia* or Sophocles' *Oedipus* cycle, we come into contact with matricides or patricides who arouse these feelings in us so that we may ultimately be relieved of them.

Besides referring to the spectator's aesthetic response to the tragic spectacle of violent death, the Greek word *katharsis* bears another, much older relation to murder as expressed in the Greek verb *kathairein*, to "cleanse" or "remove impurities." According to Lucas, these impurities could refer to "visible dirt" or to "invisible sacral contaminations," and he gives the example of the statue of Artemis among the Tauri which supposedly became polluted after it was exposed to a matricide, and which could only be cleansed by being washed in the sea.[4] Walter Burkert refers to the yearly ceremony in which the image of Athena known as the Palladion is carried "to the sea where it is purified in order to be set up once more on the ancient site of an important law court, where crimes such as homicide are tried: the condemned man is banished, but after certain purification ceremonies he may occasionally be able to return." Burkert notes that the murderer's "exile, purification, and return follows the path of the image which goes to be purified."[5] The murderer is tainted and taints others with "a peculiar, almost physically experienced pollution" known as *agos*—a word that may derive from the same root as the word *hagnos,* meaning "sacred" or "pure." Having committed an act that can be viewed both as a sacrament and as a sacrilege, the murderer must be driven from the community as a *pharmakos* in an act of *katharmos* and seek purification.[6] Vase paintings suggest that this could be accomplished through a ritual in which the murderer's head and hands are doused with the blood of a sacrificial animal such as a piglet, and then washed clean to remove the impurity.[7]

At least three centuries before Aristotle used the word *katharsis* to describe the spectator's emotional purgation in response to tragic representations of murder, and long before the term acquired its modern psychological usage by which it signifies the violent release of pent-up rage in the murderer, it designated the ritual purification required not only of the murderer, but of any person or sacred object coming into contact with him.[8] This ancient usage has largely been overshadowed by Aristotle's aesthetic adaptation of the term in the homeopathic sense of purgation, although some modern scholars insist on translating the term "purification."[9] The older meaning of the word is preserved in any case in the one other use of the term in the *Poetics* where Aristotle refers to the religious purification of Orestes after he has shed his mother's blood.[10]

The *Oresteia* is by no means the only example of the unmistakable presence in Greek tragedy of the pre-Aristotelian, pre-aesthetic cleansing ritual that seeks to remove the stain of sacrilegious murder. In the tragedy that Aristotle considered the genre's hallmark—Sophocles' *Oedipus the King*—the homeopathic catharsis of the characters' or spec-

tators' emotions is actually overshadowed by the ritual of sacral catharsis dramatized in the work itself. The people of Thebes suffer
from a plague brought about by their failure to find the murderer of
the precursor of King Oedipus and bring him to justice. Thebes must
cleanse itself of the stigma of having allowed the murderer of its
former king not only to be on the loose, but, as it turns out, to have
acceded to the throne.

Shakespearean tragedy also dramatizes the primal meaning of
catharsis in the sense of ritualistic purification in the aftermath of a
royal or sacred figure's murder. Hamlet is charged with ridding Den-
mark of the pollution brought about by his uncle's murder of the
former king. And such a dramatically charged scene as Lady Macbeth's
hand washing may derive much of its impact from its affiliation with
the ancient sense of catharsis as the cleansing of a stain, or the purification of a contagion resulting from exposure to a foul deed. Actually,
Lady Macbeth enacts the two most important cleansing rituals among
the ancient Greeks—purification by blood and purification by madness. Her delirium echoes the ancient dance of the Korybantes which
ended with each dancer succumbing to exhaustion, and finding
"release not only from his madness, but from everything which had
previously oppressed him."[11]

Christian equivalents of catharsis may be found in the ritual of
confession and in the concept of purgatory, and especially in the experience of penance through suffering—and often madness—as expressed in Dostoyevsky's writings. Through a process of atonement,
the individual who has committed a terrible crime, as well as the community affected by it, may purify themselves. Such religious rituals of
purification resemble secular artistic rituals by which the artist seeks
to purify himself in a sacrificial act, thereby transforming his life into
a work of art. Yet there is also the opposite possibility: instead of aton-
ing for his own crimes, the individual may try to cleanse the community or the state of its corruption by appearing in the role of a scourge
whose mission is to destroy a wicked, sinful people. Thus, before we
turn to the purification rituals of Hedda Gabler and Yukio Mishima,
we need to consider the dialectically opposed purgation program of
the mass murderer who, instead of purifying himself in a cathartic

ritual of self-sacrifice, takes it upon himself to purge the impurities of an entire community. From Shakespeare's Richard III to Hinckley's hero Travis Bickle to real-life killers like Mark Essex, the self-appointed scourge presents himself as an individual on a mission to "clean up" what he perceives to be a hopelessly corrupt society. This mission usually turns out to be a self-sacrificial enterprise as well, but the cathartic nature of the mass murderer's last stand has less to do with suicidal rituals of self-purification than with the all-out purgation of society as a whole. It also has less to do with Aristotle's homeopathic *katharsis*, or the purgation of the self's physiological or emotional excesses, than with the ancient Greek ritual involving a *katharsion*, or purificatory human sacrifice.

Criminal Discipline: Sade

When a man wants to murder a tiger he calls it sport: when the tiger wants to murder him he calls it ferocity. The distinction between Crime and Justice is no greater.
—Shaw, "Maxims for Revolutionists" in *Man and Superman*

I would express that what is about to take place is a murder.
—Alton Waye's last words before his 1989 execution for raping and repeatedly stabbing a woman to death

Referring to the "aesthetic rewriting of crime" and to "the discovery of the beauty and greatness of crime" in the late eighteenth century, Foucault presents the romantic concepts of poetic power and the sublime as a sublimation of the sociohistorical fact that crime has always been "the exclusive privilege of those who are really great." The criminal is the modern counterpart of the power-hungry despot of feudal times who, like Macbeth, proves his greatness through murder and appropriates the sacred by violating society's most sacred taboos. Going back to antiquity, we can find the modern artist-criminal's ancestors in the early Roman emperors, particularly Caligula and Nero, whom Leo Braudy has depicted as performance artists: "Both emphasized the element of performance in the role of the emperor and presented themselves as great artists, even entertainers, for whom approval had to be immediate." Lacking their predecessor

Augustus's achievements and abilities, these emperors could only demonstrate their sovereignty by taking crime to a theatrical extreme. "When one's inheritance was absolute power, only the striking colors of art or crime could make one truly distinctive."[12]

Of the modern figures to discover "the beauty and greatness of crime," Sade is perhaps the earliest and most notorious. His criminal excesses were a sign of his social—and, therefore, to his mind, "natural"—sovereignty; his sexual preying off actresses, prostitutes, and other women of the lower classes was an exercise of noblesse oblige. Deprived of his customary outlets for aggression during his prolonged incarceration, he developed a philosophical rationale for his libertinism that he escalated in his literate pornography to include acts of murder. Where De Quincey was to make a hard and fast distinction between moral and aesthetic judgment in his "Murder" essays, facetiously arguing that the latter was more appropriate in cases of homicide, Sade maintained in all seriousness an absolute distinction between two types of crime—legal crime, which he abhorred, and instinctual crime, which he glorified. Legal crimes take the form of laws that put constraints on individual freedom; instinctual crimes are professions like "atheism, calumny, theft, prostitution, incest, and sodomy—even murder" that, as Gilles Deleuze suggests, are Sade's admittedly ironic examples of ideal institutions that allow "only the barest minimum of laws."[13] "An addict of refined ways of execution, a theoretician of sexual crime," Camus wrote of Sade, "he was never able to tolerate legal crime."[14] Sadism was justifiable, and even made to seem admirable, when it was presented not as a despotic form of discipline or punishment, but as a sign of individual sovereignty; altogether without justification was the state's attempt to legalize its crimes in the form of imprisonment and capital punishment. "Every indulgence is allowed the murderer, none is allowed the executioner."[15]

Sade's vindication of instinctual crimes committed by sovereign individuals, in contrast to the "legal" crimes carried out by the state, finds little support in social reality. Studies of the social background of murderers who availed themselves of their alleged "right to crime" suggest that while such individuals were indeed often socially "privileged," their power and greatness was often in decline. But eigh-teenth-century aristocrats didn't have to resort to murder to fulfill their dream of sovereignty. Simone de Beauvoir has described the "one dream common to most young aristocrats of the time": "Scions of a declining class which had once possessed concrete power, but which no longer retained any real hold on the world, they tried to revive sym-bolically, in the privacy of the bedchamber the status for which they were nostalgic, that of the lone and sovereign feudal despot."[16] Indeed, this was true of Sade, who could trace his noble lineage back to the twelfth century, but who could no longer count on his estates to yield their former revenues, and who had to renounce his nobility and become an ordinary "citizen" after the Revolution.

Despite Sade's glorification of sadism as a sign of sovereignty, the aristocrats' abuses against their social inferiors were less often demon-strations of their social and sexual power than attempts to discipline and punish individuals from a lower class who were perceived to be a threat to their waning privilege and prestige. Although not tech-nically a murderer himself ("It was not murder that fulfilled de Sade's erotic nature," de Beauvoir notes; "it was literature"[17]), Sade was cer-tainly a social scourge. His treatment of Rose Keller, the beggar-woman whom he hired for a debauch and who later brought charges against him for whipping and slashing her, reveals his disciplinary motives. Between the two extremes of the mass murderer who purges society and the suicidal aesthete who seeks to purify himself, Sade is clearly closer to the former; as Stoddard Martin observes, "a suicide impulse seems to have been unknown to him."[18] As capable of taking punishment as he was of inflicting it, Sade's disciplinary dialectic may have saved him from falling into suicidal despair during his excessive confinement.

Elliott Leyton provides the following genealogy of the multiple murderer:

> In the archaic, pre-industrial period, it was the old and "noble" landed aristocracy which was most threatened by the rebellious peas-antry and the rising mercantile classes. It makes a certain terrible sense that it was among this threatened class that fantasies of disor-dered self-indulgent sexuality might turn to the torture and murder of

> the lower orders. During the industrial revolution of the late eigh-
> teenth and nineteenth centuries, while the aristocracy retired to its
> estates to lick its wounds and the rising bourgeoisie revelled in its
> ascendancy, it was the new marginal middle classes . . . who, inse-
> cure in their unaccustomed roles, would grow obsessed with a sense
> of possible exposure and failure. During that period, it would primar-
> ily be doctors, government clerks, and school teachers who might dis-
> cipline those of the lower orders—who perhaps whispered about past
> errors exposing class origins or who flaunted their indifference.
> (pp. 296–97)

During the brief heyday of romanticism, the criminal in literature may
have risen "from the streets to the drawing room," but the long-term
movement of the real-life criminal was from the manor to the garret—
from the debauched and despotic aristocrat who victimized the rebel-
lious peasantry to the newly arrived petit bourgeois who victimized
the lower orders of society which he felt to be a threat to his hard-won
ascendancy. The nineteenth century witnessed not so much the rise of
a professional criminal class as the proliferation of a criminal subculture where "middle-class functionaries—doctors, teachers, professors,
civil servants, who belonged to the class created to serve the new tri-
umphant bourgeoisie—preyed on members of the lower orders, especially prostitutes and housemaids." By the early twentieth century, as
Leyton documents, such Jack-the-Ripper killings "had become a common art form" (p. 276).

   If we consider crime as a form of social discipline exercised by a
dominant but insecure class on its potentially threatening inferiors,
the aristocratic despot of the feudal period and the bourgeois multiple
murderer of industrialized society will appear as near relations. Only
in the twentieth century has the situation shown signs of reversing
itself. As Leyton suggests, the disenfranchised proletariat began to
take its revenge on bourgeois citizens and institutions; individuals
"straddl[ing] the border between the upper-working class and the
lower-middle class" reacted to their exclusion from what they felt to be
their rightful place in society by resolving to "punish those above
them in the system—preying on unambiguously middle-class figures
such as university women" (p. 297). For the first time, spectacular
multiple murders were committed from below rather than from above

in terms of social class. Murder committed for its own sake has shifted from an elitist or disciplinary activity to a terrorist or vindictive program. Not surprisingly, where authorities may look indulgently upon murderers whose victims are their social inferiors—pardoning them as vigilantes, eccentrics, or even connoisseurs—they judge killers who prey on people of a higher social standing far more harshly, as unregenerate psycho- or sociopaths.

Orgasmic Rites: Mishima and Genet

The murderer knows that only by being murdered can he be completed, realized.

—Yukio Mishima

Among the victims found at the scene of a typical mass murder is the killer himself. Since the mass murderer is often prepared to perish during his rampage, to die in a blaze of glory, his death—and the killings that occasioned it—can be regarded as a form of suicide. Considered as cathartic events, homicide and suicide are virtually indistinguishable: by killing himself, the suicide effectively annihilates the world, and by recklessly opening fire on society, the mass murderer or gang member is fully reconciled to his own death. Often, the mass murderer will take his own life before he is killed or taken prisoner.

Closely related to mass murders which culminate in suicide are suicides performed as a means of committing mass murder, as in the case of the attacks on Allied targets by Japanese kamikaze pilots during World War II, or the more recent rash of terrorist hijackings and truck bombings in the Middle East. Mass murders and suicide attacks cannot properly be considered to be aesthetic acts because they are drastic purgative measures rather than (self-)purifying rituals. They are not pure gestures: they are neither suicide nor murder but a confused combination of the two in which the subject's desire for transcendence is made contingent upon some secondary action. In contrast, aesthetic suicides such as that of Hedda Gabler entail "doing it beautifully," taking one's life in a deliberate, willful act rather than waiting to be hit by a random bullet or seeking a worthwhile target to attack. Something of a paradox, aesthetic suicide might be called "controlled catharsis."

The clearest examples of aesthetic suicide are to be found in non-Western cultures, such as in the Japanese samurai ritual of hara-kiri, or self-disembowelling. This ritual act is an obsessive subject in the fiction of Yukio Mishima, who himself committed *seppuku* (the ceremonial term for hara-kiri) on November 29, 1970, during an unsuccessful, and highly theatrical, coup attempt in Tokyo.

On the very day that he delivered to his publishers the final installment of his tetralogy *The Sea of Fertility,* Mishima and four other members of his private army, the Tatenokai, commandeered a general's office at a base of the Japanese Self-Defense Forces. Taking General Mashita hostage, Mishima demanded to speak to the assembled soldiers at the garrison. From the balcony outside the General's office, he harangued the jeering soldiers, urging them to reject Japan's postwar constitutional government, and to restore the nation to its former status as an imperial power. At noon, he returned inside the office where he and his appointed second, his protégé Morita, committed ritual suicide in the presence of the General and the three other Tatenokai members.[19]

Mishima is related to the fictional character Hedda by virtue of their self-image as solitary aristocrats in a decadent, middle-class world. Hedda is presented, and Mishima presented himself, as exemplars of a heroic warrior code of values that no longer has a place in modern bourgeois society. The proud nobility that Hedda inherited from her father, the General, is crushed by the claustrophobic, small-mindedness of Norwegian provincial life which deprives her of any possibility of self-expression. From Mishima's reactionary perspective, the warlike code of the samurai had been destroyed once and for all after Japan's defeat in the Second World War when the Emperor had given up his claim to divinity. For all their differences, Hedda and Mishima are both obsessed with the ideal of aesthetic suicide as the supreme aristocratic gesture.

Here, however, any resemblance between the two figures ends. Hedda's suicide is principally an individualistic act of self-assertion: she shoots herself as a sign of her autonomy. While she may not have power over anyone else in the patriarchal society in which she lives, at least she has power over her own destiny. She is disgusted when she learns that Eilert has died from a wound not to the head or even the heart, but to the lower abdomen—roughly the region of the body where the knife is directed in seppuku. In contrast to Eilert, Hedda's own death is instantaneous and painless; by the decisive act of shooting herself in the head she strikes out any consciousness of pleasure or pain.

According to Mishima's various portrayals of seppuku in his writings, the individual doesn't seek to obliterate but to expand consciousness through an experience of extreme pleasure and pain that culminates in an ecstatic communion with the red Sun, the symbol of Japan. When asked about the origin of seppuku by a Western journalist, Mishima replied that this was a distinctively Japanese practice that demonstrated the individual's ability to endure pain: "it was also the symbol of the will of the soldier, the samurai; everybody knew that this was the most painful way to die. And the reason they preferred to die in the most excruciating manner was that it proved the courage of the samurai. This method of suicide was a Japanese invention and foreigners could not copy it!"

Mishima's fascination with ritual suicide was unique among mainstream Japanese authors. Significantly, his obsession with this distinctly "Japanese invention" was partly inspired by his avid interest in Western writers like Bataille, Nietzsche, Rilke, Radiguet, and Wilde. His own aesthetic death needs to be understood in the context of his repeated descriptions of ritual suicide in his fiction, where such acts are presented in both a political and an erotic aspect.

In *Runaway Horses* (1969), the second volume of his magnum opus, *The Sea of Fertility*, the basic plot is remarkably similar to the film *Taxi Driver*. In that film, we recall, a young man who is fed up with the corruption around him attempts to purify society by a political assassination; when this fails, he stages a one-man raid against some underworld figures. The hero of Mishima's tale is a reactionary terrorist named Isao who organizes a plot with other right-wing youths to assassinate Japanese business and government leaders and to blow up the Bank of Japan. Isao's father informs the authorities of the activities of his son who, as a result, is imprisoned; after he is released, Isao acts on his own and assassinates a tycoon named Kurahara who has been financing his father and who is rumored to have unwittingly profaned a holy shrine. Immediately after his deed, Isao flees to a cliff overlooking the sea where he kills himself.

Paul Schrader, the writer of *Taxi Driver*, includes a performance of this tale in his 1985 film about Mishima's life and art *(Mishima, A Life in Four Chapters)*. The dry narrative of Isao's slaying of the business-man becomes a stunning cinematic spectacle. Rather than enter Kurahara's residence through a latched door as he does in the novel, Isao sneaks up to the house through a highly artificial stage set of a for-est. A lighting change suddenly reveals him behind an enormous semitransparent painting that hangs on a wall of his victim's sump-tuous home. With a broad stroke of his knife, Isao slashes the paint-ing, steps through it into the presence of the amazed Kurahara, and swiftly stabs him. Appropriately, the painting that Isao penetrates is Delacroix's masterpiece *The Death of Sardanapalus* (1827–28). Inspired by Byron's 1821 play about the Babylonian king who resolves to die to escape his captors, the painting depicts the king reclining on an enor-mous bed atop the pyre on which he is to be burned, looking on lan-guorously and disinterestedly as his eunuchs cut the throats of his concubines, servants, and animals. As Delacroix himself described the scene, "none of the objects that have contributed to his pleasure must survive him." Schrader's incorporation into Mishima's tale of this Oriental scene of voluptuous, despotic death which had fasci-nated European romantic artists (Byron, Delacroix, Berlioz), and his allusion to Dorian Gray's suicidal slashing of his portrait in Wilde's novel, would no doubt have won the Japanese author's approval.

In the novel, the explanation Isao gives to his examiners in prison about his plot to assassinate leading politicians and businessmen applies to his own (and Mishima's) suicide: he is convinced of the necessity of performing a "pure act." "To join heaven and earth, some decisive deed of purity is necessary. To accomplish so resolute an action, you have to stake your life, giving no thought to personal gain or loss." Isao claims never to have "thought in terms of killing people, only of destroying the deadly spirit that was poisoning Japan." Far from being politically motivated, assassination was an act of ritual pur-ification, of the victim as well as of the assassin:

I had to tear away the robe of flesh with which this [deadly] spirit is garbed. By this action the souls of those whom we cut down would also become pure, and the bright, wholesome Yamato Spirit would come alive in their hearts again. And they, with my comrades and me, would rise to heaven. For we in turn, after destroying their flesh, had to commit seppuku immediately. Why? Because if we did not cast aside our own flesh as soon as possible, we could not fulfill our duty as bearers of an urgent message for heaven.[20]

Isao is determined to purify the flesh through assassination and seppuku, "to throw down [his own] life in reverence for the Imperial Will," "to tear asunder the dark clouds, climb to heaven, and plunge into the sun, plunge into the midst of the Imperial Mind."[21] He experiences such communion when, facing the spot where the sun will shortly rise from the sea, he cuts his stomach open. "The instant that the blade tore open his flesh, the bright disk of the sun soared up and exploded behind his eyelids."[22]

Graphic descriptions of seppuku appear elsewhere in Mishima's work. In the short story "Patriotism" (1961), an army lieutenant performs the act when he is not included in the Ni Ni Roku coup of 1936; his young wife looks on with adoration during his death, and then stabs herself in the throat. Mishima himself played the lieutenant's part in a 1965 film based on the story, and four years later he played the role of a samurai who disembowels himself in the film *Hitogiri*. Small wonder that in retrospect Mishima appears to one of his biographers as a man who "endlessly rehearsed his own death."[23]

It should be kept in mind, however, that these so-called rehearsals, these literary descriptions and dramatic performances of ritual suicide, are first and foremost exhibitionistic displays that are designed to be seen by a witness/beholder. This was especially evident in the case of Mishima's own death, which was staged for maximum publicity, and which he arranged to perform under the eyes of General Mashita. (Mishima specifically instructed the three other Tatenokai members present at his and Morita's deaths not to kill themselves, and to see that the General did not commit suicide.) Both in his writings and in his own death, Mishima presents seppuku as an aesthetic spectacle that is not only beautiful to behold, but that is *intended* to be beheld.

"I cannot believe in Western sincerity because it is invisible," Mishima told the foreign journalist who asked about the origin of seppuku, "but in feudal times we believed that sincerity resided in our entrails, and if we needed to show our sincerity, we had to cut our bellies and take out our *visible* sincerity."[24] It is this exhibitionistic idea of a visible display or revelation of one's inner being before a witness/beholder that constitutes the aesthetic dimension of such ritual suicide. In "Patriotism," as Lieutenant Takeyama and his wife Reiko make preparations for their *shinju*, or double suicide, they debate whether they should remove the hanging scroll, but decide to leave it "since it had been written by their go-between, Lieutenant General Ozeki, and consisted, moreover, of two Chinese characters signifying 'Sincerity.' . . . Even if it were to become stained with splashes of blood, they felt that the lieutenant general would understand."[25] Lieutenant Takeyama defies convention by arranging for his wife to take her life *after* his own death. His reason for doing so is clear: as he is about to commit seppuku with his wife looking on, he imagines himself at "the very pinnacle of good fortune . . . To have every moment of his death observed by those beautiful eyes — it was like being borne to death on a gentle, fragrant breeze. There was some special favor here. He did not understand precisely what it was, but it was a domain unknown to others: a dispensation granted to no one else had been permitted to himself" (p. 143).

In contrast, Hedda retires discreetly offstage at the end of Ibsen's play to kill herself in a private, *invisible* act. Unable to witness what she hoped would be Eilert's "beautiful" end, she at least expected to hear about it, after which she could have taken her own life in a lover's suicide. But when she learns the sordid circumstances of his demise — that he didn't deliberately take his life at all — she shoots herself in utter isolation. No one is capable of appreciating her deed as being aesthetic or sincere. Her death cannot be instructive or inspirational, a demonstration to or remonstration with the bourgeois members of her society who can only react with incomprehension. Hardly an exhibitionistic act, a sign to others of her sincerity, Hedda's suicide is a purely personal gesture, a dramatic exit performed offstage as a private, authentic act.[26]

Based on the "detail" in "Patriotism" "that the officer wants to be *watched* as he performs hara-kiri," Henry Scott-Stokes concludes that the story is "a work by an abnormal man."[27] Rather than dismiss the exhibitionistic nature of suicide in Mishima's writing as a sign of abnormality, we should view it as a necessary element in his presentation of ritual suicide as an aesthetic phenomenon. For Mishima, the aesthetic requirement that suicide be performed in the presence of a beholder is inseparable from its erotic aspect—the suicide's beholder is also his beloved. (It is suspected that Mishima's second, Morita, had been his lover; Mishima's insistence to the other Tatenokai members participating in the coup that only he and Morita take their lives has led some to regard their deaths as a shinju.)[28] Although Lieutenant Takeyama kills himself for his country in the story "Patriotism," he does so after an orgiastic night of love with his wife. His ecstasy brings him to a point at which he can no longer distinguish the act of love and the act of death: "Was it death he was now waiting for? Or a wild ecstasy of the senses? The two seemed to overlap, almost as if the object of this bodily desire was death itself" (pp. 133–34). Mishima presents seppuku as a quasi-sexual consummation that resolves all the contradictions of the individual's existence in the world by allowing him to transcend his own identity through an identification with a universal principle embodied in the Emperor, the Sun, Japan.[29]

For Mishima, ritual suicide was the cathartic moment of transcendence par excellence that he repeatedly rehearsed in his literary descriptions and cinematic enactments. But he also rehearsed them in his private orgasmic *petites morts* upon which such suicide is ultimately modeled. Shortly before his death, Mishima referred to hara-kiri as the "ultimate masturbation."[30] Elsewhere he credited "the philosopher Georges Bataille, the 'Nietzsche of eroticism,'" for inspiring the idea expressed in "Patriotism" of choosing the appropriate moment for one's death.[31] This peak erotic experience is described by Bataille in *L'Érotisme* as a sacrificial moment of "rupture," when the isolated body overcomes its discontinuity with other bodies in a burst of excess, a gushing forth of blood or sperm whereby the body loses its individual identity and re-establishes its continuity with the rest of existence. Either through one's own suicide, or through the "sacrificial" slaughter of another, violent death has an irresistible erotic appeal for certain individuals who, for cultural more than biological reasons, associate it with an explosive orgasm.[32]

In his writing, Mishima adopted the idea of eroticized death and the form of ritualized sacrifice in his own characteristic way, most notably as the homoerotic motif of the excruciating death of a handsome youth. He describes his fascination with this subject in his autobiographical *Confessions of a Mask*, explaining that it originated in his discovery as a boy of a reproduction of Guido Reni's painting of Saint Sebastian that caught his eye while he was browsing through one of his father's art books. Mishima attached a fateful significance to his encounter with this image: "Suddenly there came into view from one corner of the next page a picture that I had to believe had been lying in wait there for me, for my sake." The sight of the saint's nearly nude body pierced by arrows—"The arrows have eaten into the tense, fragrant, youthful flesh and are about to consume his body from within with flames of supreme agony and ecstasy"—overwhelmed the boy, who experienced his first ejaculation: "Suddenly it burst forth, bringing with it a blinding intoxication." As Lieutenant Takeyama considered removing the "Sincerity" wall-hanging so that it would not be "stained with splashes of blood" during his suicide, so the young Mishima made "a reflex motion of my hand to protect the picture" and "saved the book from being soiled" by the "cloudy-white splashes."[33] (In "Patriotism," the Lieutenant decides to leave the wall-hanging in place; it would be entirely appropriate if it was stained with his blood, since, in Mishima's own words, it was essential to show the sincerity that "resided in our entrails.") Always the exhibitionist, Mishima arranged in later life to be photographed in the same pose as the Reni Sebastian.

Mishima was not unique in his homoerotic, onanistic cult centered on the figure of Saint Sebastian. In the 1980s, the figure of a comely youth whose body is penetrated by needle-like arrows became a recurrent motif in the work of artists who addressed the subject of AIDS: the image of the dying saint focused attention on the two groups most vulnerable to the disease, homosexuals and intravenous drug-users.[34] A half-century earlier, the French writer-thief Jean Genet

had established his own cult of murderer-saints by affixing the photographs of these "tabloid Saint Sebastians," as Laurence Senelick calls
them, to the walls of his prison cell. Genet contrasted petty criminals
like himself with murderers whom he extolled as saintly beings partici
pating in quasi-divine mysteries of transubstantiation and transves-
tism. "Hélas, une crainte religieuse m'écarte du meurtre, et me tire à
lui" ("Alas, a religious fear turns me from murder and draws me to it"),
he writes in *Journal du Voleur*. "Il risque de faire de moi un prêtre, de la
victime Dieu" ("Murder might very well transform me into a priest, and
the victim into God").[35] Murder is not only a baptism of blood, but a
baptism of sperm, as when the youthful killer who receives the name
Notre-Dame-des-Fleurs in the 1951 novel of that title assuages the guilt
and panic he feels after his crimes by ritual masturbation. The petty
thief Genet pays homage to such killers both in his own private mastur-
batory fantasies before image/icons of these murderer/saints in his
prison/monastic cell, and in his chronicles of their lives.

As in Mishima, who developed the idea of a "murder theater" in
his writings,[36] Genet's aesthetics of violence centers on the role of the
image, the spectacle. Sartre wrote in his study of Genet that "it is the
specter of the murder, even more than the murder itself, that horrifies
people and unlooses base instincts."[37] But where Genet's onanistic
cult is inspired by the image or icon of the murderer, it is the image of
the expiring martyr that Mishima believes has been lying in wait to
seduce him. And where the exhibitionistic Mishima labored to fashion
a mask (his avowed political program) that would allow him actively
to transform himself into the martyred saint whose image he adored,
Genet was content to remain in the passive role of witness, the sub-
missive role of the murderer's ardent devotee and scribe.

Mishima's obsession with suicide and Genet's preoccupation
with murder (not with mass murderers who perish while scourging
society, but solitary killers who slay their solitary victims in a quasi-
religious ritual of betrayal/communion) are primarily aesthetic concerns that eschew conventional moral values. At a teach-in after the
assassination of Robert Kennedy in 1968, Mishima criticized students
for denouncing killing in general and for not being "able to deal with
the problem of murder objectively . . . I think about the deed, the

actual act. And there are assassinations of high quality, and assassinations of low quality. . . ."[38] Mishima's call for a return to Japanese
imperialism was less a political or ideological than an aesthetic credo,
based on the samurai perfection of both literary and martial arts *(bun-
buryodo)*. Similarly, in his *Journal du Voleur*, Genet reiterates De
Quincey's position on the irrelevance of morality "from the aesthetic
viewpoint with regard to an act."

> La bonne volonté des moralistes se brise contre ce qu'ils appellent
> ma mauvaise foi. S'ils peuvent me prouver qu'un acte est détestable
> par le mal qu'il fait, moi seul puis décider, par le chant qu'il soulève
> en moi, de sa beauté, de son élégance; moi seul puis le refuser ou
> l'accepter. On ne me ramènera pas dans la voie droite. Tout au plus
> pourrait-on entreprendre ma rééducation artistique—au risque toute-
> fois pour l'éducateur, de se laisser convaincre et gagner à ma cause si
> la beauté est prouvée par, de deux personnalités, la souveraine.

> The good will of the moralists cracks up against what they call my dis-
> honesty. Though they may prove to me that an act is detestable
> because of the harm it does, only I can decide, and that by the song it
> evokes within me, as to its beauty and elegance; only I can reject or
> accept it. No one will bring me back to the path of righteousness. At
> most, someone might undertake my artistic re-education—at the risk,
> however, of the educator's being convinced and won over to my cause
> if its beauty is proved by the more masterly of the two personalities.[39]

From a moral perspective, aesthetics and eroticism will ultimately
appear as criminal activities. But, as Bataille demonstrated, transgression cannot do away with morality altogether since it depends upon the
law to retain its allure *as* transgression. The criminal may even seek out
the law in order to heighten crime's erotic thrill. Hence Genet's flirta-
tion with a Marseilles police inspector, and hence his distaste for crime
in Nazi Germany ("Si je vole ici je n'accomplis aucune action singulière
et qui puisse me réaliser mieux: j'obéis à l'ordre habituel. Je ne le détruis
pas" ["If I steal here, I perform no singular deed that might fulfill me.
I obey the customary order; I do not destroy it"]).[40]

Suicide and murder derive their erotic appeal for Mishima and
Genet as transgressions against social norms of human conduct. From
the amoral perspective of aesthetics, however, suicide and murder cannot be considered transgressions at all; they are ritual enactments of

a higher, sacred law that combines and transcends the antitheses of the law and transgression. Ritual provides the basis for both an aesthetic and an aristocratic existence; the very acts that a bourgeois ethics, founded on individual self-interest and a closed economy, stigmatizes as scandals are precisely acts of ritual self-sacrifice and prodigality whereby the individual transcends his mundane social identity. Considered in the context either of ancient purification rituals or their modern equivalent of aesthetic action, suicide and murder no longer appear merely as transgressions against Judeo-Christian law; rather, they stand revealed as <u>ecstatic acts of transcendence</u>, or what Bataille called acts of excess that "rupture . . . the discontinuous individualities" that constitute the confined, fragmented condition of human existence.

AFTERWORD

WRITING AFTER MURDER

> The distortion of a text is not unlike a murder. The difficulty lies not
> in the execution of the deed but in the doing away with the traces.
> —Freud, *Moses and Monotheism*

What precisely is the relation between committing a murder and
writing about it? More specifically, what are the particular artistic problems that a murderer faces when he tries to write about his crimes?

The killer who has been apprehended, and who either awaits his
trial or execution or simply waits out his prison sentence, has a strong
reason to tell his story or have it told.[1] The confessional impulse is evident in the title of De Quincey's projected *Confessions of a Murderer.*
One can't help suspecting that a factor in De Quincey's failure to write
this sequel to the *Confessions of an English Opium-Eater* was the circumstance that, although he had tried opium, he had not committed
murder and therefore lacked the authority to write the authentic autobiographical "confessions" of a killer. For the memoir of an actual murderer we can turn to a writer like Pierre-François Lacenaire.

As subjects who typically have the most pressing need to confess,
murderers are logically well suited to become autobiographers. Convicted killers may be motivated to produce a text with a "confessional
intent," as Stanley Corngold calls it, a text that carries "the illocution-
ary force of a demand for exculpation."[2] However, it is more often the
case that the individual accused of murder has a compelling reason
not to tell his story as he knows it to have happened, but to distort the
facts of the case to his advantage. In such instances, we have to do not
with autobiographical confession—the purest form of autobiography

in Corngold's view, in that it conveys a sense of "the virtue, whole-ness, or intactness of the self at the order of experience"[3] – but rather with autobiographical fiction, in which the author intentionally plays with various personas of the self. The individual accused of murder may knowingly lie in his self-presentation in order to persuade a judge or jury of his innocence. In the case of a killer like Lacenaire, we have the writer of a memoir who freely admits his crimes and makes no attempt to deny them, and yet who cannot be said to have written "confessions" in the strict sense because, like other assassins of the first half of the nineteenth century, he is so obviously adopting a fictional persona and making a point of "displaying" his crimes.[4] Even in such alternately self-serving and self-incriminating fictions, one hears a Rousseau-like protestation of innocence, an appeal to future readers to exculpate and vindicate the speaker by understanding him. Whether the accused subject seeks to conceal or reveal his crimes, he addresses his reader with the implicit belief that *tout comprendre, c'est tout pardonner.*

We can better appreciate the relation between autobiographical confession and the extratextual act of murder if we turn to a text writ-ten at the same time of Lacenaire's *Mémoires* by a killer who presented himself with a good deal more modesty, although he was guilty of a far more shocking crime. The memoir of Pierre Rivière, a young peasant from Aunay, was written a month after his arrest for killing his mother, his sister, and his brother on June 3, 1835. Despite their atrocity, these acts of parricide and mass murder were overshadowed by Joseph Fieschi's attempted regicide on July 28, 1835,[5] and Lace-naire's sensational trial, memoir, and execution the following year. Rivière was rediscovered by Michel Foucault and his colleagues who in 1973 published a "dossier" consisting of the available documents per-taining to the case, along with their own "notes" and Rivière's memoir concerning the "particulars and explanation of the occurrence." As the centerpiece of the published volume, Rivière's memoir provided Foucault and his research team with a unique opportunity to study the confessional discourse of the assailant in a case of parricide and mass murder, and to situate this text in the context of the legal and medical discourses of the time.

Foucault admits at the outset to having been seduced by Rivière's memoir. His interest in it is aesthetically motivated: "Its beauty alone is sufficient justification for it today."[6] Even more than the legal and medical controversy surrounding the case, it was "simply the beauty of Rivière's memoir" that led Foucault and his fellow researchers "to spend more than a year in these documents": "The utter astonishment" that Rivière's memoir "produced in us was the starting point" (p. x).

Jack Katz has pointed out that Rivière's memoir only appears "beautiful" because its author "was motivated to construct an account that would make his viciously cruel, extremely messy act neatly reappear as a self-sacrificial, efficient blow for justice." Rivière accomplished this by devoting "less than a sentence" to what he himself calls the "particulars of the occurrence"—the actual slaughter itself—and reserving "the sixty-seven pages his 'memoir' covers" for "the background of his family biography." "By glossing over the homicidal event itself," Katz argues, Rivière "continued the attack on his mother before a new, larger audience." That audience, which includes Foucault and his colleagues as well as Rivière's own contemporaries, has tended to respond favorably to the simple peasant's account. (Although Rivière's jury found him guilty, it "petitioned the King to commute the sentence."[7]) Katz summarizes his remarks with the observation that "many of the interpreters sought to exploit too much from the murder to dwell on its gruesome lived reality." And with an oblique reference to Foucault, he writes that, although "Rivière's account was elaborately inculpating in substance, in style, it bespoke a sophisticated rationality, which in many eyes was exculpating. (Some even labeled it 'beautiful.')"[8]

Katz is undoubtedly right to put readers on guard against the seductive "beauty" of Rivière's account, beauty to which Foucault himself was not immune. Foucault's case study is most credible when it turns away from Rivière's seductive narrative about his crime and concerns itself instead with the relation between the narrative and the crime. Curiously, Rivière's contemporaries and judges were not particularly struck by this relation. As Foucault notes, "no one seemed really surprised that a humble Norman peasant 'barely able to read and write' should have been able to couple his crime with a narrative of this sort, that this triple murder should have been interwoven with the discourse of the murder, or that when Rivière undertook to kill half his family he should have conceived of writing a text which was neither confession nor defense, but rather a factor in the crime" (pp. 200–201).

Foucault implies that Rivière's memoir, published in 1836 in the *Annales d'hygiène publique et de médecine légale,* failed to arouse anything approaching the sensation caused by the publication of Lacenaire's *Mémoires* in the same year because his contemporaries were incapable of giving it a proper reading. For Rivière's contemporaries, "the fact of killing and the fact of writing, the deeds done and the things narrated, coincided since they were elements of a like nature. . . . The murder and the narrative of the murder were consubstantial" (p. 200). Memoir and murder were regarded as products of the same author, and as such, the memoir was read as evidence, as a sign either of Rivière's sanity (and hence his guilt) or his madness (and hence his "innocence"). Foucault insists, however, that Rivière's text cannot be read as a sign of the "author's" state of mind at the time of his crime. The relation between memoir and murder cannot be reduced to a simple "chronological sequence—crime and then narrative. The text does not relate directly to the deed" (p. 201). For as Rivière reveals in his narrative, he originally undertook to write about his deed *before* actually doing it. Moreover, the "memoir" he envisioned writing was not so much an account of his own life as a history of his parents' lives, since it was his mother's unremitting persecution of his father that Rivière claimed had induced him to kill her as a way of "delivering" his father from his tribulation.

> I intended at first to write down the whole life of my father and my mother practically as it is written here, to put an announcement of the deed at the beginning and my reasons for committing it at the end, and the way I intended to flout the law, that I was defying it, that I was immortalizing myself and so forth; then to commit my deed, to take my letter to the post, and then to take a gun I would hide beforehand and kill myself. (p. 107)

Rivière was obliged to change his writing plans because his sister Aimée became inquisitive, and "wanted to see what there was that had already been written"; Rivière claims that he "took great care not to show her, for it was the announcement of the beginning." When Aimée persisted in asking her brother to show her what he was writing, Rivière became fearful "that someone might read this announcement," and so he adopted what Foucault called his "second project" (p. 201). He allegedly burned the announcement, and planned to compose two texts: a memoir about his parents' life that he would write "without hiding from anyone," and a text in which "I would secretly put in the reasons of the end and the beginning" (p. 107). According to this new plan, as Foucault says, the "murder would no longer be interwoven with the text; it would be shifted from the center, placed outside, at the culminating point, and at the same time moved to the far end of the text, and would, so to speak, be finally produced by it" (p. 201).

But this plan also failed, this time because Rivière, in his own words, "got up to write a night or two but I almost always went to sleep and I could only write a little." It was then that Rivière made his final decision which he ultimately put into effect: "I gave up writing, and I thought that after the murder I would come to Vire and give myself up to the district prosecutor or the police inspector; then I would make my declarations that I would die for my father" (p. 107). Although Rivière did not give himself up immediately after his crime but wandered about aimlessly for a month, and although he gave a distorted account of his actions during his initial interrogation after his arrest, he insisted in the memoir he eventually wrote for the judge presiding over his case that he "had intended to write this history before the crime and had considered most of the words that I would put in it" (p. 107).

Commenting on "all these transformations" in which "the text and the murder kept changing places, or, to put it more precisely, moved one another around," Foucault notes that the murder itself

> has been reversed and has gradually become disengaged from the memoir; from the original intention that it should happen after the memoir was written and simply for the purpose of triggering its dispatch it has broken free and has at length arisen to stand alone and to happen first, propelled by a decision which had determined the narrating of it, word for word, but without being written down.

The murderer's confession is an *énoncé* that cannot be spoken or written beforehand, but only after the murder itself—the act of *énonciation*—has first been performed. Although he planned the very wording of his discourse before his crime, he could not write it down and fix it in narrative form until after he had actually committed the murders, at which point his threatening profession to avenge his father became a retrospective confession, his inarticulate *histoire* became a written *mémoire* claiming authorship for past events.[9] Yet as Foucault suggests, although the murders were a precondition for the writing of the memoir, they could not take place until the memoir had been conceived in Rivière's mind as a program that he could enact. This situation is not so different from that of Chapman and Hinckley who, in *The Catcher in the Rye* and *Taxi Driver*, found the scripts they needed to execute their respective assassination projects.

Prior to their homicidal attacks against Lennon and Reagan, Chapman and Hinckley both attempted suicide. (We have seen that Hinckley also half-expected to die in the act of taking the President's life.) In Rivière's original murder-scenario, suicide was to be the logical *conclusion* of his slayings; he planned first to write out his parents' history and his reasons for taking his mother's life, "then . . . commit my deed, . . . take my letter to the post, and then . . . take a gun I would hide beforehand and kill myself" (p. 107). The suicide plan had to be altered, however, because he was unable to write his statement out beforehand; he therefore resolved to give himself up after the murders, and "then . . . make my declarations that I would die for my father." Instead of being executed after writing his memoir as he expected, Rivière was reprieved by the King. Four and a half years later, he took his life by hanging himself in his cell.

Foucault's cogent analysis of the relation between Rivière's memoir and his murders neglects the equally pertinent relation between the memoir and his suicide. Because they were attracted to Rivière's text as an example of a murder memoir qua sociocultural document, Foucault and his fellow researchers ignored the fact that Rivière's text is an example of another confessional genre: the suicide note. For Rivière presents himself in his memoir as one who fully expects to die, who is preparing to die, and who even considers himself already dead. He presents the slaughter of his family not as a mass murder, but as self-sacrificial ritual. He repeatedly characterizes his triple-murder as a sacrifice to his father. Through the deaths of his mother, sister, and brother—but more significantly, through his *own* death—he will deliver his father from his many persecutions.[10] Citing as many examples of sacrificial deaths as he can recall from his reading, including that of Christ Himself, Rivière concludes that "I can deliver my father only by dying for him" (p. 106). "I should immortalize myself by dying for my father" (p. 105). When the neighbors came upon him immediately after his slaughter, he told them to look after his father and grandmother, and to "see to it" that they "do not do themselves a mischief, I die to restore them peace and quiet" (p. 112). At his trial, when he was presented with the blood-stained pruning bill that he had used to slay his victims, he reportedly responded that "I am in haste to die" (p. 140). After his death sentence was commuted to life imprisonment, it was left to him to confirm his statement that his murders had been a sacrificial act in which he had died for his father. The announcement of the suicide in a local newspaper suggests the degree to which he had been obsessed with dying.

> Rivière believed himself to be dead and refused to take any sort of care of his body; he said he wanted his head cut off, which would not hurt him at all because he was dead; and if they would not comply with this wish, he threatened to kill everybody. Because of this threat he had to be isolated from all the other prisoners, and he took advantage of this isolation to commit suicide.[11]

Given Rivière's longstanding obsession with suicide, it is surprising that Foucault and his team of researchers have virtually nothing to say about his death, or, for that matter, about his description in the memoir of the murders as a sacrificial act, or about the memoir itself as a suicide note. Their attention is directed not to Rivière's suicide but to his murders, and their interest in the memoir is not as a personal suicide note but as a text inextricably interwoven with other discourses of the period. Rather than read Rivière's memoir as an autobiographical confession, Foucault reads it as an example of the early nineteenth-century fictional subgenre of "sorrowful lamentations" or "songs of murder." This most popular of literary forms portrays the criminal in the act of calling "for both memory and execration," "speaking up when the punishment is imminent; in the very moment before death," and "rais[ing] his voice to summon the justice which is about to engulf him." Significant as this popular literary tradition may be, it fails to account adequately for Rivière's memoir which is not a "song . . . placed between two deaths—murder and execution" (pp. 207–8), but rather a *confession* written between the two deaths of murder and *suicide*. Rivière's personal account of his deeds as an act of devotion to his father needs to be distinguished in this regard from Lacenaire's blatantly self-dramatizing presentation of his murders as his revenge on society. The latter belongs to the nonconfessional genre of "fictional lyricism" described by Foucault in which the "speaker displays his murder for all to see, isolates himself in it, summons the law, and calls for both memory and execration" (p. 208). Such a description does not fit Rivière's memoir which expresses the nonfictional, confessional "demand for exculpation" to which Corngold refers, and which finds its resolution not in the public event of execution but in the private act of suicide.

For all his criticism of Foucault for being seduced by the lyrical beauty of Rivière's memoir, Katz is led to make the opposite error by reading the memoir as a cannily crafted artifice in which the "simple" peasant consciously sought to transform his ghastly deed into an act of beauty and justice. Like Foucault, Katz ignores Rivière's suicide, a crucial element of his "artistry." Even if Rivière deliberately misrepresented "his viciously cruel, extremely messy act" as "a self-sacrificial, efficient blow for justice," his subsequent suicide had the effect of validating this factitious version of the murders *as* a self-sacrificial act. If the state was unwilling to execute him, he would execute himself. If his text could not be situated between the deaths of murder and execution, then by taking his life, even after a five-year delay, Rivière would re-position it between the deaths of murder and suicide. In so doing, he retroactively—indeed, posthumously—recast his autobiographical fiction as an autobiographical confession. This explains why Rivière was so enraged in prison, insisting that he was dead, and threatening "to kill everybody" if his jailers did not cut off his head.

Having composed his fictional *histoire,* he had committed himself to death, and he could not authenticate his identity until his self-sacrificial scenario was fulfilled and his autobiographical fiction validated as confessional *mémoire.*

In light of the analysis in the preceding chapter, Rivière's case is of particular interest in that, as a real-life mass murderer and a suicide, he enacted both the role of the scourge sent to purge his family of his father's persecutor, and that of the penitent seeking to cleanse himself of his own impurities through a sacrificial act. Rivière's memoir is not merely a confession of his past murders, but an integral stage of the purification ritual that can only be completed through his own death. Suicide had been part of Rivière's plan from the time he first determined to commit murder, just as it was in other instances of artistic assassination we have seen. ("I could not help feeling sorry," wrote Berlioz as he envisioned the theatrical destruction of his fiancée and her family, "that my plans, excellent as they otherwise were, involved my own suicide";[12] "after destroying their flesh," Mishima's character Isao proclaimed about his victims, "we had to commit seppuku immediately"; even Hedda has resolved to die when she murders Eilert's and her rival's "child" by burning the manuscript the two have written together.) Rivière's case is peculiar in that he appears to have been unable to take his life until he had first written down his statement. Foucault's suggestion that Rivière could not murder half his family until he had composed the statement in his mind needs to be supplemented with the observation that Rivière could not have written down his memoir in the form he did without the expectation of his imminent death. If he was only able to write his history-as-memoir after the murders, he could only validate the memoir-as-suicide-note by dying himself. Having presented his murders in the memoir as a sacrificial act—not of his mother, brother, and sister, but of himself—Rivière was in effect writing his own sentence that no monarch could commute, a suicide note that would only become readable as such through his death.

If Rivière's murder memoir also functioned as a suicide note, it is also possible for a suicide note to function as a murder memoir. To see that this is so, we may consider Goethe's novel *Die Leiden des jungen Werthers* (1774, revised 1787), which consists of a posthumously edited series of letters composed by a sentimental youth who resolves his hopeless passion for an engaged woman by killing himself. It is well known that the composition of this novel helped the young Goethe to assuage his frustrated passion for a colleague's fiancée while he was an intern at the Imperial Chamber of Justice at Wetzlar in 1772. Sixty years before Berlioz channeled his murderous and suicidal rage at Camille Moke's betrothal to Pleyel into the composition of the *King Lear* overture, Goethe imaginatively projected his own sufferings over Charlotte Buff's engagement to Kestner onto another acquaintance, a young theological student named Karl Wilhelm von Jerusalem whose own longing for the wife of a legation secretary had ended with his suicide in October of that year.

Goethe's "use" of Jerusalem's suicide in the creation of the fictional character Werther need not have been so successful. Had Goethe been of a more impressionable disposition, Jerusalem's example might only have reinforced his youthful suicidal impulses, which he describes in his autobiographical work *Wahrheit und Dichtung*.[13] This is in fact what happens to Werther himself in his chance encounter with a minor but significant character in the revised version of the novel who, however, is a murderer rather than a suicide. This character is a servant who has had the misfortune to have fallen in love with his widowed mistress, and who has been discharged by the widow's brother for having made advances to her. The widow has since taken on another servant whom she has decided to marry in spite of her brother's opposition. The discharged servant is "fest entschlossen, das nicht zu erleben" (6:78) ("determined not to live to see it"). Instead of resolving this untenable situation through suicide, however, he murders his replacement. "'Keiner wird sie haben, sie wird keinen haben'" (6:95) ("'No one shall have her, and she shall have no one'"), he explains after his arrest to Werther, who identifies completely with the young servant in his plight:

> unüberwindlich bemächtigte sich die Teilnehmung seiner, und es ergriff ihn eine unsägliche Begierde, den Menschen zu retten. Er

fühlte ihn so unglücklich, er fand ihn als Verbrecher selbst so schuld-
los, er setzte sich so tief in seine Lage, daß er gewiß glaubte, auch
andere davon zu überzeugen. Schon wünschte er für ihn sprechen
zu können, schon drängte sich der lebhafteste Vortrag nach seinen
Lippen. (6:96)

he was overcome by an irresistible sympathy for him, and he was
seized by an indescribable urge to save the fellow. He felt him to be
wretched, he found him—even as a criminal—to be so innocent, and
he put himself so profoundly in his place, that he was convinced
others could be persuaded as well. He was already wishing for a
chance to speak on his behalf; the most forceful argument had
already leapt to his lips.

Of course, Werther's efforts to persuade others of his conviction of the
peasant's innocence are futile. When the judge tells him, "Nein, er ist
nicht zu retten!" (6:96) ("No, he cannot be saved"), Werther takes this
as his own death sentence, writing in a note, "Du bist nicht zu retten,
Unglücklicher! ich sehe wohl, daß wir nicht zu retten sind" (6:97)
("You cannot be saved, poor fellow! I plainly see that we cannot be
saved").

The incident concerning the servant-murderer has a critical function in the novel's revised version. It is Werther's last straw, his final
disillusionment with life. In the original version of 1774, Werther's letters break off somewhat inexplicably, at which point an editor claims
to give an objective report based on eyewitness accounts of the
protagonist's final days. In the 1787 version, Werther's correspondence
ends abruptly with his crusade to defend the servant.[14] Well before he
decided to take his life, he had vigorously defended suicide to
Charlotte's fiancé, Albert. But it is his identification with the servant-
murderer, and his personal involvement in the case, that makes him
resolve to take his life. As the editor reports:

Der vergebliche Versuch, den Werther zur Rettung des Unglück-
lichen gemacht hatte, war das letzte Auflodern der Flamme eines
verlöschenden Lichtes; er versank nur desto tiefer in Schmerz und
Untätigkeit; besonders kam er fast außer sich, als er hörte, daß man
ihn vielleicht gar zum Zeugen gegen den Menschen, der sich nun
aufs Leugnen legte, auffordern könnte. (6:98)

Werther's vain effort to save the unfortunate man was the last flicker in the flame of a dying light, after which he only sank ever deeper into pain and inertia. He was nearly beside himself when he heard that he might be called upon to testify against the man, who now denied any guilt.

Far from helping the servant, Werther has set a disastrous example for him. Instead of displaying an attitude of abject humility that might have won the court's sympathy and worked in his favor, the unfortunate servant has taken his cue from Werther, and arrogantly protested his innocence. To make matters worse, Werther has himself become a dupe of the legal process: instead of becoming the accused man's defender and savior, he has been set up by the court to bear witness against him, thereby hastening his conviction and execution. Werther's impulse to take up the servant's cause as if it were his own only escalates the violence initiated by the murderer's deed. The murderer's suicidal prophecy "nicht zu erleben," not to live to see his beloved's marriage to another, will indeed come to pass: his murderous deed has sealed his fate as certainly as if he had taken his own life. And Werther's prophecy—"ich sehe wohl, daß wir nicht zu retten sind"— is similarly borne out: society's decision to condemn to death a man who has committed a *crime passionnel* leads directly to Werther's decision to take his own life.

The virtual equivalence of suicide and murder in the novel is apparent in the equivocal responses of the servant and Werther to their frustrated passions. Why didn't the servant kill himself straight off, rather than commit murder and be condemned to death? Why didn't Werther kill his rival Albert instead of killing himself? In his actual suicide note which he addresses to Charlotte, Werther raises the possibility of murder: "O meine Beste! in diesem zerrissenen Herzen ist es wütend herumgeschlichen, oft—deinen Mann zu ermordern!—dich!—mich!" (6:104) ("Oh, my dearest one, slinking around this tattered heart the thought often rages—to murder your husband!—you!—myself!"). But murder is not a solution because Werther has already made up his mind to die. Just before he confesses his murderous impulse he has written:

> ich will sterben!—Ich legte mich nieder, und morgens, in der Ruhe
> des Erwachens, steht er noch fest, noch ganz stark in meinem
> Herzen: ich will sterben!—Es ist nicht Verzweiflung, es ist Gewiß-
> heit, daß ich ausgetragen habe, und daß ich mich opfere für dich. Ja,
> Lotte! warum sollte ich es verschweigen? Eins von uns dreien muß
> hinweg, und das will ich sein! (6:104)

> I want to die! I went to bed, and in the morning, in the calm of awak-
> ening, it remains firm and strong in my heart: I want to die! It is not
> out of despair, but out of certitude that I have made my decision, and
> that I sacrifice myself for you. Yes, Lotte, why should I hide it? One
> of us three must go, and I want it to be me!

Why does Werther settle on suicide rather than murder as a response
to his thwarted passion when, in a similar situation, the servant resorts
to murder, even after contemplating suicide? The principal difference
between the servant's situation and Werther's/Goethe's is that the servant was *succeeded* by another in his mistress's affections, while Werther
was *preceded* by Albert in his love for Charlotte, and Goethe was *preceded*
in his love for Charlotte Buff by her fiancé Kestner. It is as if a vestigial
code of male honor dictates the response of murder in cases where the
rival replaces the subject in his role of lover, and the response of suicide
in cases where the subject himself plays the role of the would-be
replacement, "[d]er neue Ankömmling" (9:543) ("the new arrival") as
Goethe describes himself in his autobiographical account of the Wetzlar idyll with Charlotte and Kestner.

Whatever his motive for committing suicide—rather than murder—may be, Werther responds to his own failure to plead the servant's (and his own) cause by resolving to take his own life and to
offer himself as a sacrifice to Charlotte. He begins to write the letter to
her that will become his suicide note within a week or two of learning
of the servant's deed. But since Werther by this time has virtually identified himself with the servant, the suicide note is also a kind of
murder memoir in which Werther professes/confesses his desire to
murder Charlotte and her husband. Through the servant's actual slaying of his rival, Werther has acted out the fantasy of murdering his
rival, and proceeds like Rivière to write his suicide-note/murder-
memoir in preparation for his purifying ritual of self-sacrifice.

Where Werther's suicide-note/murder-memoir is composed between the servant's act of homicide and his own suicide, Goethe's composition of the novel *Werther* took place before, as well as after, actual
suicidal events. Goethe responded to Jerusalem's suicide by creating
the fictional character of Werther as a scapegoat who allowed the
author to "save" himself from a possible episode of mimetic violence.
But if the confessional text of *Werther* had been a kind of drug or *phar-
makon* ("Hausmittel") that had enabled Goethe to get through a crisis
period in his life and to be "wieder froh und frei" (9:588), it proved to
be a lethal poison for many of its youthful readers who succumbed to
an epidemic of mimetic identification with the suicidal protagonist,
and who actually emulated Werther's dress and demeanor, and even
his unhappy end. Goethe describes this virtually unique event in literary history:

> Das alte Hausmittel war mir diesmal vortrefflich zustatten gekom-
> men. Wie ich mich nun aber dadurch erleichtert und aufgeklärt
> fühlte, die Wirklichkeit in Poesie verwandelt zu haben, so verwirrten
> sich meine Freunde daran, indem sie glaubten, man müsse die Poe-
> sie in Wirklichkeit verwandeln, einen solchen Roman nachspielen
> und sich allenfalls selbst erschießen; und was hier im Anfang unter
> wenigen vorging, ereignete sich nachher im großen Publikum und
> dieses Büchlein, was mir so viel genützt hatte, ward als höchst
> schädlich verrufen. (9:588)

> This time the old household cure had worked for me like a charm.
> But while it made me feel relieved and enlightened to have trans-
> formed reality into poetry, my friends deluded themselves into believ-
> ing that they had to turn poetry into reality to enact such a novel, and
> actually shoot themselves. What happened at first among a few
> occurred later among the general public, and this booklet that had
> been so useful to me was denounced as being extremely harmful!

If Goethe wrote *Werther* as an imaginative, posthumous suicide note
for Jerusalem, it became an actual suicide note for all the sentimental
youths who took their lives in imitation of the work's protagonist. As
a text framed by extratextual acts of suicide, the novel *Werther* repli-
cates its own subtext—its protagonist's suicide note—which in its
revised version is itself framed by the intratextual events of the
servant's murderous deed and Werther's own death.[15]

Leaving aside the issues of Goethe's intention in writing *Werther* and the effect of its composition on him, we are confronted by a work that was received by many of its original readers as a suicidal "script" that they themselves proceeded to enact. These readers adopted Werther's suicide note as their own, provoking the novel's censure by Pastor Goeze, Nicolai, and other moralists. As a murderous text that mediated a number of its readers' deaths, *Werther* played a role similar to that of Eugène Sue's novel *Le Juif errant* in the case of the Alsatian journeyman Jean-Baptiste Troppmann, whose obsession with this work inspired his 1869 slaughter of a family of eight.[16] And one is of course reminded of those more recent instances of media-mediated violence: the role of the novel *The Catcher in the Rye* in Chapman's slaying of John Lennon, and of the film *Taxi Driver* in Hinckley's attempted assassination of President Reagan. In all these instances, a fictional work becomes a script for a "purifying" act of violence.

The reason that texts like *Werther* and *The Catcher in the Rye* exert such a compelling and seductive effect on their readers surely has a great deal to do with the fact that they are autobiographical fictions written in the first person and featuring young, sensitive, alienated protagonists. Such texts lend themselves to the identification fantasies of impressionable, noncritical readers who, unable to produce any artistic fiction of their own, emulate a fiction provided by the media. Himself an aspiring artist who is unable to give expression to his feelings in a pictorial form, Werther is drawn into the dramas of the other characters he encounters—Albert's courtship of Charlotte, the servant-murderer's defense. Where Goethe countered his dangerous identification with the suicide Jerusalem by writing *Werther*, his blocked hero can only react to his identification with the servant-murderer ("unüberwindlich bemächtigte sich die Teilnehmung seiner," "er setzte sich so tief in seine Lage") by accepting the unhappy man's fate as his own: "ich sehe wohl, daß wir nicht zu retten sind." One may suppose that the suicidal readers of Goethe's novel, failing to respond to their identification with Werther by producing a counterfiction of their own, became inextricably implicated in his fatal narrative.

Pierre Rivière seems to have suffered from a similar case of writer's block. He tried to write down the circumstances behind his decision to kill his mother, sister, and brother *before* committing the deed, but for one reason or another, he was unable to do so. As Goethe could only write *Werther* after Jerusalem's suicide, and as Werther could only write his suicide note after the servant's murder of his successor and rival, so Rivière was only able to write about his actions *after* his crime when he was asked to do so by the judge presiding at his trial. Regardless of whether they are fictional or factual, these texts originated in acts of violence and in turn gave rise to such acts. It took nothing less than suicide or murder for these blocked artists to find it within themselves to write. In contrast to Foucault's view that Rivière's memoir is an instance of a tradition of criminal songs in which the "use of the first person" made it possible for "everyone . . . to sing it as his own crime, by a lyrical fiction" (pp. 207–8), we need to recognize that Rivière's ability to produce his memoir was a consequence of his inability, as a literalist, to participate in the cultural game of singing criminal songs about legendary figures as if they were his own. Had he joined everyone else in singing (or writing) fictional songs of murder, he may never have felt compelled to commit his crime. Instead, he slaughtered half his family, an act that made it possible for him to compose his own, original autobiographical song.

But even Rivière's written memoir, like Lacenaire's, is curiously *tactful* regarding the actual slaughter, to which (as Katz says) he devotes "less than a sentence." Rather than rush to accuse Rivière of having deliberately glossed over the atrocity of his act, we ought to consider the plausible alternative that for the killer/confessor, the act itself is literally "unspeakable." Narrators of murder fictions may be expected to be less tactful in this regard than autobiographical confessors; the narrator's tact in De Quincey's "Postscript," verging on paralysis, sets this artistic treatment of murder apart from the general run of lurid, sensational fictions.

My sense that Rivière's memoir should be considered an autobiographical confession rather than an autobiographical fiction stems not only from the relation the memoir bears to a murderous act in the past and a suicidal act in the future, both of which it "announces" in a disturbingly tactful way, but also from a basic difference in the popular reception of the two autobiographical forms. Both types of first-person narrative are intended not as scripts to be enacted or performed, but simply as texts to be recited or read. Nevertheless, readers have shown a surprising readiness to identify with the made-up narrators of autobiographical fictions, more so than with the nonfictional narrators of autobiographical confessions. It is hard to think of someone enacting Rivière's own first-person memoir (although, as I have suggested, by describing his murders as a self-sacrifice, the author was composing his *own* script, his *own* suicide note), or even the much-publicized *Mémoires* of Lacenaire. But readers have proven quite prepared to identify with the first-person narrators in novels like *Werther* and *The Catcher in the Rye,* and to commit acts of violence as a direct result of their identification fantasies. Literary masterworks ranging from the *Inferno* (the Paolo and Francesca episode) to *Don Quixote* to *Madame Bovary* to *Notes from Underground* have thematized this mimetic tendency of readers of fiction and its disastrous consequences.[17] Something about fictional discourse seems to invite readers and moviegoers to identify more closely with its narrators and characters than with those of nonfiction. Consumers of literature and film are able to read themselves into fictional characters and situations more readily than they are in the case of real-life personalities and events. This is why Chapman turned against Lennon and toward Holden Caulfield, and why Hinckley took *Taxi Driver* rather than Bremer's diary as his primary script. But it isn't only criminal sociopaths and fanatics who are liable to confuse cinematic fictions with the real thing. As Leo Braudy has remarked, the acting experience of Hinckley's victim Reagan enabled him to appeal to an entire nation, and made him far more popular than his presidential predecessor because "[l]ittle could be read into Carter, while Reagan, like any good performer, suggested a host of possibilities and 'personal' messages that could be read as desired by any fan."[18]

At least since the romantic era, the media have worked to transform the "true confessions" of real-life personalities and events into the more powerful stuff of fiction. An outstanding early example was the death of Goethe's literary rival Heinrich von Kleist, who carefully planned his suicide with Henriette Vogel in 1811. The couple prepared for death by composing letters in which they took their leave of the world; then Kleist shot his companion, after which he took his own life. The highly sensationalized and often fictionalized coverage of this incident triggered a second "suicide epidemic" after the earlier devastation caused by *Werther's* publication. But Kleist had already anticipated his dramatic end in his own fiction. In his 1808 play *Penthesilea* — dedicated to a revolted Goethe "on the knees of my heart"—he had "scripted" the Amazon queen's orgiastic slaughter of Achilles followed by her own suicide upon realizing what she had done.[19] Rivière wrote his confession/suicide-note after committing murder and before committing suicide; the fictional character Werther composed his suicide letter after the murder committed by the servant and before his own suicide; and the author Kleist created a work of art that prefigured his combined acts of murder and suicide. (One article about the Kleist scandal was called "Public Beatification and Deification of Murder and Suicide in Germany."[20]) While apparently no one was inspired to violence by Rivière's autobiographical confession, Goethe's autobiographical fiction, and the media's fictionalization of Kleist's end, set off a wave of imitative suicides.

Because of their mediated and mediating nature, autobiographical fictions are more seductive than nonfictional autobiographical confessions, even though the latter are based on fact and would thus seem to offer the more compelling model to follow. This is why it is really unjustified to contrast Goethe's "strengths" as the artist-author of *Werther* with the "weaknesses" of the novel's protagonist or of the novel's readers who imitated him by taking their lives. Werther and his imitators may have been blocked artists who, unable to produce any fictions of their own, enacted a ready-made script provided by someone else; Goethe, in contrast, was the true artist who, rather than succumb to Jerusalem's example, went on to write the script that the young suicide might have followed, and that *Werther's* suicidal readers did follow. But then Goethe had only to contend with the straightforward circumstances of Jerusalem's actual fate, while his readers had to confront the potentially irresistible fiction of a literary character's demise.

NOTES

Introduction

1. Henrik Ibsen, *Plays: Two*, trans. Michael Meyer (London: Eyre Methuen, 1980), p. 316. Subsequent references are in the text.

2. Werther illustrates what Eric A. Blackall calls "the contrast between heroic intent and feeble execution" (*Goethe and the Novel* [Ithaca: Cornell University Press, 1976], p. 38). Before he shoots himself, moreover, Werther attaches great significance to the circumstance that his beloved Lotte has given his servant the pistols that he requested from her husband with her own hand. Unlike Hedda, however, Lotta was reluctant to give the servant the pistols, perhaps suspecting (and dreading) Werther's suicidal intentions.

3. *The Collected Writings of Thomas De Quincey*, ed. David Masson (Edinburgh: Adam & Charles Black, 1890), 13:13. Subsequent citations from De Quincey's writings will be followed in parentheses by the volume and page number in this edition.

4. Originally appearing in 1790, and translated several times into French, Kant's third critique was not translated into English for over a century.

5. Taking his cue from De Quincey's anglicizing of the German word *Ästhetik*, Laurence Senelick suggests in passing that "connoisseurship in murder may be regarded as a direct ancestor of 'art for art's sake'" (*The Prestige of Evil: The Murderer as Romantic Hero from Sade to Lacenaire* [New York: Garland, 1987], p. 131). I explore this insight at some length in this study, taking it well beyond the late nineteenth-century *l'art pour l'art* movement.

6. Edmund Burke, *A Philosophical Enquiry into the Origin of Our Ideas of the Sublime and Beautiful*, ed. J. T. Boulton (London: Routledge & Kegan Paul, 1958), p. 47.

7. Jack Henry Abbott, *In the Belly of the Beast* (New York: Random House, 1981), pp. 72–73.

8. Burke, p. 47.

9. Jean-Paul Sartre, *Saint Genet: Actor and Martyr*, trans. Bernard Frechtman (New York: George Braziller, 1963), pp. 490–92.

10. This circle is situated between the six larger circles of upper Hell where the more venial sins of incontinence are punished, and the narrower, bottom two circles that are restricted to the most heinous sins of fraud, "the vice of which man alone is capable" and which God consequently "loathes [the] most" (John Ciardi's translation).

11. W. H. Auden, "The Guilty Vicarage," in *The Dyer's Hand, and Other Essays* (1948; rpt. New York: Vintage, 1968), p. 149.

12. Auden glosses over the important distinction between private and public vengeance here. In the shame mentality of despotic or aristocratic cultures, the murder victim would be avenged by his dishonored family or companions who would pursue the assailant themselves; in bourgeois society, the victim would be "avenged" by society as a whole in the form of a police force that would hunt the assailant down, a legal institution that would pronounce the murderer's "guilt," and a penal institution that would administer his appropriate punishment.

13. Albert Camus, *The Rebel: An Essay on Man in Revolt*, trans. Anthony Bower (New York: Knopf, 1956), p. 4.

14. W. Wolfgang Holdheim, "Reflections on the Detective Story," unpublished paper.

15. Anthony Burgess: "It is unfair—and unsophisticated—to demand of a detective fiction the exhaustive moral imagination that one demands of that serious branch of letters to which we accord the honorific 'literature'" (*Atlantic* 266, no. 2 [August 1990]: 89).

16. John Fraser appears to make this argument when he contrasts the "almost *respectable* [moral] ambiguousness" of a film like *The Godfather* with the less violent, but "far from respectable" ambiguities of *A Clockwork Orange* which is a representative example of a genre he calls "the Violation Movie" (*Violence in the Arts* [New York: Cambridge University Press, 1974], pp. 16–17). Fraser's distinction between violence and violation demonstrates how murder can be appreciated aesthetically in contrast to rape scenes like the one in *A Clockwork Orange;* such scenes are troubling, according to Fraser, because they "reinforce and in a sense confirm the psychopathological vision of the violators" (p. 24).

17. Ian Watt, *The Rise of the Novel: Studies in Defoe, Richardson and Fielding* (London: Chatto & Windus, 1957), p. 243.

18. *Sir Charles Grandison* (6:315); cited in Watt, pp. 243–44.

19. Senelick discusses Lacenaire and related examples in the context of the rise of the *roman-feuilleton* in *The Prestige of Evil* (chap. 5). He finds that Marie Lafarge's "inveterate habit of novel-reading [which] she contracted when a girl" (p. 296) provided her with the fantasies that led her to poison her husband in 1840, and he discusses how Lacenaire "carefully made himself into a

recreation of the models presented in his reading; his image was the result of a painstakingly groomed personality" (p. 278). Moreover, Senelick suggests that Lacenaire may have taken Julien Sorel, the hero of Stendhal's *Le Rouge et le Noir*, as his literary model in his own *Mémoires* (pp. 319-20); it is known that Lacenaire himself was the model for the character Valbayre in Stendhal's final, unfinished novel *Lamiel* (pp. 320-23).

20. See Samuel H. Monk's classic study, *The Sublime: A Study of Critical Theories in Eighteenth-Century England* (1935; rpt. Ann Arbor: University of Michigan Press, 1960).

21. *The New Science of Giambattista Vico* (3d ed. of 1744), eds. Thomas Goddard Bergin and Max Harold Fisch (1948; rev. ed., Ithaca: Cornell University Press, 1984), p. 120.

22. Burke, p. 39.

23. Ernst Cassirer, *The Philosophy of the Enlightenment*, trans. Fritz C. A. Koelln and James P. Pettegrove (Princeton: Princeton University Press, 1951), p. 330. The example of Vico points up the inaccuracy, however, in crediting Burke with having introduced the element of fear as "the one new element in the theory of the sublime in the period between Boileau and Kant", see Paul H. Fry, "The Possession of the Sublime," *Studies in Romanticism* 26, no. 2 (1987): 189.

24. Kant, *Critique of Judgment*, trans. J. H. Bernard (New York: Hafner, 1951), sec. 26, p. 91.

25. Ibid., sec. 28, p. 102.

26. Ibid., sec. 26, p. 91.

27. For a recent collection of essays that address this problem in contemporary culture, see *Ethics/Aesthetics: Post-Modern Positions*, ed. Robert Merrill (Washington, D.C.: Maisonneuve Press, 1988).

28. Dennis Porter, *The Pursuit of Crime: Art and Ideology in Detective Fiction* (New Haven: Yale University Press, 1981), pp. 22-23. See also p. 25: "Poe's first detective story inverts De Quincey's aesthetics of murder by imagining a comparable art of detection, but in both cases the central unsettling irony is the simultaneous presence of extreme brutality and an unusual refinement of taste and perception."

29. Walter Benjamin, "On the Mimetic Faculty" (1955), in Peter Demetz, ed., *Reflections: Essays, Aphorisms, Autobiographical Writings*, trans. Edmund Jephcott (New York: Harcourt Brace Jovanovich, 1978).

30. Benjamin, "Critique of Violence" (1920-21), in *Reflections*.

31. Walter Benjamin, "The Work of Art in the Age of Mechanical Reproduction" (1936), in Hannah Arendt, ed., *Illuminations*, trans. Harry Zohn (New York: Schocken, 1969).

32. See Paul Virilio's investigation of "the systematic use of cinema techniques in the conflicts of the twentieth century" in *War and Cinema: The Logistics of Perception*, trans. Patrick Camiller (New York: Verso, 1989), and Friedrich Kittler, *Grammophon Film Typewriter* (Berlin: Brinkmann & Bose, 1986), who writes that "[d]ie Geschichte der Filmkamera fällt also zusammen mit der Ge-

schichte automatischer Waffen" (p. 190). See also Thomas Pynchon's reference in *Vineland* (Boston: Little, Brown, 1990) to the Death to the Pig Nihilist Film Kollective's "doomed attempt to live out the metaphor of movie camera as weapon." A revamped version of the Kollective's manifesto declares that "'A camera is a gun. An image taken is a death performed. Images put together are the substructure of an afterlife and a Judgment'" (p. 197). Already in *Gravity's Rainbow* (New York: Viking, 1973), Pynchon had noted that the "countdown as we know it, 10-9-8- etc., was invented by Fritz Lang in 1929 for the Ufa film *Die Frau in Mond.* He put it into the launch scene to heighten the suspense" (p. 753).

33. For a detailed, frame-by-frame analysis of five early Hitchcock films in this regard, see William Rothman's study *Hitchcock: The Murderous Gaze* (Cambridge: Harvard University Press, 1982).

34. Cf. Gilles Deleuze and Felix Guattari, *Anti-Oedipus: Capitalism and Schizophrenia,* trans. Robert Hurley, Mark Seem, and Helen R. Lane (Minneapolis: University of Minnesota Press, 1983): "fantasy is never individual: it is *group fantasy*—as institutional analysis has successfully demonstrated" (p. 30).

35. Marcia Pally's interview with De Palma, *Film Comment* 20 (September-October 1984): 15.

36. Auden, pp. 150-53.

37. Camus, p. 105.

38. In order to suggest the atrocity of abortion, some "pro-life" lobbyists have drawn a comparison with Nazi genocide; however, abortion was in fact outlawed by Hitler as well as by Stalin as a criminal offense. See Marcia E. Bedard, "Profamilialism and the New Right: A Feminist Analysis of Fascist Family Ideology," *Psychohistory Review,* 15, no. 2 (1986-87): 77-108; see pp. 85-86.

39. Jack Levin and James Alan Fox, *Mass Murder: America's Growing Menace* (New York: Plenum Press, 1985), p. 91.

40. Levin and Fox, p. 92, n.

41. Michel Foucault, ed., *I, Pierre Rivière, Having Slaughtered My Mother, My Sister, and My Brother . . . : A Case of Parricide in the Nineteenth Century,* trans. Frank Jellinek (New York: Pantheon, 1975), pp. 205-6.

42. Foucault, p. 206.

43. *Newsweek* (August 14, 1989), p. 16.

44. Jorge Luis Borges, "The Gospel According to Mark," in *Doctor Brodie's Report,* trans. Norman Thomas di Giovanni (New York: Dutton, 1972).

45. See the *Final Report of the Attorney General's Commission on Pornography* (1986; rpt. Nashville, Tenn.: Rutledge Hill Press, 1986), esp. chap. 5 ("The Question of Harm"). The most urgent recommendation of the Meese Commission's report concerned legislation regulating child pornography. Yet Meese was opposed to child-abuse laws that attempted to stop the physical violence against children that often precedes its appearance in pornographic representations. (Regarding the New Right's proposed legislation of the Family Protection Act of 1979, Marcia Bedard [p. 83] has commented, "We must ask what

purpose is served by prohibiting federal legislation to prevent child abuse. Yet the New Right has presented this as legislation that 'protects' the American family.")

46. Namely, intervening on behalf of the Wedtech corporation, planning payoffs to Israeli officials in order to promote the billion-dollar Iraqi pipeline project, and blocking investigations by the Miami U.S. attorney into covert arms shipments to Nicaraguan rebels.

47. Helms's campaigns against sex and violence have not met with equal success. A 1989 bill that would limit violence on television was overwhelmingly approved by both houses of Congress, but lost support when Senator Helms amended it to include "sexually explicit material."

48. Susan Stewart, "The Marquis de Meese," *Critical Inquiry* 15 (Autumn 1988): 162-92; p. 167. Stewart calls attention to the Meese Commission's assumption of a Kantian "sex (in) itself" beyond all representation: "this problematic acquires its particular depth from the fact that a 'sex itself' is unimaginable without visualization, scopic desire, anticipation, and projection" (p. 181).

49. Tom Mathews, "Fine Art or Foul?" *Newsweek* (July 2, 1990), p. 51.

50. See Mark Hertsgaard, *On Bended Knee: The Press and the Reagan Presidency* (New York: Farrar, Straus & Giroux, 1988).

One: Murder as (Fine) Art

1. Porter, *The Pursuit of Crime*, p. 12.

2. Porter, pp. 12-13.

3. Senelick, *The Prestige of Evil*, p. 366.

4. Porter, p. 11. Similarly, Senelick (pp. xxix, xii) asserts that "romantic literature is, *par excellence*, the literature of crime," and that the "glorification of crime was a prerogative of the romantics."

5. Camus, *The Rebel*, p. 26. Cf. also Camus's statement that "the heritage of [French] romanticism was not claimed by Victor Hugo, the epitome of France, but by Baudelaire and Lacenaire, the poets of crime" (p. 52).

6. Cf. Philippe Lacoue-Labarthe and Jean-Luc Nancy's claim that romanticism "marks the moment . . . when 'literature' is raised to an art"—that is, the moment when the term "'literature' ceases to refer, within the totality of written things, to the ensemble of lettered (or 'classical') culture that should form the basis of every completed education (the equivalent of the future 'humanities' of our academic systems), and begins to name the art of writing in general" (*The Literary Absolute: The Theory of Literature in German Romanticism*, trans. Philip Barnard and Cheryl Lester [Albany: State University of New York Press, 1988], p. 82).

7. Michel Foucault, "What is an Author?" in *Language, Counter-Memory, Practice: Selected Essays and Interviews*, ed. Donald F. Bouchard, trans. Donald F. Bouchard and Sherry Simon (Ithaca: Cornell University Press, 1977), pp. 113-38; see pp. 124-25.

8. Foucault, ed., *I, Pierre Rivière*, pp. 207-8.

9. Theodore Ziolkowski, "A Portrait of the Artist as a Criminal," in *Dimensions of the Modern Novel: German Texts and European Contexts* (Princeton: Princeton University Press, 1969), pp. 290–91.

10. See Senelick, chap. 4, and Keith Hollingsworth's study, *The Newgate Novel, 1830–1847: Bulwer, Ainsworth, Dickens, and Thackeray* (Detroit: Wayne State University Press, 1963).

11. Although his authorship has not been conclusively established, Daniel Defoe is credited with having also written a pamphlet giving a scathing, first-hand history of this figure, "The True and Genuine Account of the Life and Actions of the Late Jonathan Wild."

12. Gerald Howson, *Thief-Taker General: The Rise and Fall of Jonathan Wild* (New York: St. Martin's Press, 1970).

13. Senelick (p. xvii) mentions as one of the earliest such reports the *Select Trials for Murder, Robbery, Rape, Sodomy, Coining, Fraud, and other Offences at the Old Bailey* which appeared in the same year—1734—that Gayot de Pitaval began his *Causes célèbres et intéressantes*.

14. Raymond Williams, *Communications* (1962; rpt. Harmondsworth: Penguin, 1976), p. 15. Williams reports that daily papers were being read by one adult in eighty in 1850, while the Sunday papers were read by one adult in twenty. "By 1900 the daily papers were read by one adult in five or six, the Sunday papers by one adult in three."

15. Ziolkowski, p. 291.

16. Edmund Gosse, *Father and Son: A Study of Two Temperaments* (1907; rpt. New York: Norton, 1963), p. 91.

17. Senelick, p. xix.

18. Michel Foucault, *Discipline and Punish: The Birth of the Prison*, trans. Alan Sheridan (New York: Pantheon, 1977), pp. 68–69.

19. *Schillers Werke* (Weimar, 1962), 20:244; English trans.: *Aesthetical and Philosophical Essays*, vol. 1, ed. N. H. Dole (Boston: Aldine, 1910), p. 265.

20. Denis Diderot, *Le Neveu de Rameau, Satire seconde*, ed. Jacques Chouillet (Paris: Imprimerie nationale, 1982), p. 136; trans. Leonard Tancock (*Rameau's Nephew and D'Alembert's Dream*, [Harmondsworth: Penguin, 1966], p. 93). See also this remark in Diderot's *Salon de 1765*:

Je hais toutes ces petites bassesses qui ne montrent qu'une âme abjecte; mais je ne hais pas les grands crimes: premièrement, parce qu'on en fait de beaux tableaux et de belles tragédies; et puis, c'est que les grandes et sublimes actions et les grands crimes, portent le même caractère d'énergie.

(Diderot, *Salons*, 2nd ed., ed. Jean Seznec [New York: Oxford University Press, 1979], 2:144.)

21. Diderot, *Le Neveu de Rameau*, p. 140; *Rameau's Nephew*, p. 97. In the twentieth century, the writer-thief Jean Genet has echoed Diderot's and Schiller's observations that theft appears a more base crime than murder when considered from an aesthetic perspective (*The Thief's Journal* [1949], trans. Bernard Frechtman [New York: Grove Press, 1964], p. 107):

Murder is not the most effective means of reaching the subterranean world of abjection. Quite the contrary. The blood he has shed, the constant danger to which his body is exposed of eventually losing its head (the murderer withdraws but his withdrawal is upward), and the attraction he exerts—for he is assumed to possess, in view of the way he defies the laws of life, the most easily imagined attributes of exceptional strength—prevent people from despising the criminal. Other crimes are more degrading: theft, begging, treason, breach of trust, etc.; these are the ones I chose to commit, though I was always haunted by the idea of a murder which would cut me off irremediably from your world.

22. *The Complete Works of Oscar Wilde* (New York: Harper & Row, 1989), p. 993.

23. See Jeffrey N. Cox, "Killing Kotzebue: Nerval's *Léo Burckart* and the Romantic Ideology of Death," *European Romantic Review* 1, no. 1 (Summer 1990), pp. 27–58.

24. *Mémoires de Hector Berlioz* (Paris: Michel Lévy, 1870), pp. 124–26. In his marginalia to *Le Rouge et le Noir*, which was published in the same year as Berlioz's escapade, Stendhal remarked on the parallel between this incident and Julien Sorel's actions. See Stendhal, *Oeuvres complètes* (Paris: Le Divan, 1936), 70:140.

25. Letter to William Hayley, 28 May 1804, in *The Letters of William Blake, with Related Documents*, ed. Geoffrey Keynes, 3rd ed. (New York: Oxford University Press, 1980), p. 93.

26. The New York City sculptor Carl Andre was accused of killing his wife Ana Mendieta by pushing her out of their thirty-second-floor apartment on 8 September 1985. The prosecution argued that the Minimalist artist Andre was jealous of his wife, who was sixteen years younger than he and who had also been a sculptor. Mendieta's work belonged to a more contemporary style than her husband's, and was steadily gaining recognition at the time of her death, while the taste for Andre's Minimalist art had substantially declined. After a nine-day trial in 1988 consisting in large part of the testimony of New York artists and art critics, Andre was acquitted. See Jan Hoffman, "Rear Window: The Mystery of the Carl Andre Murder Case," *Village Voice* (March 29, 1988), pp. 25–32, and Robert Katz, *Naked by the Window: The Fatal Marriage of Carl Andre and Ana Mendieta* (New York: Atlantic Monthly Press, 1990).

27. J. P. Stern has described Hitler as an artist manqué in *Hitler: The Führer and the People* (Berkeley and Los Angeles: University of California Press, 1975), pp. 45f. See also Stoddard Martin, *Art, Messianism and Crime: A Study of Antinomianism in Modern Literature and Lives* (New York: St. Martin's Press, 1986), p. 5.

28. Ziolkowski, p. 309.

29. The general reluctance of critics to explore the criminal-as-artist theme, and their preference for the artist-as-criminal theme, is evident not only in Sartre's chapter title, but also in Ziolkowski's ("A Portrait of the Artist as a Criminal"), and in the title of A. S. Plumtree's study of De Quincey's "Murder" essays: "The Artist as Murderer," in Robert L. Snyder, ed., *Thomas De Quincey: Bicentenary Studies* (Norman: University of Oklahoma Press, 1985).

30. Cf. Plumtree (p. 161): "I would propose that De Quincey's conception of the murderer as artist springs from an intuition of the artist as murderer." See also Margo Ann Sullivan, who, on the basis of a passing statement in De Quincey's essay on Coleridge—"My mind almost demanded mysteries in so mysterious a system as those which connect us with another world"—implies that De Quincey portrayed Williams as "a distinctively Romantic artist" for the purpose of deepening the mysteries of murder and art (*Murder and Art: Thomas De Quincey and the Ratcliffe Highway Murders* [New York: Garland, 1987], p. 44).

31. Sartre, *Saint Genet*, p. 485.

32. Ziolkowski, p. 290; Ernest Mandel, *Delightful Murder: A Social History of the Crime Story* (Minneapolis: University of Minnesota Press, 1984), p. 5.

33. Ian Ousby, *Bloodhounds of Heaven: The Detective in English Fiction from Godwin to Doyle* (Cambridge: Harvard University Press, 1976).

34. See Senelick, Appendix 3 ("Vidocq or Vautrin?"), pp. 400–407, and Ousby, chap. 3 ("Vidocq Translated").

35. Ziolkowski, p. 293.

36. Mandel, p. 10.

37. See Ousby, pp. 66–73, and Ziolkowski, p. 293.

38. Ziolkowski, p. 292.

39. Ziolkowski, p. 293.

40. Ousby, p. 18.

41. Philip John Stead, *Vidocq: A Biography* (London: Staples Press, 1953), p. 59.

42. "In Poe's detective stories," remarks Stefano Tani, "there is no fully rounded, 'realistic' criminal and thus no room for the tragic implications of crime" (*The Doomed Detective: The Contribution of the Detective Novel to Postmodern American and Italian Fiction* [Carbondale: Southern Illinois University Press, 1984], p. 9). Tani notes further (p. 7) that Poe's criminals are never brought to justice or sent to jail; they are less evildoers who must be punished than irrational agents who must be controlled or "caged," like the orangutan in "The Murders in the Rue Morgue."

43. David Lehman, *The Perfect Murder: A Study in Detection* (New York: Free Press, 1989), p. xiii.

44. Mary Hottinger, *Mord: Angelsächsische Kriminalgeschichten von Edgar Allan Poe bis Agatha Christie* (Zurich, 1959); cited in Helmut Heissenbüttel, "Rules of the Game of the Crime Novel," trans. Glenn W. Most and William W. Stowe, in Most and Stowe, eds., *The Poetics of Murder: Detective Fiction and Literary Theory* (New York: Harcourt Brace Jovanovich, 1983), pp. 79–92; p. 82.

45. Jacques Barzun, *The Delights of Detection* (New York: Criterion Books, 1961), p. 23.

46. Ousby, p. 20.

47. Cited by Ousby (p. 21), who winds up agreeing with De Quincey's judgment: "Rather than being the overreacher which his narrative tone at times suggests, Caleb the detective is more the Peeping Tom and the gossip, a figure who invites criticism" (p. 29).

48. Cf. Heissenbüttel, p. 82: "The difference between a case of the sort solved by the literary detective and one of the legal practice of any country is, above all, that the real case results from complexities that only permit violent solutions, while the case in a novel must be constructed with a view towards its plausible solubility."

49. The only study of which I am aware that develops in any detail the distinction between detective fiction and crime literature to the latter's advantage is Tony Hilfer's *The Crime Novel: A Deviant Genre* (Austin: University of Texas Press, 1990), which was about to appear at the time of this writing.

50. Letter of 24 October 1822; cited in Grevel Lindop, *The Opium-Eater: A Life of Thomas De Quincey* (New York: Taplinger, 1981), p. 258.

51. See Senelick, p. 71.

52. De Quincey's biographer Grevel Lindop (p. 317) has suggested that the exposé of Coleridge after his death in the series of articles appearing in *Tait's Edinburgh Magazine* (1834–35) may have been just such a case of "murdering a sham." The idea of murdering one's double had already been tried out by E. T. A. Hoffmann in *Die Elixiere des Teufels* (1815–16), and again in his tale "Die Doppeltgänger" (1822). It would be a recurrent theme in the psychological studies of such later writers as Poe in "William Wilson," Dostoyevsky in *The Double*, Stevenson in *Dr. Jekyll and Mr. Hyde*, Marcel Schwob in "The Veiled Man," and Nabokov in *Despair*.

53. Senelick, pp. 132–33.

54. Cited by George Frederick Drinka in *The Birth of Neurosis: Myth, Malady, and the Victorians* (New York: Simon & Schuster, 1984), p. 153.

55. Burke, *A Philosophical Enquiry* (part 1, sec. 3), pp. 34–35.

56. Burke, p. 136.

57. Actually, as Thomas Weiskel has noted, the translation by Pope used by Burke is a mistranslation of the *Iliad*. The hunted murderer is not "conscious of his crime" and haunted by guilt; he has instead committed his crime in a state of confusion or temporary insanity (*ate*): "*ate* is the cause of the crime and not its result." Weiskel suggests that Pope and Burke's "post-Homeric" reading which presents *ate* as punishment is more appropriate to modern guilt-cultures than to early shame-cultures. Moreover, it is not the murderer who, escaping apprehension, is "All gaze, all wonder!," but the strangers in the land to which the murderer flees who are filled with amazement (Thomas Weiskel, *The Romantic Sublime: Studies in the Structure and Psychology of Transcendence* [Baltimore: Johns Hopkins University Press, 1976], p. 89). Both of these considerations are pertinent, as Weiskel shows, to the situation in the *Iliad* which the simile is intended to illuminate, namely Priam's startling appearance in Achilles' camp to plead for the return of Hector's corpse. For it is the murderous Achilles' amazement at Priam's presence that "is in fact the point of Homer's simile"; "for the moment," Achilles' anger at his enemy, which shortly is to surge up again, "is suspended—sublimated—into wonder" (Weiskel, p. 90).

58. See Marmontel's account of the sublime in the *Encyclopédie* as a state of suspension: "Tout ce qui porte nos idées au plus haut degré possible d'étendue & d'élévation, tout ce qui se saisit de notre ame & l'affecte si vivement que sa sensibilité réunie en un point laisse toutes ses facultés comme interdites & suspendues; tout cela, dis-je, sois qu'il opere successivement ou subitement, est *sublime* dans les choses" (Diderot et al., *Encyclopédie, ou dictionnaire raisonné des sciences, des arts et des métiers* (Lausanne and Bern, 1781), 31:797.

59. Weiskel, p. 89.

60. Jean Genet, *Oeuvres complètes* (Paris: Gallimard, 1951), p. 105; English translation by Bernard Frechtman: *Our Lady of the Flowers* (New York: Grove Press, 1963), pp. 186–87.

61. Jack Katz, *Seductions of Crime: Moral and Sensual Attractions in Doing Evil* (New York: Basic Books, 1988), p. 31.

62. Suzi Gablik, *Magritte* (Greenwich, Conn.: New York Graphic Society, 1970), pp. 47–48.

63. Two other works in which a gramophone figures prominently in a murder or series of murders are the television series *Twin Peaks* and Christian de Chalonge's 1990 film *Docteur Petiot*. In contrast to the scene portrayed in Magritte's painting, however, the killer's behavior before the gramaphone in each of these works is hardly serene, but unmistakably manic.

64. Albert Cook, *Dimensions of the Sign in Art* (Hanover, N.H.: University Press of New England, 1989), pp. 200–201. It's hard to see how anyone could downplay or deny the narrative nature of this painting which is so clearly based on the literary and cinematic genres of the detective story and the thriller. Moreover, *L'assassin menacé* has played a crucial role in Robbe-Grillet's novel *La Belle Captive*, which incorporates seventy-seven of Magritte's paintings. "Many central elements of the narrative," observes Leslie Ortquist, "including the abduction and death of a young woman, a suspected assailant, witnesses to the crime and investigators, are suggested by this painting" ("Magritte's Captivity in Robbe-Grillet's *La Belle Captive*: The Subjugation of the Image by the Word," *Visible Language* 23, no. 2/3 [1989]: 243). While Ortquist argues that Robbe-Grillet's incorporation of selected paintings by the Belgian surrealist in his novel "creates the illusion of a narrative order in Magritte's work and represses many of Magritte's own very different artistic concerns" (p. 245), Bruce Morrissette finds this "diegetic order" to be "illusionary yet convincing. It is almost as if Magritte, over a period of many years, had continued to develop and extend his early theme of the threatened assassin" (*Intertextual Assemblage in Robbe-Grillet from Topology to the Golden Triangle* [Fredericton, N.B.: York Press, 1979], p. 40; cited in Ortquist, pp. 250–51).

65. Gablik, pp. 47–48. In Magritte's painting, Gablik finds a suggestion of "the possibility of disguise or escape" in the killer's nearby hat, coat, and valise (p. 61). Moreover, she cites a written description by Magritte, published shortly after *L'assassin menacé* was painted, of Fantômas's pursuit by an accomplished inspector of the Sûreté, in which the wily criminal is caught and

bound while sleeping, but nevertheless is able to escape. The inspector realizes that only "one means remains for him to achieve his end", he "will have to get into one of Fantômas's dreams—he will try to take part as one of its characters" (p. 48).

66. At a colloquium held at the opening of the School of Criticism and Theory at Northwestern University in May 1981.

67. The finale of Mozart's opera *Don Giovanni* comes to mind in this regard: the pounding chords that accompany the awesome paternal-figure of the Commander's statue and that signal Don Giovanni's doom invite comparison with the gate-knocking motif in *Macbeth*. Weiskel detects a similar situation at the end of the *Iliad* when Achilles' anger at Priam "is suspended—sublimated—into wonder" because "Priam has cleverly assumed the role of the father in Achilles' mind" (p. 90). The encounter between Achilles and Priam, murderer and father-figure, is the occasion for Homer's simile of the fleeing killer which Burke cites in order to show that the removal of pain or danger results in a "delightful horror, a sort of tranquillity tinged with terror" that is altogether different from the mere sensation of pleasure (see above, n. 57). Weiskel suggests that the "latent reference" of Burke's "'delight' is to submission to a father figure. I think we may infer," he adds, "that the 'imminent danger' to which we are exposed and from which we are then released in the sublime moment is an unconscious fantasy of parricide" (p. 92). Following Freud's insight that "the categorical imperative of Kant is thus a direct inheritance from the Oedipus-complex" (p. 93), Weiskel argues that "an Oedipal fantasy enters into the deep structure of the terrible sublime" (p. 92).

68. Porter, p. 22.

69. For an objective account of the Williams murders as compiled from contemporary newspaper reports and criminal records, see Senelick, pp. 133-38.

70. See the passage in the "Affliction of Childhood" section of the *Suspiria de Profundis* where De Quincey's narrative of his visit as a child to his sister's bedside is interrupted by a digression on the relation between death and summer at the very moment he is about to behold his sister's corpse. I discuss this digression's effect on the narrative in "Confession, Digression, Gravitation: Thomas De Quincey's German Connection," in *Thomas De Quincey, Bicentenary Studies*, ed. R. L. Snyder (Norman: University of Oklahoma Press, 1985), pp. 308-37; esp. pp. 324-32. See also Erich Auerbach's classic discussion of Homer's interruption of his narrative in book 19 of the *Odyssey* at a "moment of crisis"—namely, when the old housekeeper Euryclea recognizes his scar (*Mimesis: The Representation of Reality in Western Literature*, trans. Willard R. Trask [Princeton: Princeton University Press, 1953], p. 4).

71. In this tale that describes a series of murders of entire families, De Quincey had already worked up elements of the Williams murders into a fictional form. A witness to one of the murders is a "journeyman currier" (12:254). And in the climactic scene, a thirteen-year-old girl happens by chance to spy the leg of the concealed murderer while rummaging in a closet at her boarding

school. She coolly manages to withdraw from the closet without letting the murderer think she has seen him. As her older sister is just then about to enter the same closet, the young girl quickly has to devise a means of diverting her without giving her cause for alarm and the murderer cause for suspicion. Barely suppressing her own hysteria, she at last succeeds in hurrying her sister to a room upstairs where she throws the bolt of the door—only a split second before the murderer, who by this time has realized he has been spotted, arrives at the door.

> Already he was on the topmost stair—already he was throwing himself at a bound against the door, when Louisa, having dragged her sister into the room, closed the door and sent the bolt home in the very instant that the murderer's hand came into contact with the handle. Then, from the violence of her emotions, she fell down in a fit, with her arm around the sister whom she had saved. (12:259)

Senelick (pp. 139–40) quotes this passage at length in order to point out its similarities to key scenes in the "Postscript."

72. Auden, p. 147.

73. Auden, p. 158; cited in Ziolkowski, p. 331.

74. See n. 57 above.

75. Actually, Dostoyevsky plays with two opposed arrangements in the murder scene. First Raskolnikov rings the bell of the old woman's apartment, and when she fails to answer right away, he listens with his ear to the door and becomes aware of her presence. "Someone was standing silently just inside the door and listening, just as he was doing outside it, holding her breath and probably also with her ear to the door" (Feodor Dostoevsky, *Crime and Punishment*, ed. George Gibian, trans. Jessie Coulson [1964; rev., New York: Norton, 1989], p. 64). Later, after he has killed the woman, he again listens at the door—this time from inside the apartment—to the approach of the unknown visitor: "They were standing now, opposite one another, as he and the old woman had stood, with the door dividing them, when he had listened there a short time ago" (p. 70). In both cases, the killer Raskolnikov assumes Mary's role in the "Postscript" of the listener—first in a state of suspense as he tries to hear his victim inside the apartment, and then in a state of terror as he hears the visitor outside.

76. Carol J. Clover, "Her Body, Himself: Gender in the Slasher Film," *Representations* 20 (Fall 1987): 187–228; p. 201.

77. Clover, p. 198.

78. Clover, p. 219.

79. In his 1984 film *Body Double,* De Palma takes this technique a step further by recording Gloria Revelle's brutal death-by-drilling from the agonizing point of view of her would-be rescuer, the ineffectual voyeur Jake Scully. In this film, the "penetration scene" in which the drill is shown breaking through the ceiling is not "inevitably seen from the victim's point of view" as in the slasher films discussed by Clover (p. 198), but from the vantage of a voyeuristic witness.

80. It is true, however, that De Palma heightens the terror of the actual stabbing in *Dressed to Kill* by having the camera record Kate's horror at the fatal
instant—just before the hooker appears to witness her final agony. Similarly,
Gloria's desperate struggle with her assailant, which precedes the actual death
scene in *Body Double*, is shown both from her point of view as well as from
Jake's. De Palma uses cinematic montage to cut back and forth rapidly between
the points of view of the victim and her would-be rescuer/witness.

81. Similarly, in *Body Double*, Jake partially redeems his failure to prevent
Gloria's death by discovering and overcoming her murderer.

82. Pierre Boileau and Thomas Narcejac, the prolific authors of suspense
tales including *D'Entre les Morts*—the 1954 novel upon which Hitchcock's film
Vertigo was based—have characterized the victim in the suspense story not as
someone who "is hunted and directly threatened," but as someone who

is present at events whose definitive meaning one is unable to decipher,
as soon as the real becomes a trap, as soon as everyday life is turned
upside down. One becomes a victim because one seeks vainly for truth,
and because the truth one obtains is not the genuine article, and so on
and so forth, and the more one thinks rationally the more one goes astray.
*The crime story, instead of signalling the triumph of logic, has then to consecrate
the failure of rational thought:* it is precisely for this reason that its hero is a
victim.

(Boileau and Narcejac, *Le Roman Policier* [Paris, 1975], p. 178; cited in Mandel,
pp. 87–88.) In light of this observation, we might extend Auden's characteriza-
tion of the chief interest offered by the suspense thriller—the "ethical and eris-
tic conflict between good and evil, between Us and Them"—to include the
pure, paranoiac antagonism between Reason and Unreason itself. The detective story celebrates deductive brilliance and is the appropriate genre for periods of clear-headed enlightenment, for times of reason. The suspense thriller,
in contrast, appears to have greater appeal during periods of crisis—in our century, the years up to and including the Second World War, and during and
after the Vietnam conflict—when the hero is portrayed as a victim by virtue of
the fact that he or she alone is thinking and behaving rationally in a world of
madness. Thus Richard M. Levine ("Murder, They Write," *New York Times Magazine* [November 16, 1986]) has explained the boom in the 1980s of books dealing with the subject of murder—not only the traditional fictional genres of
detective stories and murder mysteries, but nonfictional journalistic accounts
of sensational murder "events" that have proliferated in record numbers and
that are regularly adapted into films and television miniseries—with the observation that "[t]hese are conservative genres for a conservative time. They mirror the public's paranoia over violent crime and reflect its hope that the social
fabric, however badly rent, will mend itself" (p. 133).

83. In his study of detective fiction, Dennis Porter has insisted that "all narrative, from the most popular to the most subtle . . . traditionally depends for
its success with a reader to some extent on its power to generate suspense,"

and he explains that "suspense involves . . . the experience of suspension: it occurs wherever a perceived sequence is begun but remains unfinished" (*The Pursuit of Crime*, p. 29). This observation is even more pertinent to the genres of suspense thrillers and psychological dramas than to detective fiction. Cf. Gilles Deleuze's observation that "the art of suspense always places us on the side of the victim and forces us to identify with him"; in contrast to this masochistic experience, "the gathering momentum of repetition tends to force us onto the side of the torturer and make us identify with the sadistic hero" ("Coldness and Cruelty," in *Masochism* [New York: Zone, 1989], p. 34). As I suggest, however, the suspense associated with the victim's point of view needs to be distinguished from the aesthetic state of suspension experienced by the victimizer. In the thriller the reader becomes engrossed in what is about to happen to the victim, while in the psychological drama the reader is made to participate in the murderer's own vertiginous experience of suspension from worldly reality and moral law.

84. See John C. Whale, *Thomas De Quincey's Reluctant Autobiography* (Totowa, N.J.: Barnes & Noble, 1984), chap. 4 ("Suspended Moments").

85. In this story, subtitled "A Study of Duty," the protagonist feels a moral obligation to commit murder after learning from a palm-reader that he is fated to do so. Only by killing someone can he marry the woman he loves with a clear conscience:

> Ardently though he loved the girl, and the mere touch of her fingers, when they sat together, made each nerve of his body thrill with exquisite joy, he recognised none the less clearly where his duty lay, and was fully conscious of the fact that he had no right to marry until he had committed the murder. This done, he could stand before the altar with Sybil Merton, and give his life into her hands without the terror of wrong-doing.

(*The Complete Works of Oscar Wilde* [New York: Harper & Row, 1989], p. 178.)

86. In contemporary fiction, a notable instance of the technique of portraying a "crime" from the bystander's point of view is depicted in Julio Cortázar's story "Las babas del diablo" (1964), later adapted by Michelangelo Antonioni in his film *Blow-up* (1966) about an unwitting witness to a murder, and still later reworked by De Palma into his film *Blow Out* (1981). Cf. also Marcel Schwob's short *récit* "The Veiled Man" from his collection *Coeur double* (1891), which I discuss below.

A particularly interesting film with respect to the problem of point of view in a murder story is *Witness* (1985). Despite the film's title, the protagonist is not the young Amish boy who is the sole witness to a murder, but the police detective who—after the initial investigation in which the boy identifies the murderer as the detective's colleague—is threatened along with the boy as a potential victim of the criminal's attempted cover-up. Thus, the film is a hybrid example of a detective-thriller in which the protagonist is not the boy-witness, but his protector—first in the role of detective, and then in the role of victim.

87. It should be said that many critics have flatly denied the possibility of the

feminine gaze in De Palma's films. Arguing that "the idea of a female who out-smarts, much less outfights—or outgazes—her assailant is unthinkable in the films of De Palma and Hitchcock," the chief practitioners of "the higher genres of horror," Carol Clover credits the "low" genre of the slasher film for allowing the heroine to assume what she calls the "active investigating gaze": "she exactly reverses the look, making a spectacle of the killer and a spectator of herself. . . . The gaze becomes, at least for a while, female" (p. 219). Unfortunately, Clover's analysis ignores the way in which "the higher genres of horror" employ the feminine gaze of the witness as well as of the victim. Thus, although the victim in De Palma's *Casualties of War* (1989) is a Vietnamese girl and the witness to her gang-rape and murder a U.S. serviceman, Michael J. Fox's distinctly *feminine* appearance in this role underscores his nonvoyeuristic role as horrified and sympathetic spectator.

88. Clover, pp. 212-13.

89. Georges Bataille, *L'Érotisme* (Paris: Minuit, 1957), p. 42; English translation: *Death and Sensuality: A Study of Eroticism and the Taboo* (New York: Walker & Co., 1962), p. 36.

90. Joseph Conrad, *Heart of Darkness*, ed. R. Kimbrough (1963; rev., New York: Norton, 1971), p. 67.

91. *Kants gesammelte Schriften*, hgg. von der Königlich Preußischen Akademie der Wissenschaften (Berlin, 1902-23), 5:250; English translation by J. H. Bernard (New York: Hafner, 1951), p. 89. Subsequent references to the original text and the translation will be followed by the volume and page number from these editions in parentheses.

92. Sigmund K. Proctor, *Thomas De Quincey's Theory of Literature* (1943; rpt., New York: Octagon Books, 1966), p. 91.

93. Proctor (p. 90) notes that for De Quincey as well as for Kant, the sublime involves an "expansion of the soul." However, in the case of De Quincey, this expansive feeling appears

> to have a different source from that of the similar expansion which Kant attributes to the experience. There is nothing whatsoever in De Quincey to indicate that there are two stages in the experience—one a recoil in "a momentary check to the vital forces," caused by the temporary bafflement of the imagination and a realization of man's relative insignificance in comparison with the might and greatness of objects in nature, the other "a discharge all the more powerful" in a moment of expansion caused by the mind's sense of triumph in its realization of its own dignity and majesty as a portion of the moral infinite of the universe.

Proctor claims that instead of experiencing its own moral greatness by recoiling "upon itself after failure to encompass the object," the mind discovers its apotheosis in De Quincey's presentation of the sublime "through the sense of its kinship to the object" (p. 81). However, Proctor elsewhere admits that De Quincey's truly significant contribution to the theory of the sublime is his demonic concept of the "dark sublime."

94. Horace A. Eaton, *Thomas De Quincey: A Biography* (London: Oxford University Press, 1936), p. 374, n.; cited in Lindop, p. 329.

95. At the close of the same autobiographical sketch ("German Studies and Kant in Particular") where he assails Kant for degrading the human spirit, De Quincey even avers that his disenchantment with the German philosopher led him to cancel his plans to move to the "profound solitude" of the New World, where he had intended to commune with the sublime in nature: "Had the transcendental philosophy corresponded to my expectations, and had it left important openings for further pursuit, my purpose then was to have retired, after a few years spent in Oxford, to the woods of Lower Canada. I had even marked out the situation for a cottage and a considerable library, about seventeen miles from Quebec" (2:108). In the solitude of the great Canadian forests, De Quincey expected to discover the tremendous "forces of nature" that were unknown "in England, and in all moderate climates."

> Great heats, or great colds (and in Canada there are both), or great hurricanes, as in the West Indian latitudes, recall us continually to the sense of a powerful presence, investing our paths on every side; whereas in England it is possible to forget that we live amongst greater agencies than those of men and human institutions. (2:108)

By renouncing the "spirit of German abstraction" represented by Kant, De Quincey also renounced his quest for the sublimity of solitude, and, at least by his own account, became a somewhat more social being.

96. René Wellek, *Immanuel Kant in England, 1793–1838* (Princeton, N.J.: Princeton University Press, 1931), p. 177.

97. My suggestion that De Quincey, in his aesthetic analyses and portrayals of murder, transferred the point of view over the course of his career from the murderer to the murder witness should be read in conjunction with Laurence Senelick's observation (p. 126) that, at "the moment of the crime, De Quincey, who can very easily sympathize with the meek and inoffensive murderee, suddenly switches allegiance to the murderer." Senelick finds De Quincey's abrupt identification with the murderer to be psychologically motivated: "Such a tactic argues a defense mechanism; the artist and the murderer must combine, if the artist is not to go under." This is quite true, but it should be added that De Quincey discovered a happy and influential solution to the problem of the presentation of murder in the "Postscript"—namely, by assuming neither the victim's nor the murderer's point of view, but that of the witness as a potential murder victim who is ultimately spared.

Two: Murder as (Pure) Action

1. See Senelick, *Prestige of Evil*, pp. 136–37.
2. See above, Chap. 1, n. 26.
3. See above, Chap. 1, nn. 20, 21.
4. Katz, *Seductions of Crime*, p. 275.
5. Katz, p. 300. A remark by Genet comes to mind in this context: "In order

to destroy the efficacy of murder, perhaps I need only reduce it to the extreme by the practical necessity of a criminal act. I can kill a man for a few million francs. The glamour of gold can combat that of murder" (*Journal of a Thief*, p. 212).

6. Senclick, p. 142.

7. Cf. these remarks in *Der Wille zur Macht*: "Seit Plato ist die Philosophie unter der Herrschaft der Moral"; "Durch moralische Hinterabsichten ist der Gang der Philosophie bisher am meisten aufgehalten worden" (Friedrich Nietzsche, *Gesammelte Werke* [Munich: Musarion, 1926], 18:288 [secs. 412, 413]; "Since Plato, philosophy has been dominated by morality"; "Ulterior moral motives have hitherto most obstructed the course of philosophy" [*The Will to Power*, trans. Walter Kaufmann and R. J. Hollingdale (New York: Vintage, 1968), p. 222]). Subsequent references in the original German to Nietzsche's writings will be followed by the volume and page numbers from this edition.

8. Nietzsche, *The Gay Science*, trans. Walter Kaufmann (New York: Vintage, 1974), p. 265 [335].

9. Ibid., pp. 265f. [335].

10. See, e.g., Randolph Hughes, "Vers la contrée du rêve: Balzac, Gautier, et Baudelaire, disciples de De Quincey," *Mercure de France* 293 (1939): 545–93.

11. Proctor, *Thomas De Quincey's Theory of Literature*, p. 269. In his appendix to Proctor's study, Clarence D. Thorpe suggests that De Quincey's fervent moral convictions would have prevented him from accepting the radical disinterestedness associated with the art-for-art's-sake movement (Proctor, pp. 281f.). Although De Quincey may well have exercised considerable influence on nineteenth-century aestheticism in France (see Hughes), there is every indication that he himself would have been quick to repudiate the art-for-art's-sake program, a claim made by Edward Sackville-West in *A Flame in Sunlight: The Life and Work of Thomas De Quincey* (London: Cassell, 1936).

12. Nietzsche, *On the Genealogy of Morals*, essay 3, sec. 6; trans. Walter Kaufmann and R. J. Hollingdale (New York: Vintage, 1969), p. 104 ("Ohne Interesse! Man vergleiche mit dieser Definition jene andre, die an wirklicher 'Zuschauer' und Artist gemacht hat,—Stendhal, der das Schöne einmal une promesse de bonheur nennt. Hier ist jedenfalls gerade das *abgelehnt* und ausgestrichen, was Kant allein am ästhetischen Zustande hervorhebt: le désintéressement. Wer hat recht, Kant oder Stendhal?" [15:379]).

13. Ibid., pp. 103–4 ("dass Kant, gleich allen Philosophen, statt von den Erfahrungen des Künstlers [des Schaffenden] aus das ästhetische Problem zu visiren, allein vom 'Zuschauer' aus über die Kunst und das Schöne nachgedacht und dabei unvermerkt den 'Zuschauer' selber in den Begriff 'schön' hinein bekommen hat" [15:379]).

14. Much the same view of judgment as mental action would be held by Freud, for whom "judging is the intellectual action which decides the choice of motor action, which puts an end to the postponement due to thought and which leads from thinking to acting" ("Die Verneinung" ["Negation"], cited in

Stuart Schneiderman, *Jacques Lacan: The Death of an Intellectual Hero* [Cambridge, Mass.: Harvard University Press, 1983], p. 100).

15. Nietzsche, *On the Genealogy of Morals*, essay 2, sec. 6; p. 66.

16. Ziolkowski, *Dimensions of the Modern Novel*, p. 300.

17. Ibid., p. 309.

18. Foucault, *Discipline and Punish*, p. 68.

19. Benjamin, "The Work of Art in the Age of Mechanical Reproduction," p. 242. Martin Jay ("'The Aesthetic Ideology' as Ideology; or What Does It Mean to Aestheticize Politics?," unpub. paper, 1989) situates Benjamin's 1936 insight in the context of the Symbolist poet Laurent Tailhade's response to the anarchist bombing of the French Chamber of Deputies in 1893 ("What do the victims matter if the gesture is beautiful?"), and F. T. Marinetti's glorification of war as "the world's only hygiene," and his reference to "beautiful ideas worth dying for" in the 1909 "Futurist Manifesto." Benjamin quotes Marinetti in the epilogue of his essay to exemplify the fascistic credo of "*Fiat ars—pereat mundus*" which he finds to be the "consummation of *'l'art pour l'art.'*"

20. Even in such a turbulent work as *The English Mail-Coach* (1849), De Quincey provides an essentially *aesthetic* presentation of the sublime, potentially destructive power of the hurtling coach; its demonic fury is presented from the passive perspective of a helpless onlooker or victim (in this case, De Quincey in his capacity as narrator, and the series of female figures who are brought within a hair's breadth of annihilation by a vehicle that is out of control). V. A. De Luca (*Thomas De Quincey: The Prose of Vision* [Toronto: University of Toronto Press, 1980], p. 114) rightly points to the passive, aesthetic mode of this work. In contrast to its biblical counterpart, the Fall for De Quincey

consists not in proud self-assertion but . . . in passive acquiescence to destructive power, and the trials which God visits upon the innocent are designed apparently not to strengthen their moral resistance in a fallen world but to engrave such a world upon their imaginations, to expand their conscious apprehension of a pattern composed of multiple contradictions. . . . God's task is so to intensify human sensitivity to the contradictions of history and of personal experience that they are heard as a kind of fugal music.

21. Sander L. Gilman, "The Nietzsche Murder Case," *NLH* 14 (Winter 1983): 359–72; p. 360.

22. Scott's journal of 4 April 1829, cited in Senelick, p. 84.

23. Senelick, pp. 83–84.

24. See Iain White's introduction to his translation of *The King in the Golden Mask and Other Writings by Marcel Schwob* (Manchester, England: Carcanet New Press, 1982), p. 11. Translated passages from Schwob's work hereafter cited in the text will be followed by the page number in parentheses from this edition.

25. Jorge Luis Borges, *The Aleph and Other Stories, 1933–1969*, ed. and trans. Norman Thomas di Giovanni, in collaboration with the author (New York: Dutton, 1978), p. 222.

26. Senelick, p. 83.

27. William Bolitho, "The Science of William Burke," in *Murder for Profit* (1926; rpt. New York: Time, 1964), p. 16.

28. Ibid., pp. 30–31.

29. Marcel Schwob, *Oeuvres complètes* (Paris: François Bernouard, 1927), 1–2:187. Subsequent references to Schwob's work in the original French will be followed by the page number from this edition and volume.

30. Maureen McKernan, *The Amazing Crime and Trial of Leopold and Loeb*, with an introduction by Clarence Darrow and Walter Bachrach (New York: New American Library, 1957), p. 22. According to the defense attorneys Darrow and Bachrach, the trial of Leopold and Loeb is of historical importance because it made "possible for the first time in the history of medical jurisprudence a completely scientific investigation in a court of law of the mental condition of persons accused of crime" (p. ix).

31. My use of the term "pure" murder is intended to avoid the confusion that is bound to result when the term "perfect" murder is used to designate homicides that are "artistically conceived" as well as homicides that are "insoluble." (See Lehman, *The Perfect Murder*, p. xix.)

32. It is noteworthy that the most sensational murders tend to be those committed without an apparent motive by upper-middle-class prep-school types; besides the Leopold-Loeb slaying, and their assorted fictional take-offs, one thinks more recently during the "yuppified" '80s of the 1984 "Billionaire Boys Club" murders in California, or the 1986 "preppy murder" of Jennifer Levin by Robert Chambers during a bout of rough sex in Central Park—a case of *crime passionnel par excellence*. For all the surface similarities between the "BBC" slayings and the Leopold and Loeb murder, the motive for the two killings allegedly committed by Joe Hunt and the fellow prep schoolers in his investment fraternity was nothing more than financial gain; such a motive, however, is a good deal more than no motive at all.

33. *Oeuvres complètes d'André Gide* (Paris: NRF, 1932), 7:350; *Lafcadio's Adventures*, trans. Dorothy Bussy (1925; rpt., New York: Random House, 1953), p. 197. Subsequent references to Gide's novel will be followed by the page numbers from these editions.

34. Fyodor Dostoyevsky, *Notes from Underground*, trans. Mirra Ginsburg (1974; rpt., New York: Bantam, 1981), p. 28.

35. The technique of presenting a novelist-in-a-novel in order to expose his fraudulence is even more in evidence in Gide's *The Counterfeiters*. Because this work, in John Johnston's words, "investigates the conditions and limitations of its own artistic conventions, it must be taken as a more genuine or authentic representation than the naturalistic novel it criticizes, which is seen as 'false' to life, a degraded copy of a copy" (*Carnival of Repetition: Gaddis's The Recognitions and Postmodern Theory* [Philadelphia: University of Pennsylvania Press, 1990], p. 14).

36. A. D. Nuttall, *Dostoyevsky's Crime and Punishment: Murder as Philosophic Experiment* (Edinburgh: Sussex University Press, 1978), p. 23.

37. Ironically, the rationale behind the *acte gratuit*—namely, the absolute freedom of the agent who commits a crime without any need, reason, or motive— has been inverted in the realm of social reality by the legal-medical establishment. Sander L. Gilman has noted that the *Criminal Code of the German Empire* set forth the provision that the accused was not guilty of "a punishable deed . . . if . . . at the time of the commission of his deed [he was] in a state of unconsciousness or in a state of a morbid disruption of his mental faculties through which free choice is made impossible" (cited in Gilman, p. 364). Thus, when a young German law student stood trial at the beginning of the present century for the slaying of his lover, he was found guilty of manslaughter rather than of the crime of murder because he was believed to have fallen under the "baneful influence" of the "dangerous philosophy" of Schopenhauer and Nietzsche. Supposedly, the student's susceptibility to the teachings of these philosophers severely limited his free choice; consequently, the charge of murder was deemed inapplicable. In this instance, then, society ruled that a violent killing had been influenced by Nietzsche's philosophy and that it was therefore not a crime—*not* because it had been a pure act free from moral constraint, an *acte gratuit* inspired by a reading of Nietzsche, but on the contrary, because the killer had been *deprived* of free choice through his exposure to this philosopher.

38. Alain Robbe-Grillet, "The Secret Room," in *Snapshots* (*Instantanés,* 1962), trans. Bruce Morrissette (Evanston, Ill.: Northwestern University Press, 1986), p. 65.

39. See Chap. 1, n. 64.

40. A work like Magritte's *The Menaced Assassin* should be contrasted in this respect with the depictions of the brutality of murder by the early modernist Cézanne (in *The Murder* and *Woman Being Strangled*), and the images of butchery in Francis Bacon's work. (Bacon's *Figure with Meat* is the one painting that Jack Nicholson in his role as the homicidal artist, the Joker, stops his goons from defacing during their rampage in the art museum in Tim Burton's 1989 film *Batman*.) When one thinks of the portrayal of murderous violence in modern art, however, it is the wartime atrocities depicted by the Spanish painters Goya (in *Desastres de la guerra,* 1810–13) and Picasso (*Guernica,* 1937) that typically come to mind.

41. Saint Augustine, *Confessions* [II, 5], trans. R. S. Pine-Coffin (Baltimore: Penguin, 1961), pp. 48–49.

42. Note found "on the cover of a copy of Crombie on Philosophical Necessity" by Shadworth H. Hodgson, *Outcast Essays and Verse Translations* (London: Longmans, Green, 1881), p. 32; cited in Proctor, p. 51.

43. Cited by Senelick, p. 119.

44. See Arden Reed, *Romantic Weather: The Climates of Coleridge and Baudelaire* (Hanover, N.H.: University Press of New England, 1983).

45. Senelick, pp. 119–20.

46. Ibid., p. 123. Senelick cites De Quincey's tale "The Avenger" as an exam-

ple where a "seemingly unmotivated series of murders . . . disrupt [a] small town, leaving the noblest or most defenceless of citizens weltering in gore," and where the killings "cannot easily be ascribed to any mortal, for they lack sequential logic" (p. 128).

47. Ibid., p. 374.

48. Schwob, *Oeuvres complètes*, 3–4:64.

49. Thomas Pynchon, *Gravity's Rainbow* (New York: Viking, 1973), p. 703.

50. Senelick, p. 119.

51. James Hogg, "Nights and Days with De Quincey," *Harper's Monthly* (February 1890): 447; cited in Senelick, p. 122.

52. Senelick, pp. 122 23.

53. Senelick observes that Balzac's murderers "destroy . . . their victims over a long . . . period of time," in "oblique ways, often at many removes from the actual scene of death" (p. 325).

54. J.-K. Huysmans, *A Rebours* (Paris: Fasquelle, 1972), pp. 104–106; English translation by Robert Baldick. *Against Nature* (Baltimore: Penguin, 1959), pp. 81–83.

55. Punning on the different senses of the word, Sterne in *Tristram Shandy* has Tristram mock Locke and his followers as men of "great gravity" and "false wit," "men of wit and genius" who "have all along confounded this [straight] line, with the [curved] line of GRAVITATION" (6:40). Sigurd Burckhardt ("*Tristram Shandy's* Law of Gravity," *English Literary History* 28 [1961]: 70–88) has shown that for Tristram, the solemn lack of humor of sages like Locke prevented them from seeing that the movement of physical objects in the act of falling, and of human beings in the act of living, was by no means a straightforward, linear motion, but an erratic trajectory that is repeated in the digressive movement of Tristram's own narrative description of planetary motion and human action.

What Sterne did to Locke, De Quincey did to Kant in his essay "On Murder," ridiculing him as the exemplary instance of the type of readers who may be expected to take offense at his satire. In the "Postscript," De Quincey defended "the gaiety" of his satire which "trespasses a little into the province of the extravagant"; he offered no apologies to those "readers of so saturnine and gloomy a class that they cannot enter with genial sympathy into any gaiety whatever" (13:70). Such unsympathetic readers belong to the same moralizing audience that Sterne mocks in *Tristram Shandy*.

56. See Donald Ault, *Visionary Physics: Blake's Response to Newton* (Chicago: University of Chicago Press, 1974).

57. Gilles Deleuze, *Nietzsche et la philosophie* (Paris: P.U.F., 1962), chap. 2.

Three: Murder as (Carnal) Knowledge

1. Porter, *The Pursuit of Crime*, p. 22.

2. An exemplary instance of such complicity between the witness to and the agent of a criminal act occurs in Malcolm Lowry's novel, *Under the Volcano*

(1947). The Consul "innocently" happens to bear witness to some foul play involving a mortally injured Indian who has been left to die on a deserted Mexican road. The Consul becomes obsessed by this scene, and is plagued by his own helplessness (under Mexican law as well as under the spell of his own drunkenness) to do anything about it. He imagines a number of possible motives for the Indian's murder—assuming that this *was* in fact a case of murder—without there being any means of determining what was the "real" motive. Ultimately, the Consul becomes implicated in the affair, making the discovery that he has been both the dying Indian's comrade *(compañero)* as well as his tormentor *(pelado)*, both a commiserating Jesus and a treacherous Judas. The Consul only gains this insight, however, when at the novel's conclusion he himself becomes, like the Indian, the arbitrary victim of a senseless, apparently unmotivated, possibly sacrificial, murder.

3. As an example of life's many coincidences, the narrator of G. K. Chesterton's story "The Blue Cross" (1910) observes that "a man named Williams does quite accidentally murder a man named Williamson," adding that "it sounds like a sort of infanticide." Martin Gardner notes that Chesterton uses the same example in another essay in which he writes, "A man named Williams did walk into a strange house and murder a man named Williamson; it sounds like a sort of infanticide" (*The Annotated Innocence of Father Brown*, ed. Martin Gardner [New York: Oxford University Press, 1988], p. 20, n. 14). Gardner comments that he doesn't "know whether G. K. wrote this sentence before or after the similar sentence in 'The Blue Cross,' but the wording suggests that he had in mind an actual crime." It seems he did indeed.

4. Susanne Kappeler, *The Pornography of Representation* (Minneapolis: University of Minnesota Press, 1986), p. 8. Subsequent references are in the text.

5. Bataille, *Death and Sensuality,* pp. 11f.

6. Bataille, *L'Érotisme,* p. 19; *Death and Sensuality,* pp. 12–13.

7. Bataille, *L'Érotisme,* pp. 26, 103; *Death and Sensuality,* pp. 19, 93.

8. For De Quincey's identification of God and Death, see De Luca, *Thomas De Quincey,* p. 84.

9. See Black, "Confession, Digression, Gravitation," pp. 324–38.

10. *Mémoires de Lacenaire, avec ses poèmes et ses lettres,* ed. Monique Lebailly (Paris: Albin Michel, 1968), pp. 68f.; the English translation, *The Memoirs of Lacenaire,* is by Philip John Stead (New York: Staples Press, 1952), pp. 114f. Subsequent citations from Lacenaire's *Mémoires* in the original and in translation are to these editions and are in the text.

11. Senelick, *The Prestige of Evil,* p. 285.

12. Anonymous critic in the *Revue de Paris;* cited by Monique Lebailly in *Mémoires de Lacenaire,* p. 23.

13. Other examples of this subgenre dealing with hands are Nerval's tale "La Main enchantée" ("The Charmed Hand," 1852) and Maupassant's "La Main d'écorché" ("The Flayed Hand," 1875) and its later version "La Main" (1883). (See Sima Godfrey's essay, "Lending a Hand: Nerval, Gautier, Maupassant

and the Fantastic," *Romanic Review* 78, no. 1 [1987]: 74-83.) In Balzac's story "Le Chef-d'oeuvre inconnu" ("The Unknown Masterpiece," 1831; revised, 1837)—on which Gautier himself collaborated—the painter Frenhofer's masterpiece "La Belle Noiseuse," created by the artist's hand, depicts nothing more than an idealized foot. The narrator of Gautier's own tale "Le Pied de Momie" ("The Mummy's Foot," 1840) dreams of exchanging a mummified foot that he has actually purchased in a curio shop for the hand (in marriage) of the Egyptian princess to whom the foot belongs. (See Godfrey's earlier study, "Mummy Dearest: Cryptic Codes in Gautier's 'Pied de Momie,'" *Romanic Review* 75, no. 3 [1984]: 302-11.)

14. See Nerval's "La Main enchantée," which originally (1832) was called "La Main de gloire." In his 1919 essay "The 'Uncanny,'" Freud alludes to a curious variation of the "main de gloire" tradition—a story from Herodotus in which a fleeing thief leaves his brother's severed hand in the clutches of the princess who tries to detain him. Freud compares this story with a scene of dancing hands in a fairy tale by Hauff. As Tobin Siebers (*The Romantic Fantastic* [Ithaca: Cornell University Press, 1984], p. 48) observes, the hands in the Hauff tale produce an uncanny effect according to Freud because "the reader identifies with the witness of the marvelous event"; in contrast, "the severed hand in Herodotus produces no uncanny feelings because the reader," whose attention is focused on the thief, "is not allowed to identify with the person terrified by the phenomenon"—namely, the princess.

15. Bataille, *Death and Sensuality*, pp. 17, 90.

16. Théophile Gautier, *Émaux et Camées*, ed. Claudine Gothot-Mersch (Paris: Gallimard, 1981), pp. 32-35; p. 33.

17. See Ousby, *Bloodhounds of Heaven*, pp. 47f.

18. Thomas De Quincey, *Confessions of an English Opium-Eater and Suspiria de Profundis* (Boston: Ticknor, Reed, & Fields, 1851), p. 39.

19. Jan Kott, *Shakespeare Our Contemporary*, trans. Boleslaw Taborski (New York: Norton, 1974), pp. 90f.

20. Bataille, *Sur Nietzsche*; cited in Derrida, "From Restricted to General Economy: A Hegelianism without Reserve," in *Writing and Difference*, trans. Alan Bass (Chicago: University of Chicago Press, 1978), p. 263.

21. Unpublished letter from Jack Abbott to Norman Mailer, April 18, 1983; my thanks to Lidia Berger for making this letter available to me. I am unable to quote directly from this letter, however, as Mr. Abbott has refused me permission to do so.

22. Abbott, *In the Belly of the Beast*, p. 74.

23. Jack Henry Abbott with Naomi Zack, *My Return* (Buffalo: Prometheus Books, 1987), pp. 163-64. Subsequent references to this book will be followed by the page number in parentheses.

24. Abbott, *In the Belly of the Beast*, pp. 75-76.

25. Nietzsche, *The Gay Science*, p. 265 [335].

26. Abbott, *In the Belly of the Beast*, p. 78.

27. Genet, *Journal du Voleur* (Paris: Gallimard, 1949), pp. 210, 100, 259; *The Thief's Journal*, pp. 197-98, 94, 243.

28. Gregor von Rezzori, *The Death of My Brother Abel*, trans. Joachim Neugroschel (New York: Viking Penguin, 1985), pp. 371-72.

29. "En exigeant (avec quelle ferveur!) que chacun de mes amis possédât son double dans le police, à quel obscur désir obéissais-je?" ("What obscure desire was I obeying in requiring (and so fervently!) that each of my friends have his double in the police?" [*Journal de Voleur*, p. 205; *The Thief's Journal*, p. 194]).

30. Bataille, "Hegel, la mort et le sacrifice"; cited by Derrida in "From Restricted to General Economy," p. 257.

31. Abbott, *In the Belly of the Beast*, p. 73.

32. René Girard, *Violence and the Sacred*, trans. Patrick Gregory (Baltimore: Johns Hopkins University Press, 1977), p. 5. Subsequent references are in the text.

33. René Girard, *Des Choses cachées depuis la fondation du monde* (Paris: Grasset, 1978), p. 184; my translation.

34. Girard, *Des Choses cachées*, p. 79.

Four: Mimesis and Murder

1. James W. Clarke notes that between 1963 and 1989 eight assassination attempts were made against national political figures—"as many assassination attempts in 25 years as were recorded in all the previous 174 years of the nation's presidential history" (*On Being Mad or Merely Angry: John W. Hinckley, Jr., and Other Dangerous People* [Princeton: Princeton University Press, 1990], p. 125). Elliott Leyton (*Compulsive Killers: The Story of Modern Multiple Murder* [New York: New York University Press, 1986]) provides statistical documentation (pp. 288-89) that indicates a steady rise in the rate of multiple murder beginning in the 1960s, and increasing exponentially during the '70s and '80s. Subsequent references to Leyton's study are cited in the text.

2. Clarke suggests that the influence of television "figures prominently in the motives of most recent assassins," and "that the anticipation of this kind of exposure is also a factor in the growing incidence of mass public murder during the same era" (*On Being Mad*, p. 113).

3. My chronology and categorization differ slightly from that of Clarke, who finds a new type of assassin already emerging with Lee Harvey Oswald in the 1960s: "Before 1963 American assassins were usually either rational political extremists or utterly insane" (*On Being Mad*, p. 81)—individuals whom Clarke labels Type I and Type IV subjects. Clarke contends that most of the attacks on American presidents since Oswald's slaying of Kennedy have been made by "emotionally disturbed, but sane" individuals belonging to Types II or III (p. 82). (Type II assassins settle on a scapegoat to be their victim who is often a political figure; "Type III assassins choose their political victims because of their prominence and visibility, *not* their political views" [p. 84]). I set 1980, the eve of the Reagan presidency, as the date when the break occurred between tra-

ditional assassins who were either political extremists or psychotics, and a new type of killer who is especially susceptible to the media.

4. See Franklin L. Ford, *Political Murder: From Tyrannicide to Terrorism* (Cambridge, Mass.: Harvard University Press, 1985), chaps. 13 and 15, and William J. Crotty, ed., *Assassinations and the Political Order* (New York: Harper & Row, 1971).

5. See Lincoln Caplan, *The Insanity Defense and the Trial of John W. Hinckley, Jr.* (Boston: Godine, 1984); and Peter W. Low, John Calvin Jeffries, Jr., and Richard J. Bonnie, *The Trial of John W. Hinckley, Jr.: A Case Study in the Insanity Defense* (Mineola, N.Y.: Foundation Press, 1986), hereafter cited as *LJB*. From a sociological perspective, James Clarke explains Hinckley's rampage less as an act of madness than as an expression of "a decade's accumulation of anger" directed at his parents whom he wanted to embarrass for "the way they had treated him all these years" (*On Being Mad*, p. 40). Clarke's treatment of Hinckley's case as a pathological family romance downplays the crucial role played by the media. Moreover, Clarke's analysis of Hinckley is based in large part on his similarity to Arthur Bremer as an apolitical sociopath who chose a political figure as his victim; my approach will focus instead on the close relation between Hinckley's case and that of the celebrity assassin Mark David Chapman, and on the more direct effect that the film *Taxi Driver*—which was based on Bremer's diary—rather than the diary itself, exerted on Hinckley.

6. Christopher Lasch, *The Minimal Self: Psychic Survival in Troubled Times* (New York: Norton, 1984), p. 141.

7. Laurence Senelick's paraphrase of Camus's argument in *L'Homme révolté* (Senelick, *The Prestige of Evil*, p. 375).

8. Greil Marcus, *Lipstick Traces: A Secret History of the Twentieth Century* (Cambridge, Mass.: Harvard University Press, 1989), p. 17.

9. Not to mention exporting cigarettes and tobacco products that have become less marketable domestically as public awareness of their harmful effects has grown. The extent to which U.S. trade in drugs and arms was related, and even interdependent, has never been fully revealed. During the 1980s, the U.S. military repeatedly expressed its aversion to involve itself directly in the "war" on drugs, a suspicious policy considering the Reagan administration's tolerance of Central American drug lords and its attempts to engage them in its covert efforts to supply arms to the Nicaraguan contras. Such activities first came to light as early as 1984 when the journalist Manuel Buendia was assassinated while researching the CIA's relations with Mexican politicians and drug traffickers, and were more widely publicized during the Iran-Contra investigation. The 1989 report of the Senate Subcommittee on Narcotics, Terrorism, and International Operations headed by Senator John Kerry presented clear evidence of CIA collaboration with the drug lords. Only with the U.S. raid on Panama in the same year, and with the electoral defeat of the Sandinistas in Nicaragua the following year and the declaration that the cold war in Europe was at an end, did the Pentagon become a willing partner in the

campaign against drug traffickers. (For a study that presents the drug "war" not as an anticriminal crusade but as a geopolitical operation in which the U.S. has deliberately or inadvertently financed terrorist activities abroad, see Rachel Ehrenfeld's *Narcoterrorism* [New York: Basic Books, 1990].)

As the superpowers disarm in the 1990s, the emerging tie-in between arms and entertainment that has brought us such motion pictures as *Top Gun*, *The Hunt for Red October*, *Fire Birds*, and *Navy Seals* may be expected to continue. Besides serving as recruiting films for the armed forces, these movies afford a simulacrum of postmodern warfare as well as an opportunity to deploy new state-of-the-art weapons before they become obsolete.

10. Leo Braudy, *The Frenzy of Renown: Fame and Its History* (New York: Oxford University Press, 1986), p. 4.

11. Braudy, p. 4.

12. I follow Leyton's terminology here, which identifies "mass" and "serial" murder as the two categories of "multiple murder," in contrast to Jack Levin and James Alan Fox's practice (*Mass Murder*, p. 13) of calling these categories "simultaneous" and "serial" murder and designating the umbrella term "mass murder."

13. Associated Press, 12 February 1978; cited in Braudy (p. 3), who adds the murderer's observation that "only with his sixth killing . . . had he begun to get his due in publicity."

14. Clarke, *On Being Mad*, p. 72.

15. Thus after Bundy's death, rock star Deborah Harry claimed she had been picked up and attacked by the killer in New York in the early 1970s, and had just barely managed to escape (*Atlanta Journal and Constitution* [Nov. 8, 1989], A-2).

16. Malcolm's essays in *The New Yorker* (March 13 and 20, 1989) were subsequently published in book form as *The Journalist and the Murderer* (New York: Knopf, 1990).

17. Genet, *The Thief's Journal*, p. 213.

18. For a sample, see *People Weekly* (July 31, 1989), p. 64.

19. The psychiatrist Donald T. Lunde states that "the most important single contrast between mass murderers and murderers of a single person is a difference in their relationships to the victims" (*Murder and Madness* [New York: Norton, 1979], p. 48; cited in Leyton [p. 263], who adds, "the former killing strangers, the latter killing intimates"). Leyton furthermore notes that it "is in modern, industrializing societies that stranger-murder becomes a major homicidal theme."

20. Leyton draws a sharp distinction between murder in general and the specific phenomenon of multiple murder on the grounds that the latter entails an aesthetic sensibility or orientation on the part of the assailant: "The multiple murderer, who sacrifices his own life to make an art form out of killing strangers, is qualitatively a very different man from the slum husband who, driven beyond endurance by poverty and humiliation, beats his wife or neighbour to death in some drunken brawl" (p. 23). Leyton later clarifies this rather

general assertion, explaining that it is specifically the mass murderer who regards himself as a sacrificial victim, while the serial killer is more concerned with attaining celebrity status and with making "an art form out of killing strangers." Both types of multiple murderer nevertheless share an aesthetic awareness; they are engaged in "a kind of primitive rebellion against the social order which has become an increasingly fashionable form of social art" (pp. 26-27). I would only add in this regard that the celebrity murderer has at least an equal, if not a greater, claim to "artistry" as the multiple murderer. Assassinating a public figure is not only a way of creating an identity, but of becoming a celebrity in the process—and in one deft stroke as well.

21. Interview of John W. Hinckley, Jr., by Allan Sonnenschein, *Penthouse* (March 1983), p. 164.

22. As reported by James R. Gaines in the second installment of his three-part account, "In the Shadows A Killer Waited," *People Weekly* (March 2, 1987), p. 59. In subsequent citations, the three parts of this article will be referred to as follows: PW 1 (February 23, 1987: "The Man Who Shot Lennon"), PW 2 (March 2, 1987: "In the Shadows A Killer Waited"), and PW 3 (March 9, 1987: "The Killer Takes His Fall").

23. Sonnenschein's interview with Hinckley, p. 164.

24. "Answers from John Hinckley," *Newsweek* (Oct. 12, 1981), p. 51.

25. From the transcript of Hinckley's trial, *U.S. v. John Hinckley, Jr.*, May 13, 1982, p. 3204. My thanks to the prosecuting attorney, Mr. Roger Adelman, for giving me access to the transcript of the trial.

26. *U.S. v. John Hinckley, Jr.*, p. 3204.

27. *U.S. v. John Hinckley, Jr.*, p. 3640. This wasn't Hinckley's only attempt at suicide. He claimed to have played Russian roulette at least twice in 1979, and allegedly took an overdose of antidepressants the following year (*LJB*, pp. 24, 26).

28. Gaines, PW 2, p. 60.

29. Actually, as part of a plea-bargaining maneuver, Hinckley offered to plead guilty to all counts against him "in exchange for a recommendation by the Justice Department that his sentence be served concurrently, not consecutively, so that he might be eligible for parole in fifteen years rather than serving in prison for life" (Caplan, p. 125).

30. Clarke, p. 4.

31. Gaines, PW 1, p. 65.

32. *Newsweek* (Oct. 12, 1981), p. 51.

33. Cited in *LJB*, p. 45.

34. Caplan, p. 72.

35. Gaines, PW 1, p. 68.

36. In his closing argument, defense attorney Vincent Fuller referred to this term which had been used by Dr. Carpenter to describe Hinckley's perception of his victims. "But in his delusion," Fuller told the jurors, "he is not aware of the humanity of those victims. They play a very minor role in his delusional

state. They are merely means to the end, to the end he wishes to accomplish: To win the love and affection and establish the relationship with Jodie Foster" (*LJB*, pp. 102–03).

37. One of the most sensational examples of a scripted murder is the case of Lyle and Erik Menendez, who were accused of the 1989 killing of their parents in Beverly Hills. Two years before the murders, the younger son Erik had collaborated on a screenplay about an eighteen-year-old who killed his parents for money. Whether or not this script served to motivate or mediate Erik's alleged violence, it was presented as crucial evidence at the brothers' trial. In an article called "The Hottest Show in Hollywood," *Time* reporters described the trial itself as a ready-made screenplay, and found themselves "speculating about who should play the various characters when the movie is made. Sean Penn as Lyle? Rob Lowe as Erik?" ([Oct. 1, 1990], p. 46).

38. Gaines, *PW* 1, p. 60.

39. Gaines, *PW* 3, p. 63.

40. Gaines, *PW* 1, p. 60.

41. Gaines, *PW* 1, p. 60.

42. Gaines, *PW* 2, p. 63.

43. Gaines, *PW* 3, p. 67.

44. Quoted in Gaines, *PW* 1, p. 59.

45. Gaines, *PW* 3, p. 62.

46. Gaines, *PW* 2, p. 59.

47. Gaines, *PW* 3, p. 62.

48. Gaines, *PW* 3, p. 67.

49. Gaines, *PW* 3, p. 69.

50. Gaines, *PW* 3, p. 70.

51. Gaines, *PW* 3, p. 74.

52. Cf. Dietz's testimony: "His ability to wait, when he did not have a clear shot of the President on the President's way into the Hilton is further evidence of his ability to conform his behavior. A man driven, a man out of control, would not have the capacity to wait at that moment for the best shot" (*LJB*, p. 81).

53. Gaines, *PW* 3, p. 74.

54. The year following Hinckley's assassination attempt, Scorsese wrote and directed *The King of Comedy*, a film about a man who resorts to crime in a desperate effort to turn his fantasized image of himself as a celebrated comedian into reality. Thus, in the ten-year period extending back from 1982 to 1972, matters came around full circle: art *(The King of Comedy)* imitated life (Hinckley's assassination attempt), which itself imitated art *(Taxi Driver)*, which in turn imitated life (Bremer's assassination attempt). We may only imagine how far this interplay of fiction and reality as each other's simulacrum may extend back in time before 1972 or forward in time since 1982.

55. Cited in Caplan, pp. 70–71.

56. *U.S. v. John Hinckley, Jr.*, p. 3839.

57. By Chapman in a photograph taken by Harry Benson for Gaines, *PW* 1, pp. 58–59; by Hinckley in a photograph he took of himself in early 1980 which was presented as evidence at his trial and in which he held an actual gun up to his head.

58. *U.S. v. John Hinckley, Jr.*, p. 1492.

59. *U.S. v. John Hinckley, Jr.*, p. 3258. To the side of the note he jotted the single word, "Impotent!"

60. *LJB*, p. 103; also see p. 78. During Hinckley's trial, Dr. Carpenter repeatedly insisted that the defendant's "primary purpose" in shooting the President was "to terminate his own experience, his own existence"; this was "the predominant mental motivation that he [was] experiencing" at the time of his crime (*LJB*, p. 34; see also p. 60).

61. Cited in Caplan, p. 16.

62. Caplan, p. 77.

63. Clarke, pp. 53–55.

64. Gregory B. Craig, *U.S. v. John Hinckley, Jr.*, p. 59.

65. *U.S. v. John Hinckley, Jr.*, p. 3147.

66. *U.S. v. John Hinckley, Jr.*, p. 3181.

67. *U.S. v. John Hinckley, Jr.*, p. 3177.

68. Cited in Caplan, p. 77.

69. Clarke, pp. 90–91.

70. Clarke, p. 90.

71. Cited in Caplan, pp. 42–43.

72. *U.S. v. John Hinckley, Jr.*, pp. 3251–52.

73. *U.S. v. John Hinckley, Jr.*, p. 3887.

74. *U.S. v. John Hinckley, Jr.*, p. 3847.

75. Gaines, *PW* 2, p. 63.

76. *U.S. v. John Hinckley, Jr.*, p. 3622.

77. *U.S. v. John Hinckley, Jr.*, p. 3246.

78. Caplan, p. 40.

79. See René Girard's concept of "mimetic" or "triangular desire" in *Deceit, Desire, and the Novel*, trans. Yvonne Freccero (Baltimore: Johns Hopkins University Press, 1965), chap. 1.

80. *U.S. v. John Hinckley, Jr.*, p. 3250.

81. *U.S. v. John Hinckley, Jr.*, p. 3859.

82. *U.S. v. John Hinckley, Jr.*, p. 3846.

83. More plausible, however, is the realistic scene between Caulfield and the prostitute in *The Catcher in the Rye* which describes a situation antithetical to that portrayed in *Taxi Driver*. The prostitute Sunny returns to Caulfield's hotel room with her pimp, and both demand more payment from Caulfield than he originally agreed to pay. When he refuses to give them more money, the pimp beats Caulfield up.

84. *U.S. v. John Hinckley, Jr.*, pp. 3844, 3850.

85. Consider the case of Theodore Streleski, a Stanford University graduate

student who bludgeoned his faculty advisor to death in 1978, and who repeatedly refused parole as his seven-year sentence drew to a close. Streleski insisted that he felt no remorse for his deed, which he described as "a rational act" that he had been planning to commit since 1970 in order "'to somehow redress the matter' of his struggle in the university" (cited in the *San Francisco Chronicle*, Aug. 18, 1985, A-20). Where Hinckley imagined Yale University as a prison from which he sought to liberate Foster, Streleski referred to the Vacaville Correctional Medical Facility as a state institution in which he was pursuing his mathematical studies, and from which he maintained he could not be "evicted."

86. *U.S. v. John Hinckley, Jr.*, p. 3852.

87. *U.S. v. John Hinckley, Jr.*, p. 56.

88. *U.S. v. John Hinckley, Jr.*, p. 3850.

89. *U.S. v. John Hinckley, Jr.*, p. 3183.

90. Sigmund Freud, *Sexuality and the Psychology of Love*, ed. Philip Rieff (New York: Macmillan, 1974), p. 52.

91. Freud, p. 57.

92. Clarke, p. 52.

93. Paul Schrader, the author of the book on which Scorsese's film *Taxi Driver* was based, also wrote the script for Brian De Palma's *Obsession*, a film that appeared in the same year as *Taxi Driver* (1976) and that explored the compulsive desire of a man for a woman who appears to be the exact double of his long-dead wife.

94. Clarke, p. 53.

95. Clarke, p. 53.

96. Angela Carter, "Our Lady of the Massacre," in *Saints and Strangers* (New York: Viking, 1986), pp. 54–55.

97. Carter does an explicit take-off of the American director in her story "'Tis Pity She's a Whore" (*Granta* 25 [Autumn 1988]: 179–97) in which she overlaps the "New World John Ford" with his namesake, the "Old World John Ford" — the seventeenth-century English dramatist who authored the play *'Tis Pity She's a Whore*.

98. Ford returned to this theme five years later in another western, *Two Rode Together*. In this film—which Brian De Palma has called a "film noir of *The Searchers*" (*Film Comment* 23, no. 3 [May-June 1987], p. 53)—James Stewart and Richard Widmark set out after some children who have been abducted by Indians and who have become murderous savages.

99. Stuart Byron, "'The Searchers': Cult Movie of the New Hollywood," *New York* (March 5, 1979), pp. 45–48. In a curious inversion of Ford's western, *Taxi Driver* shows Travis Bickle preparing for his one-man war against society by adopting a mohawk hairstyle.

100. Clover, "Her Body, Himself," p. 218.

101. Clover, pp. 218–19.

102. For a review of Schrader's and others' retellings of the Hearst story,

including Patty's own, in the context of social and political events of the 1970s, see Duncan Webster, "'Nobody's Patsy': Versions of Patty Hearst," *Critical Quarterly* 32, no. 1 (1990): 3–21.

103. "Answers from John Hinckley," *Newsweek* (October 12, 1981), p. 50. This statement invites comparison with a remark attributed to Jean-Baptiste Troppmann, the twenty-year-old Alsatian who slaughtered a family of eight in 1869: "He who reads many novels, and has them in his head, falls asleep, but he who reads only one, has a fixed idea" (Bolitho, p. 63). The inspiration for Troppmann's deed, which he committed in order to possess the Kinck family fortune, came from a mediocre novel by Eugène Sue, *Le Juif errant*. Troppmann became obsessed with this novel, which describes the Jesuits' extermination of the Rennefont family in order to gain its inheritance. Bolitho offers this rather dramatic description of Troppmann's initial encounter with his victims: "At the first meeting, when he saw the family, the first fortune he had ever seen, the Book bounded into his mind. With the parallel of the Rennefont family of the Book, his Book, *The Wandering Jew*, the Kincks' doom was settled" (p. 70). Where Hinckley implies that his inability to distinguish life from art was the result of having read and seen *too many* books and films, Troppmann maintains that his delusion has been caused by his monomaniacal obsession with a *single* book. Had he been exposed to other books, he presumably would have been released from his obsession and fallen asleep. Like Hinckley's lawyers, Troppmann's attorney defended his client by citing the media's influence. However, where Hinckley's attorneys referred at length to his readings and movie viewings in an effort to show his insanity, Troppmann's attorney used the occasion to condemn the pernicious effect of "bad books" (cf. Senelick, p. xxxiii, n. 19).

104. See, e.g., his dialogue with Sancho in part 2, chap. 12.

105. Aaron Latham, "The Dark Side of the American Dream," *Rolling Stone* (August 5, 1982), p. 18.

106. Lincoln had himself seen Booth in a performance of *The Marble Heart* less than two years before Booth was to shoot him during a performance of *Our American Cousin* at Ford's Theater (Stanley Kimmel, *The Mad Booths of Maryland* [1940; rpt., New York: Dover, 1969], p. 173). At Hinckley's trial, prosecuting attorney Roger Adelman produced a photograph of the defendant standing in front of Ford's Theater, telling the jurors that "it is not the time for you to draw conclusions, but I suggest to you it is the time to bear that in mind when we discuss the matters of thought, planning and intent, if you will" (*U.S. v. John Hinckley, Jr.*, p. 1468).

107. Louis J. Weichmann, *A True History of the Assassination of Abraham Lincoln and of the Conspiracy of 1865*, ed. Floyd E. Risvold (New York: Knopf, 1975), p. 41.

108. Girard introduces the concepts of "mimetic desire" and "double mediation" in *Deceit, Desire, and the Novel*. He moves his treatment of these issues from a literary to a cultural context in *Violence and the Sacred*, where he develops

the idea of mimetic violence – a bold attempt to render the violence of murder intelligible by revealing its affiliation with ritual sacrifice. The institution of sacrifice and the idea of the sacred to which it gives rise invest the violence of murder with an anthropological and religious significance that is beyond the aesthetic, media-mediated area of my concern. But Girard's analysis of violence as a mimetic phenomenon (which has been developed in Jean Baudrillard's study of the play of simulacra in contemporary culture and the mass media), and his research into the scapegoat phenomenon, or the arbitrarily chosen victim of such mimetic violence, is clearly pertinent to a study of the aesthetics of murder.

109. James W. Clarke, *American Assassins: The Darker Side of Politics* (Princeton, N.J.: Princeton University Press, 1982), p. 24. Subsequent references are in the text.

110. Weichmann (p. 69) reports that "Booth in all his operations and talk seemed from the start to have Ford's Theater in his mind as an objective point from which to work. At one time he kept two horses in the stable and the buggy in which the President was to be placed in the event of his capture at the theater."

111. Antonin Artaud, *The Theater and Its Double,* trans. Mary Caroline Richards (New York: Grove Press, 1958), p. 25.

112. See Gerald Langford, *The Murder of Stanford White* (Indianapolis: Bobbs-Merrill, 1962). E. L. Doctorow's historical novel *Ragtime* (1974) is based in part on this incident and its aftermath.

113. Jorge Luis Borges, "Theme of the Traitor and the Hero," trans. J. E. Irby, in *Labyrinths,* pp. 72–75; p. 75. Subsequent references are in the text.

114. Don DeLillo, *Libra* (New York: Viking, 1988), p. 370.

115. *LJB,* p. 33.

116. DeLillo, p. 370.

117. John Robert Nash and Stanley Ralph Ross, *The Motion Picture Guide* (Chicago: Cinebooks, 1987), 7:3194.

118. DeLillo, p. 370.

119. Braudy, p. 143.

120. Braudy, p. 145.

121. Braudy, p. 591.

122. *Newsweek* (July 8, 1985), p. 60.

Five: Catharsis and Murder

1. Leyton, *Compulsive Killers,* p. 261. Subsequent references are in the text.

2. Katz, *Seductions of Crime,* p. 9. Subsequent references are in the text.

3. D. W. Lucas, *Aristotle's Poetics* (Oxford: Clarendon Press, 1968), p. 276. My description of catharsis follows Lucas's discussion in his second appendix ("Pity, Fear, and *Katharsis*"), pp. 273–90. Aristotle's reference in the *Politics* (1342a7–16) to the purgative effect of music on listeners ("under the influence of sacred music we see these people, when they use tunes that violently arouse

the soul, being thrown into a state as if they had received medicinal treatment and taken a purge" [Aristotle, *Politics*, trans. H. Rackham (Cambridge, Mass.: Harvard University Press, 1967), p. 671]) appears to be closely related to his concept in the *Poetics* of the cathartic effect of tragedy.

4. Lucas, p. 276.

5 Walter Burkert, *Greek Religion, Archaic and Classical*, trans. John Raffan (Oxford: Basil Blackwell, 1985), p. 79.

6. Burkert, pp. 82–84.

7. Burkert, p. 81.

8. Cf. Burkert, p. 77: "The problem of murder and the murderer, especially its power to cast a shadow over later generations and the means of overcoming this by purification, seems to have become increasingly urgent during the course of the seventh century."

9. In his translation of Aristotle's phrase, Gerald Else applies the phrase "pity and fear" to elements in the tragedy itself rather than to the audience: "through a course of pity and fear [tragedy] complet[es] the purification of tragic acts which have those emotional characteristics" (*Aristotle: Poetics*, trans. with an introduction and notes by Gerald F. Else [Ann Arbor: University of Michigan Press, 1967], p. 25). Cf. Else's statement that "catharsis is not a change or end-product in the spectator's soul, or in the fear and pity (i.e., the dispositions to them) in his soul, but a process carried forward in the emotional material of the play by its structural elements, above all by the recognition" (*Aristotle's Poetics: The Argument* [Cambridge, Mass.: Harvard University Press, 1957], p. 439).

Besides the interpretations of catharsis as purgation and purification, Leon Goldman has proposed that the term refers to a "clarification" of the understanding ("Catharsis," *Transactions and Proceedings of the American Philological Association* 113 [1962]: 51–60). And in *Catharsis in Literature* (Bloomington: Indiana University Press, 1985), Adnan K. Abdulla endorses Ernst Cassirer's rejection of both purgation and purification as meanings for catharsis: "neither pity nor fear are changed nor are they expelled. Cassirer maintains that the change in the reader that occurs during the cathartic process is a change in the reader's soul" (p. 6).

10. Elder Olson, *The Theory of Comedy* (Bloomington: Indiana University Press, 1968), p. 34, n.

11. Burkert, p. 80.

12. Braudy, *The Frenzy of Renown*, p. 144.

13. Gilles Deleuze, "Coldness and Cruelty," in *Masochism* (New York: Zone, 1989), p. 79.

14. Camus, *The Rebel*, p. 40.

15. Camus, p. 58.

16. Simone de Beauvoir, *Must We Burn de Sade?*, trans. Annette Michelson (New York: Peter Nevill, 1953), p. 15.

17. De Beauvoir, p. 48.

18. Martin, *Art, Messianism and Crime*, p. 27.

19. Technically, only Mishima performed seppuku; Morita was unable to carry it out and had to be beheaded by a third member of the group.

20. Yukio Mishima, *Runaway Horses*, trans. Michael Gallagher (New York: Knopf, 1973), pp. 394–95.

21. *Runaway Horses*, p. 395.

22. *Runaway Horses*, p. 421.

23. Henry Scott-Stokes, *The Life and Death of Yukio Mishima* (New York: Farrar, Straus & Giroux, 1974), p. 26. Another biographer, John Nathan, reports that during the summer before his death, Mishima asked a friend at Japan National Broadcasting about the possibility of live television coverage in the event he should decide to commit seppuku. Nathan comments that "there must have been a place somewhere in consciousness where there was no distinction between death as a reality and death as a *coup de théâtre* on which the curtain would never fall (*Mishima, A Biography* [Boston and Toronto: Little, Brown, 1974], p. 265).

24. Quoted in Scott-Stokes, p. 5. In the essay *Sun and Steel*, Mishima postulates a "logical gap between seeing and existing" that he illustrates with the example of an apple's relation to its core:

> The apple certainly exists, but to the core this existence as yet seems inadequate; if words cannot endorse it, then the only way to endorse it is with the eyes. Indeed, for the core, the only sure mode of existence is to exist and to see at the same time. There is only one method of solving this contradiction. It is for a knife to be plunged deep into the apple so that it is split open and the core is exposed to the light. . . . Yet then the existence of the cut apple falls to pieces; the core of the apple sacrifices existence for the sake of seeing.

(Cited in Nathan, p. 237).

25. Yukio Mishima, "Patriotism," trans. Geoffrey W. Sargent, in *Death in Midsummer and other Stories* (London: Secker & Warburg, 1967), p. 142. Subsequent page references will follow the citations.

26. I borrow this distinction from Lionel Trilling, *Sincerity and Authenticity* (Cambridge, Mass.: Harvard University Press, 1972).

27. Scott-Stokes, p. 234.

28. See Scott-Stokes, pp. 302–5. While Nathan finds "no evidence" to prove "that Mishima had finally found the lover he had been awaiting all his life, and had contrived to die a violent warrior's death with him, as in 'Patriotism,'" he writes that "surely it was true for Mishima, whether or not he and Morita were physical lovers. At the very least, Mishima must have felt a strong sexual attraction to Morita or he would not have chosen him for his executioner" (p. 259). In contrast, Marguerite Yourcenar believes any love relationship that might have developed between Morita and Mishima to have been an incidental occurrence arising out of the latter's dream of transcendence through death: "It is natural for two beings who have decided to die together, and one at the hands

of the other, to want to meet in bed at least once, and this is a notion to which
the samurai spirit would not have objected" (*Mishima: A Vision of the Void*,
trans. Alberto Manguel in collaboration with the author [New York: Farrar,
Straus & Giroux, 1986], p. 142).

29. In this respect too Mishima's suicide differs markedly from that of
Hedda. It is true that Hedda plays a tarantella on the piano just before she
shoots herself, an orgiastic bacchanal in which the dancer's identity becomes
indistinguishable from the dance. But Hedda dances alone; there is no partner, and certainly no god, in whom she may find release.

30. Scott-Stokes, p. 308.

31. Postscript to the *Ni Ni Roku* trilogy; see Scott-Stokes, pp. 234-35.

32. Nathan notes that in the same month that the story "Patriotism" was published, a story titled "Seventeen" appeared by a young novelist, Kenzaburo
Oe. The tale is about a seventeen-year-old "chronic masturbator" who
becomes enraged when he suspects that others are aware of his habit, and
vows to "kill them, every one of them, with a machine gun." The young
paranoiac's dilemma, as Nathan describes it, is that "he cannot stop masturbat-
ing, because he needs the 'sense of power' he experiences on ejaculation" (p.
182).

According to Levin and Fox (*Mass Murder*, p. 67), in the 18 percent of mass
murders that "involve sex and sadism," the killer is sometimes motivated by
the prospect of an orgasmic payoff. Thus, the serial killer Edmund Kemper
anticipated the "reward" of "the exceptional orgasm that only the act of killing
could provide for him" (p. 34), while Douglas Clark, the "Sunset Strip Killer,"
was reportedly "striving to fulfill his fantasy of cutting the throat of a woman
during intercourse to feel the contractions of her vagina during death spasms"
(p. 74). Levin and Fox rather dubiously suggest that this obsession with orgasm
on the part of mass murderers of the 1970s may have been a consequence of
the emphasis in the pop psychology at this time "on eliminating guilty feelings," and on overcoming what the author of the best-selling *Everything You
Always Wanted to Know about Sex* called the "fear of doing wrong" as a way of
dealing with "the absence of orgasm as well as many other sexual hangups"
(p. 73). However, a work like Thomas Pynchon's novel *Gravity's Rainbow* (New
York: Viking, 1973), in which the Pavlovian linkage between sexual arousal and
imminent extermination is a recurring theme, and in which it is speculated
that Western man "might be in love, in sexual love, with his, and his race's,
death" (p. 738), suggests some of the profound, cultural factors underlying the
concern at this time with the relation between sexual orgasm and violent
death. And Mishima's repeated references before his 1970 Eastern-style suicide
to Bataille and other Western writers similarly point to the significance of such
cultural determinants. (See also John Money, David Hingsburger, and Gordon
Wainwright, *The Breathless Orgasm: A Lovemap Biography of Asphyxiophilia* [New
York: Prometheus, 1991].)

33. Yukio Mishima, *Confessions of a Mask*, trans. Meredith Weatherby (New York: New Directions, 1958), pp. 38–41.

34. Cf., e.g., the exhibit, "The Subject is AIDS," at the Nexus Gallery in Atlanta, Georgia, in February 1989).

35. Genet, *Journal du voleur*, p. 225; *The Thief's Journal*, p. 212.

36. See the story "Yakata" ("Mansion," 1939) and *Confessions of a Mask*; also, Scott-Stokes, pp. 83–84.

37. Sartre, *Saint Genet*, p. 485.

38. Quoted in Nathan, p. 247.

39. Genet, *Journal du voleur*, p. 204; *The Thief's Journal*, pp. 192–93.

40. Genet, *Journal du voleur*, p. 131; *The Thief's Journal*, p. 123. Cf. Primo Levi's observation that in the Nazi concentration camps "there are no criminals . . . because there is no moral law to contravene" (*Survival in Auschwitz: The Nazi Assault on Humanity* [*Se questo è un uomo* (1958)], trans. Stuart Woolf [New York: Macmillan/Collier, 1961], p. 89).

Afterword

1. The problems that may arise when a professional writer undertakes to narrate the story of a convicted murderer can be seen from the examples of Truman Capote's "non-fiction novel" *In Cold Blood*, where Capote was censured by some critics for exploiting the story of his condemned subjects instead of working to avert their death sentence, and most recently in the case of Joe McGinniss's book *Fatal Vision*, in which the author's subject Jeff MacDonald, who is serving a life sentence for murdering his wife and children, sued McGinniss for betraying his trust, and presenting him as his family's killer instead of a wrongly accused victim.

2. Stanley Corngold, *The Fate of the Self: German Writers and French Theory* (New York: Columbia University Press, 1986), p. 222.

3. Corngold, p. 226. One needs to bear in mind, however, that what Corngold calls "intactness of the self" is itself often made possible by a scandalous misdeed that compels the subject to confess, and that enables the subject to establish its selfhood in the first place.

4. As Laurence Senelick shows, Lacenaire carefully crafted his persona on the romantic image of the Byronic hero.

Three years after the sensation caused by Lacenaire's trial and execution, Nerval published *Léo Burckart*. Jeffrey N. Cox has observed that although Nerval based his play on the 1819 assassination of Kotzebue by the radical student Karl Sand, he drew on other historical events such as Loening's attempt on President Ibell's life in 1820, Louis Alibaud's attempted assassination of Louis-Philippe in 1836, and even Charlotte Corday's "archetypal revolutionary murder" of Marat in 1789. According to Cox, Nerval was acutely sensitive to how a particular historical act can "spark emulators," and how early nineteenth-century assassins both set and followed historical precedents. "What concerns Nerval as he surveys these repeated killings is the dangerous tendency to use prior historical events as models for one's actions – a Loening imitating a Sand, or a Sand modeling himself on a Corday, or a Corday seeing herself as a female Brutus" ("Killing Kotzebue," pp. 34–35). With respect to Brutus as a model, see Albert Furtwangler's *Assassin on Stage: Brutus, Hamlet, and the Death of Lincoln* (Champaign, Ill.: University of Illinois Press, 1991) and Manfredi Piccolomini's *The Brutus Revival: Parricide and Tyrannicide During the Renaissance* (Carbondale, Ill.: Southern Illinois University Press, 1991).

5. King Louis-Philippe survived, but eighteen persons were killed by Fieschi's "infernal machine," which consisted of twenty-five rifles rigged to fire at once.

6. Foucault, *I, Pierre Rivière*, p. 199. Subsequent references to Rivière's memoir and the accompanying texts in Foucault's volume are in the text.

7. *Annales d'hygiène publique et de médecine légale*, 1836, cited in Foucault, p. 212

8. Katz, *Seductions of Crime*, pp. 310–11.

9. I make use here of Louis Marin's adaptation of Benveniste's distinction between *histoire* and *discours* ("The Autobiographical Interruption: About Stendhal's *Life of Henry Brulard*," *MLN* 93 [1978]: 599); since Rivière's narrative (*histoire*) could not be written until after his crime, it is necessary to make an additional distinction between *histoire* and *mémoire*, between narrative fiction and narrative confession.

10. The slaying of his brother, who had not taken sides against his father as his mother and sister had, underscores Rivière's sense of his murders as an act of self-sacrifice: "I determined to kill all three of them, the first two because they were leagued to make my father suffer, as to the little boy I had two reasons, one because he loved my mother and my sister, the other because I feared that if I only killed the other two, my father though greatly horrified by it might yet regret me when he knew that I was dying for him, I knew that he loved that child who was very intelligent, I thought to myself he will hold me in such abhorrence that he will rejoice in my death, and so he will live happier being free from regrets" (p. 106).

11. *Pilote du Calvados*, Oct. 22, 1840, cited in Foucault, p. 171.

12. *Memoirs of Hector Berlioz*, p. 129.

13. See *Goethes Werke* (Hamburg: Christian Wegner, 1967), 9:585–87. Subsequent citations from Goethe's writings are in the text.

14. As Eric Blackall has shown, the editor who resumes the narrative in the later version is concerned less with distancing himself from his subject than with imaginatively trying to reconstruct Werther's disturbed state of mind from his final letter (*Goethe and the Novel*, chap. 3, esp. pp. 50–53).

15. Goethe's principal revision of the novel concerned the story of the servant-murderer and the concluding narrative by the fictional editor (see Blackall, p. 50). In contrast to the editor of the first version, the editor in the revised version "reveals that Werther's situation springs only from inside himself." Blackall suggests that "Goethe is most anxious, in this second version of his novel, that we shall see the sickness of Werther and not identify him with his author, nor ourselves with him *totally*" (p. 53). In the wake of the suicide epi-

demic that followed the initial publication of the novel, Goethe no doubt found it desirable to lessen the reader's identification with Werther in the revised version.

16. William Bolitho devotes a chapter to Troppmann in his 1926 study *Murder for Profit*. As the title of Bolitho's study indicates, Troppmann's motive for killing the Kinck family was for his own benefit, while Rivière presents his slaughter of half his own family as an act of self-sacrifice.

17. See René Girard, "The Mimetic Desire of Paolo and Francesca," chap. 1 of *"To Double Business Bound": Essays on Literature, Mimesis, and Anthropology* (Baltimore: Johns Hopkins University Press, 1978).

18. Braudy, *The Frenzy of Renown*, p. 567. According to Braudy, "Reagan's experience as an actor . . . far from trivializing his performance as president, allowed him to project a much more complicated character than he may have actually possessed."

19. In his tale *Die Verlobung in San Domingo* (1811), Kleist again presented a lover who takes his own life after slaying his beloved whom he mistakenly believed had betrayed him.

20. Joachim Maass, *Kleist: A Biography*, trans. Ralph Manheim (New York: Farrar, Straus & Giroux, 1983), p. 295.

INDEX